Family History for the Older and Wiser

Find Your Roots with Online Tools

Susan Fifer

WILEY

This edition first published 2010
© 2010 John Wiley & Sons, Ltd

Registered office
John Wiley & Sons Ltd, The Atrium, Southern Gate, Chichester, West Sussex, PO19 8SQ, United Kingdom

For details of our global editorial offices, for customer services and for information about how to apply for permission to reuse the copyright material in this book please see our website at www.wiley.com.

Library of Congress Cataloging-in-Publication Data

Fifer, Susan.

   Family history for the older and wiser : find your roots with online tools / Susan Fifer.

       p. cm.—(The Third Age Trust series)

   Includes index.

   ISBN 978-0-470-68612-6 (paper : alk. paper) 1. Great Britain—Genealogy—Computer network resources. 2. Genealogy—Computer network resources. 3. Internet—Handbooks, manuals, etc. 4. Middle-aged persons—Computer network resources. I. Title.

   CS415.F54 2010

   929'.10285—dc22

2009049237

ISBN 978-0-470-68612-6

A catalogue record for this book is available from the British Library.

Set in 11/13 Zapf Humanist 601 BT by Laserwords Private Limited, Chennai, India
Printed in Great Britain by Bell and Bain, Glasgow.

Contents

Contents

Contents

The Third Age Trust

The Third Age Trust is the body which represents all U3As in the UK. The U3A movement is made up of over 700 self-governing groups of older men and women who organise for themselves activities which may be educational, recreational or social in kind. Calling on their own experience and knowledge they demand no qualifications nor do they offer any. The movement has grown at a remarkable pace and offers opportunities to thousands of people to demonstrate their own worth to one another and to the community. Their interests are astonishingly varied but the members all value the opportunity to share experiences and learning with like-minded people. The Third Age Trust's endorsement of the Older and Wiser series hints at some of that width of interest.

THE THIRD AGE TRUST

THE UNIVERSITY OF THE THIRD AGE

About the Author

Susan Fifer has been researching her family history since 1994 when she purchased a computer program and started inputting information about her mother's many cousins. Her interest in both computers and family history has continued and she pursues both actively in her retirement, teaching computer skills to older learners and remaining obsessive about genealogy. She has been involved in international projects to index Jewish records from Poland. She is a member of Barnet U3A, where she co-ordinates the Mah Jong groups and started a Family History group whose activities were based on the material developed for this book. In common with many researchers, she hopes one day to complete and publish her own family history research.

Acknowledgements

Gemma Richardson and Frances McDarby of the National Archives for their help in reviewing Chapter 7 (any omissions and errors remain the property of the author!)

Barnet U3A Family History Group for their support and enthusiasm.

This book is dedicated to Robin (Bob) Segal for preserving the Milstone family history and for introducing me to U3A.

Publisher's Acknowledgements

Some of the people who helped bring this book to market include the following:

Editorial and Production
VP Consumer and Technology Publishing Director: Michelle Leete
Associate Director–Book Content Management: Martin Tribe
Associate Publisher: Chris Webb
Assistant Editor: Colleen Goldring
Publishing Assistant: Ellie Scott
Content Editor: Claire Spinks
Project Editor: Juliet Booker
Development Editor: Sydney Jones
Copy Editor: Grace Fairley

Marketing:
Senior Marketing Manager: Louise Breinholt
Marketing Executive: Chloe Tunnicliffe

Composition Services:
Compositor: Laserwords Private Limited
Proof Reader: Richard Walshe
Indexer: Geraldine Begley

With thanks to U3A member, Mrs Gillian Brown, for naming our Older and Wiser owl "Steady Stanley". This was the winning entry from the U3A News competition held in October 2009.

Icons used in this book

Throughout the book you will notice symbolic images. These have been introduced to help focus your attention on certain information and are summarised as follows:

	Equipment needed	Lets you know in advance the equipment you will need to hand as you progress through the chapter.
	Skills needed	Placed at the beginning to help identify the skills you'll need for the chapter ahead.
	Tip	Tips and suggestions to help make life easier.
	Note	Take note of these little extras to avoid confusion.
	Warning	Read carefully, a few things could go wrong at this point.
	Try It	Go on, enjoy yourself; you won't break it.
	Trivia	A little bit of fun to bring a smile to your face.
	Summary	Recap at the end of each chapter with the short summary.
	Brain Training	Brain training, test out your memory.

PRACTICE MAKES PERFECT

To build upon the lessons learnt in this book, visit www.pcwisdom.co.uk

- More training tutorials

- Links to resources

- Advice through frequently asked questions

- Author videos and podcasts

- Author blogs

PART I
Getting Started

Getting your granddad to recall his childhood memories is costing us a fortune in brown ale.

Introduction

Equipment needed: A computer, printer, Internet access; the earliest marriage certificate among your family papers.

Skills needed: Patience, persistence and a liking for detective stories.

I was recently at a one-day family history event in central London. It was not surprising that the queues for entry started forming half an hour before the doors opened, even for those who had pre-bought tickets. Inside the hall, individuals who had developed materials while undertaking their own research had set up stalls. There were some 30 regional or themed interest groups, most of which operate as membership societies with charitable status. Finally, there were the big commercial organisations, global in scope and often with project links to government agencies. Family history is clearly an activity that operates at a number of levels.

What was most striking, however, was the extent to which technology formed an expected and accepted part of what was on offer. Every stand had a computer, many linked to the Internet. While many books were for sale, they were complemented by hundreds of CDs, many of which were the result of cooperative indexing projects undertaken by members of various societies wishing to share their research with a much wider audience of both new and more experienced family historians.

It wasn't always like this. When I first started my family history research in 1994, computing was a minority interest in genealogical circles. Rather like digital cameras among the photographic community, it was somehow seen as cheating. As in photography, attitudes have now changed and there is an appreciation of how technology can enhance the sharing of data, ideas and resources. While the individual still has to do groundwork in relation to his/her family tree, few researchers deny the benefits that technology has brought. It saves them time, effort and cost, and makes them feel part of a much broader activity.

When I run family history sessions, I often tell the participants that I am envious of the fact that they are at the beginning of their journey with all the excitement of discovery still to come. For many of my generation, this family history journey is also accompanied by an exploration of what we can accomplish using the new technology. The computer no longer has to be seen as a solution looking for a problem – family history research and the computer are ideal marriage partners.

Enjoy your journey!

How to use this book

This book aims to take you through the stages of researching and writing your family history using online sources. These sources are growing in number on a daily basis, so the emphasis is on the major sites where you can access information and records, and the techniques for deciding whether you have found family members. The primary focus is on resources in England and Wales, with sections on Scottish and Irish records where these have significant differences.

Some of you are already experienced computer users; other may have done some research into your family history. I have organised the material in a similar way to the courses I have run in the University of the Third Age (U3A) and with other local groups. This book can be used by individuals or as a course book for groups who want to support each other in the early stages of learning to research their families and who may not have an experienced family historian among their membership.

All researchers need some basic core knowledge to do research. As groups progress, interests diverge and become more specialised. You may develop an interest in a particular geographical location, need to research relatives who have moved to Australia or find Jewish family originating in Eastern Europe, military ancestors or those in particular professions. Once you need to start researching in these directions, you will find an enormous amount of information on the Web: people with similar interests, websites and one-name studies all help you take your research to the next stage.

The rest of this introductory section looks at the benefits of using a computer for your research, and some of the associated costs. It also introduces the case study, which provides a means for all the members of a group to work together on the same material. At the end of each chapter, there are usually two research activities: one uses the case study family to test the methods and sources covered; the second asks you to apply these techniques to your own family research.

Part II looks at the basic genealogical building blocks: birth, marriage, death and census records. You look at how to start reviewing and evaluating the evidence you find in these sources.

Part III focuses on three of the major resources for online research: the Latter Day Saints' (LDS, also known as the Mormons) FamilySearch website; Ancestry, an ever-growing repository of databases and documents; and the National Archives. This is followed by an overview of a range of other resources available to you.

Part IV sets out how you can record your research using spreadsheets. Family history software will then allow you to produce reports in many different formats, all from the same data you have collected. You also look at using photographs to bring life and interest to the names and dates you are collecting.

Part V examines how research can be shared, whether with your family or with other researchers. This may be in the form of presentations, online information or printed material.

What, why and how much?

What is the difference between family history and genealogy? It is probably true to say that these terms are now used interchangeably by those undertaking their own research. Most of the societies exhibiting at the event I mentioned earlier called themselves 'family history societies'. There were some exceptions, such as the Society of Genealogists. If a distinction were to be made, it would probably give genealogy a focus on the academic study of lineage and the creation of pedigrees with names, dates and sometimes places. Much of this work was initially undertaken for royal and noble families. Evidence from wills, marriage settlements and land registries is focused on those who had land and significant possessions to pass on to their heirs.

Family history, by contrast, supplements this work through a broader consideration of social, economic and political history. Examples of this would be the movement of people from the country to the land at the time of the Industrial Revolution, the impact of the development of the railways on the creation of the London suburbs and the migration of large numbers of Irish families to the United States following the potato famine of the mid-1800s. By its nature, this covers the lives of families from more modest backgrounds where there may be less documentary evidence available of the pure genealogical variety. The recent increase in the numbers of people researching has meant that these aspects overlap. Both terms are used in this book.

Why use a computer for family history?

People were collecting and recording information about their ancestors long before computers were invented. It is, of course, still possible to do this work in the traditional way, and much of the research involves looking at a variety of evidence and deciding whether you have found members of your family. This has to be based on your own knowledge and judgement.

> Your work is similar to that of the detective. You need to look for clues, put forward your hypothesis, and find and weigh up the evidence.

Modern detectives are assisted in their work by databases of DNA, criminal records, fingerprints and car numbers. Such records no longer need to be searched manually, which speeds up the detection process. Databases can also highlight connections that might otherwise have been missed.

In the same way, the computer can act as a tool for speeding up your research and allowing you to record your findings in a variety of ways.

How much is it going to cost?

Most hobbies have some form of associated cost, and this may increase as you delve deeper into your family history. Costs could include:

- computer, printer and Internet access
- software for recording family history and for associated tasks such as editing photographs
- copies of birth, marriage and death certificates
- subscriptions to websites with genealogical databases such as census indexes
- subscriptions to family history societies
- books and magazines
- research trips to archives, libraries and locations where your family lived.

Not all of these are essential and there are a number of ways to keep down costs:

- Make use of computer and Internet access in your local library.
- Collect or copy documents and photos in your possession or held by other members of your family.
- Use free software on your computer for recording your family history and for other tasks. Some free software, such as spreadsheets and photo editing programs, helps you record your research.
- Don't buy a certificate unless you are reasonably certain that it relates to your family. As these cost several pounds each, it can be expensive if it turns out not to be your relative.
- Only buy certificates if they give you important information that is not available in any other way. Look for proxies. For example, an old passport gives you a date, place of birth and full name. The person had to submit a birth certificate to get the passport, so it's a good alternative to buying the certificate.
- Use any free databases that are available online. Even where you may need to pay for access to records, develop strategies to get the maximum information from any free index searches that you are allowed.
- Many libraries now have subscriptions to paid websites, which you can access for free using your library card.

- Visit the websites of family history societies to decide whether they are worth joining.
- Get involved with indexing projects. You will get an early sight of data not yet generally available and you may be given a copy of the data for your personal use once the project is completed.

Case study

Researching your family history is a very individual activity. There are common resources and techniques but the paths down which these will lead you diverge very rapidly. Much also depends on the amount of background knowledge that you have or can glean from your family and their documents before you actually start. Many are fortunate to begin with a wealth of information; others feel overwhelmed by the resources available and concerned that their own knowledge is so minimal.

I decided that I would run a U3A family history group based on a single 1890 marriage certificate (shown in Figure 1.1) that I had purchased at an antiques fair. The certificate has no connection with any of the families I am researching and my subsequent investigations have failed to find any links. This makes it a perfect case study for a family history group to adopt. You have no background knowledge of the family, no supporting documentation, no family myths to prove or disprove. But you can use the information on this certificate and available resources to try to build a history for the two families identified.

Each time I look at an available resource, I try it out first of all with this 'adopted' family and scrutinise the reliability of the information I find. I show you how to test assumptions about what you know and the accuracy of your results. This then allows you to undertake the same research tasks with your own families, using the skills and questioning techniques that you have learned.

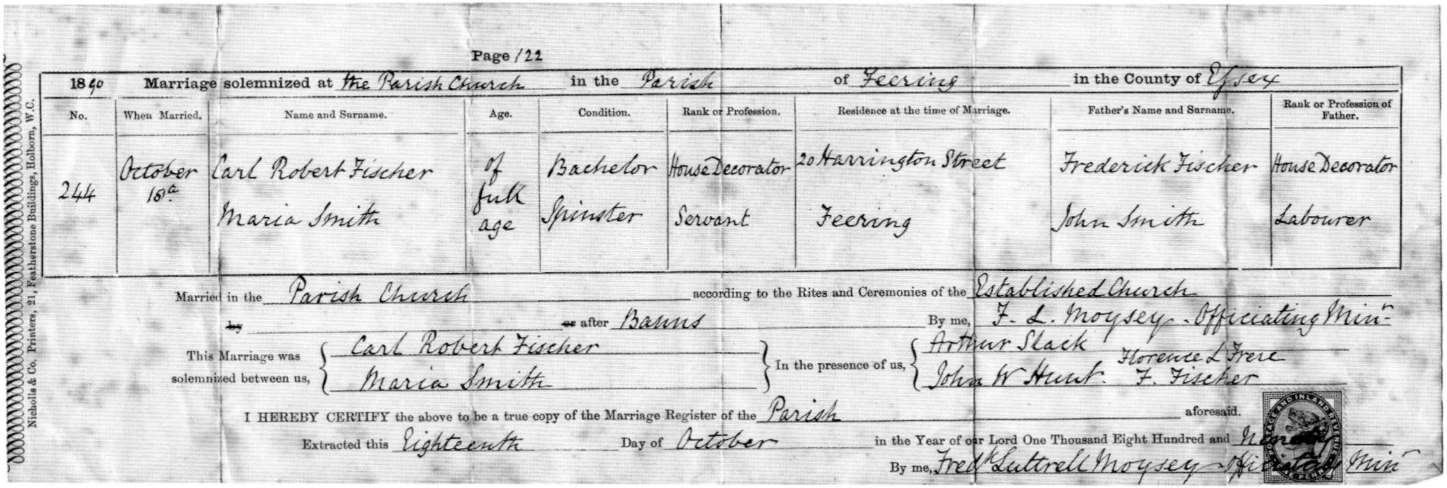

Page /22

Marriage solemnized at The Parish Church in the Parish of Fecoriz in the County of Jersey

No.	When Married.	Name and Surname.	Age.	Condition.	Rank or Profession.	Residence at the time of Marriage.	Father's Name and Surname.	Rank or Profession of Father.
1840								
244	October 18ᵗᵃ	Carl Robert Fischer	full age	Bachelor	House Decorator	20 Harrington Street	Frederick Fischer	House Decorator
		Maria Smith	full age	Spinster	Servant	Fecorey	John Smith	Labourer

Married in the Parish Church according to the Rites and Ceremonies of the Established Church after Banns By me, F. L. Morysey Officiating Minister

This Marriage was solemnized between us, { Carl Robert Fischer / Maria Smith } In the presence of us, { Arthur Mack, Florence Frere / John W Mack, F. Fischer }

I HEREBY CERTIFY the above to be a true copy of the Marriage Register of the Parish aforesaid. in the Year of our Lord One Thousand Eight Hundred and

Extracted this Eighteenth Day of October

By me, Fred Lutorell Morysey

Figure 1.1

Research task: Fischer/Smith family

How much information can you get from the facts recorded on this certificate, and can you use them to make certain deductions that will then inform other research that you can undertake to build up a tree for this family?

- Carl Robert Fischer married Maria Smith on 18 October 1890 in Feering, Essex.
- Carl, a house decorator, was the son of Frederick Fischer, also a house decorator.
- Maria, a servant, was the daughter of John Smith, a labourer.
- Carl's address is given as 20 Harrington Street.
- Maria's address is just given as Feering.
- The bride and groom were both 'of full age', which means over 21. Neither had apparently been married before.

Before reading the next section, can you draw up a list of at least five questions and assumptions that arise from studying this certificate more closely?

My U3A family history group recorded the following observations. This is not necessarily the order in which you might undertake the research.

- If the couple is 'of full age,' this means that they were both born before 1869. Start here and work backwards if looking for their birth certificates.
- There is no indication that the fathers are deceased. (It usually says so if this is the case.)
- F. Fischer is shown as one of the witnesses. This might be Carl's father but could also be a brother named after their father.
- Is Harrington Street in Feering? Why does Carl have a street name and house number but Maria doesn't? Is Harrington Street in a larger town?
- How difficult will it be to research Maria's father, John Smith? (More than 21,000 people with this name are listed on the 1901 census for England and Wales.) It will help if you can show that he was born and lived in Feering, which seems to be a relatively small place.

continued

- The spelling of the Fischer surname, together with the forenames Carl and Frederick, might mean a German connection.

- Be prepared for Fischer to be written in the form of Fisher in some documents. Carl might also be in the form of Karl.

Research task: Your family

Using the investigation of the Fischer/Smith marriage as a template, find the earliest marriage certificate among your family papers and apply the same techniques.

Summary

- Family history and genealogy are used synonymously throughout this book.

- Technology can save you enormous amounts of time but you still need to evaluate carefully the data it gives you.

- Costs can mount up. Don't rush out and buy/subscribe to everything at once. Investigate free resources first.

- When you have a certificate, extract all the obvious information and then start speculating about things not recorded on the document.

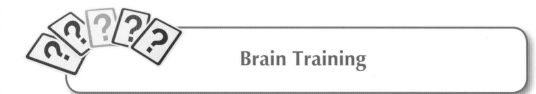

Brain Training

There may be more than one correct answer to some of these questions.

1. Which of the following pieces of information would you expect to find on a full English marriage certificate?

a) Groom's date of birth

b) Name of bride's father

c) Name of groom's mother

d) Occupation of groom

2. Which of the following is the best proxy (in genealogical terms) for a birth certificate?

a) Credit card

b) Driving licence

c) Passport

d) School leaving certificate

3. What is the minimum number of witnesses required on a marriage certificate?

4. A marriage witness can't be related to the bride or groom. True or false?

5. By what initials is the Mormon Church also known?

Answers

Q1 – b and d   **Q2** – c   **Q3** – Two   **Q4** – False

Q5 – LDS

What you need to begin

2

Equipment needed: Contact list for living relatives, family photos, certificates and any family papers giving names, dates and other personal information. Computer, printer and Internet access.

Skills needed: Interviewing techniques, tact, document organising ability. Knowledge of how to access the Web.

You might be surprised that a book looking at online techniques for family history is going to start with a section on materials and sources that have nothing to do with your computer and the Internet. When people get access to the Web, often the first thing they do is type in their own name or that of a family member they are researching to see what comes up. Because they have heard a great deal about how you can find anything with a computer, it seems the natural place to start.

The results of such a search can be disappointing and/or overwhelming, depending on how common the name is and whether it is already known for other reasons. For example, if you are a well-known chef, your name will come up hundreds of times but most of these will have little to do with the research you want to undertake.

To make sense of these results, you have to do some basic thinking and researching before you even sit down in front of the computer. If you have watched any of the TV series *Who Do You Think You Are?*, you will remember the first four activities for all the participants:

● think about what you already know

● start from yourself and work backwards

- gather any documents and photos you have at home

- go and discuss these with close members of your family who may themselves have other materials you can use.

Getting information from relatives

There is a saying in family history circles that 'documents last, people don't'. Many people start their family history research later in life, when they are retired and have fewer work and family commitments. The problem is that, by the time they are in a position to do some serious research, they no longer have many family members from earlier generations to ask for details. Very often, in family history groups, you hear people say that they started too late and that there is no one left to ask.

The first priority, therefore, is to interview the oldest living member(s) of your family. You may be lucky and still have parents and even grandparents living. If not, are there still siblings or cousins of these relatives around? If not, what about your own cousins? My mother was born in the 1920s: her oldest first cousin was born in 1900 and one of the youngest was born in 1940. In the course of my research I have been able to talk with her cousin (born 1912), who had a close knowledge of my maternal grandfather and his parents – my great-grandparents. Because of the difference in age between this cousin and my mother, he was able to tell me things from a time that she was too young to remember.

You need to think about the following:

- Who am I going to interview?

- What things could I reasonably expect this person to know?

- Is there a single key piece of information that I need to get from this person that would unlock the rest of my research at this stage?

Techniques for interviewing relatives

Not everyone in your family is necessarily going to share your new-found enthusiasm for digging up the past. Some people have amazing recall for individuals, details and places and will be more than willing to share this with you. Others could be more reticent. There may have been long-standing family disputes, often stemming from arguments between members of earlier generations. The causes of such disputes may have been long forgotten but the aftertaste lingers on.

In some families, events that are now regarded as commonplace or socially acceptable may have carried with them a sense of stigma and disgrace. This meant that they were never discussed openly by these older relatives and certainly not with more junior members of the family. Divorce and illegitimacy were much more common than you would think and many marriages took place less than nine months before the birth of the first child. Adoptions, whether formal or informal, may also have been kept secret, perhaps from the adopted child him/herself.

All of these things affect the willingness of the person to help you. The following suggestions may help:

- Don't start by saying baldly that you want information about the family. Take a collection of photos with you, and say that you are trying to identify who they are. (In any case, you should already have sorted all the photos in your biscuit tin/chocolate box into those you know, those you think you know and those you don't know at all.)

- Although it might seem a good idea to use a cassette recorder to capture all the information you are being given, this can be quite intimidating for the person being interviewed. If someone does agree to be recorded, they might ask you to stop the machine at sensitive moments.

- If someone refuses or is reluctant to talk to you directly, see if you can enlist the help of a younger member of the family such as the person's grandchild.

Consider interviewing two relatives at one time. Sometimes they can spark each other off (let's hope in a good way) and remind each other about things they thought they'd forgotten.

Dealing with difficult issues

You, too, may have certain preconceived ideas about the family and its probity, which your research quickly demolishes. You need to be prepared to look at the facts as they are. The president of the genealogical society to which I belong has

15

a phrase that he often uses to preface family history presentations: 'If you mind what you find, don't look'. If you're going to get upset because great-aunt Alice was a bigamist or because someone in the late nineteenth century was convicted of a crime, then you need to take up a more soothing hobby.

On the other hand, you need to be very sensitive about such matters the nearer they are in time to the present and the more directly they concern living people. The advice is usually to record such information in your own notes but to suppress such revelations where you are going to be making your material available to a wider audience, whether in book form or on the Web.

Obtaining certificates

The basic building blocks of family history are records of births, marriages and deaths (BMD). Most people have their own birth certificate or get a copy when they need to apply for something like a passport. Couples also have their marriage certificates. Immediate family, or those executing a relative's will, should have a copy of the death certificate. Certificates of baptism may also contain some (though not all) of the same information as a birth certificate. If your relatives were born overseas, a certificate of naturalisation (if they went through this process) is very useful. These official documents should be preserved carefully, and you should make copies of them to take with you to archives and libraries.

The further back in time you research, the more difficult it becomes to assemble this documentation. Papers may have been lost or destroyed when families moved house or in the clearance of someone's effects after their death. While it is sometimes possible to obtain copies, there are time and financial costs involved.

It may help to work through the following checklist to see if you can trace these documents, particularly for families in the late nineteenth and early twentieth centuries:

- If there were a large number of children in the family, who was still living at home when the surviving parent died? The parent may have moved to live with a married child. Unmarried children may have stayed at home to look after elderly parents.
- Who dealt with the deceased parent's estate/papers?
- If those children have subsequently died, who would have carried out the same task for them?

- Is there anyone in the family who has already made a start on creating a family tree? He/she may have been given copies, or even the originals, to help their research.

Gleaning information from photographs

I have already suggested that sorting out family photos will be one of your major jobs in researching your family history. As a child, I was fascinated by the collection of family pictures my parents had amassed. Most of them, unfortunately, were not in albums. Some had names and dates on the back but some of these references, to people who had died before I was born, were cryptic to say the least. 'To my dear pal Issy, from Herman,' one read. It took me many years of research to work out that Issy (Isaac) was actually Abraham Isaac, known to me as (great) Uncle Arthur. I now have reason to believe that Herman was not only his 'pal' but might also have been his cousin.

As someone in the family pointed out to me, you didn't need to write down who these people were. When you went through the boxes of photographs at family gatherings, there were always several of your older relatives present who knew and could tell you. Now that these relatives have gone, neither you nor others of your generation can remember.

There are a number of books that can help you to identify and preserve old photographs. For research purposes, the following tips may help:

- Scan photographs so that you handle the originals as little as possible.

- Write on the back in pencil.

- Don't just write 'Mum, 1940.' It might be clear to you that it's your mother, but this won't be clear to your great-grandchildren. Write the person's full name and, if it's a married woman, give her maiden name, particularly if the picture was taken before her marriage.

Hyphenated surnames were often used as a way of preserving the family name of the female line, particularly when there were no sons to carry on the name.

- Take copies of your scanned unknown photographs to family gatherings and pass them around. Ask your relatives to write on them who they think the pictures show and then see if there is any agreement. If nothing else, it may bring out the fact that people have copies of other photographs at home that they may be willing to share with you.

- If you think there are other photographs that you don't have, use the same method for working out who might have them as you did for finding certificates. Unfortunately, people are probably more likely to preserve an official certificate than keep large quantities of photographs when they sort out someone's papers and effects. Many end up at antique fairs, interesting examples of the photographer's art and/or period fashion but unlikely ever to find their way into the hands of the relevant family researcher. A named photograph may, at least, have a fighting chance in this respect.

Collecting family records

A quick look around my office, while typing this, confirms that we are probably the most documented generation ever. Not only are we recorded by the authorities but we create and collect such information ourselves. The following list is far from exhaustive but it should give you some idea of the sources that can provide the basis both for your research and for subsequent confirmation of the material you find once you start to research online:

- address books

- autograph books

- condolence cards

- copies of wills

- diaries

- examination certificates

- family bibles

- inscribed jewellery

- insurance policies

- letters
- newspaper cuttings
- old savings books
- passports
- payslips/pension records
- professional qualifications
- ration books/ID cards
- school reports
- scrapbooks
- sports trophies/certificates
- wedding invitations
- work testimonials.

The details from each of these sources will naturally vary. In some cases, they may provide evidence of where a person was living and/or working at a particular time. This can be cross-referenced with, for example, a marriage certificate, which gives addresses and occupations for the bride and groom.

Computing requirements

Interviewing relatives and collecting family documents gives you one half of the materials and tools you need to begin your research. You now need to consider the computing requirements for your task.

Computer

Since you are reading a book about online family history, it is probably reasonable to assume that you already have a computer, plan to acquire one soon or have access to one, perhaps through your local library. Any laptop or desktop machine you are likely to use should be sufficient for all the tasks that you'll need to undertake.

Nowadays, you see many people in record offices with laptop computers. Archives and libraries are now quite relaxed about letting you bring one in (sometimes more relaxed than if you take in a pen). Often, the archive or library has power sockets accessible from desks and microfilm readers. There are some very portable and lightweight computers, known as netbooks or 'subcompact notebook computers', costing around £200. These are small enough to go in a bag with your papers and files. They can use all the same software programs as your main machine, store photographs and usually have a wireless connection. This means you can access the Internet on your own machine if a network connection is available to you in the library or archive.

There are pros and cons to having and using such a machine.

Advantages of using a netbook

Since netbooks are inexpensive, you might want to consider these other advantages:

- They are much easier to carry about with you than larger laptops.

- You can reduce the amount of paperwork you have to print out and take with you to the library or archive.

- You can use it for presentations at family events – admittedly only on a one to one basis, unless you have access to a projector as well.

- If you are going to be away from home and undertaking research, you may want to enter data at the end of each day, to review what you have done and to keep the task manageable.

Disadvantages of using a netbook

On the flipside, netbooks do have some disadvantages:

- If you already have a desktop or large laptop computer, can you justify the additional expense?

- It requires some effort to keep a netbook secure in record offices, when you go to get something from the shelves. If it is very portable, it can be a target for thieves.

One solution to the security problem is to require a password for access. You can also buy something called a 'Kensington lock', which works in a similar way to a bicycle lock. It fits into a tiny socket found on most laptop computers. (Ask the salesperson to show you where this socket is.) The chain from the lock is secured around something heavy like a table leg or a chair, which makes it more difficult for someone to slip your netbook into their bag.

- The batteries are not always necessarily as long-lasting as they are advertised to be. You can buy additional battery power. You may need to take your power cable and adaptor with you, which somewhat negates the lightweight/portability advantages.

- The keyboard may be much smaller than you are used to and therefore you should not plan to do large amounts of data entry using the machine.

- The screen may be much smaller than you are used to and it may be tiring to read for long periods.

Printer/scanner

Most libraries and record offices have printing and copying facilities. The costs are not usually great, though they can mount up and it can be time-consuming if you have dozens of records to print, particularly if they are in different books or on different frames of a microfilm/fiche.

If you are able to capture data electronically, then having your own printer allows you much more flexibility. The best printer for family history purposes is an inkjet multi-function machine. This looks like a miniature photocopier and it will, in fact, allow you to make colour or black and white copies from books and documents. It also lets you print records, images and reports from your computer. Its final function is to allow you to scan documents and photographs directly into your computer. These can later be included in family history material, combined into collages and presented on web pages.

Printers are relatively cheap to buy. Currently, £50 gets you a good machine and there are often special deals in computer and department stores or in high street stationery shops. Many computers can be purchased with a package that includes a printer. For most of the printouts you produce, you do not need high quality paper unless you want to create photo montages, perhaps as a gift to family members on special occasions or as a thank you for their help in your research. For these purposes, you could also use the print services now available in many photographic shops, department stores or supermarkets.

The main ongoing expense will be the cost of ink cartridges. Unless you plan to do extensive printing of photographic quality material, there is no reason why you should not look for cheaper alternatives (compatible or remanufactured cartridges) rather than buying the much higher priced originals produced by the printer manufacturer.

> When using cheaper ink alternatives, your printer may produce a message querying your decision but, as is best when dealing with machines, you should assure it that all is well (and basically that it should mind its own business).

Gaining Internet access and email

If you want access to the Internet on your home computer, then you need to sign up with an Internet Service Provider (ISP.) Your Internet connection uses your phone line. Nowadays, nearly all such connections are 'broadband', which means you can search the Internet and still keep your phone line available for calls. You will also be given an email address. There are as many ISPs as there are providers of telephone and mobile services. In fact, many telephone and mobile providers can also include a broadband connection in the package they supply to you. Check out articles in consumer magazines, talk to friends and work out the best deal for your requirements.

Even if you don't have a computer at home, you can still have an email address that you can use at libraries, Internet cafes and on the computers of any friends and family who are willing to give you some access time. This is the whole basis on which gap year students keep in touch with their friends and parents.

Signing up to discussion groups, subscription databases, family history societies and newspaper archives usually requires you to register and provide an email address, together with a password. Should you forget the password, then there is usually a facility on the website to request a reminder to be sent to your email account. Many of these 'webmail' accounts are free. Well-known accounts include Yahoo!, Hotmail (from Microsoft) and Gmail (from Google).

Even if you have an email account from your Internet service provider, you can still sign up for additional webmail accounts such as Hotmail. You might want to use such an account exclusively for your family history research, leaving other email accounts for personal and/or business use.

Internet access also allows you to contact other researchers and to post messages on discussion groups. The archives of such groups are often available to search online. You can check these to see if names and places in which you are interested have been mentioned by researchers in earlier postings.

Searching the Web

You will be searching online for websites connected with family history, and viewing them. For this, you need to use a program called an Internet browser. Browsers contain all the features you need to go to websites, save and print information and mark web pages for future reference.

Your Internet browser

When you turn on your computer, you need to go into your Internet browser. This is a program that allows you to access the millions of pages that make up the World Wide Web (www). Your browser is probably Internet Explorer, or it may be Mozilla Firefox or some other program. If you have a Mac computer, it could be Safari. These all work in a similar way. There should be an icon on your main computer screen for the browser. Internet Explorer, for example, looks like a large blue letter 'e'. If the icon is not on your main screen, try the Start menu, where other programs are listed.

Home pages

Most browsers are set up so that the first page you come to (known as the 'home page') will allow you to search for things on the Web. This function is known as a 'search engine.' If your home page doesn't allow you to search, it is possible to change it (ask a computer-savvy friend or family member to help you). One of the best known search engines is Google, which is shown in Figure 2.1.

Typing in a known website address

If you know the exact address of a website, then you can type it into the long address box at the top of the page. In Figure 2.1, the address in the box is for the

Reproduced by permission of Google™ © 2009

Figure 2.1

Google home page. If you click in the box it changes colour and you can start typing the address you want. This usually starts with 'www'. Web addresses have 'dots' instead of spaces and must be typed exactly if the browser is to find them.

 Some web pages have long and complicated addresses and it is easy to make a typing mistake.

Searching if you don't know the address

The other way to search is to type some words into the search box. On Google this is in the middle of the page. In other home pages it may be nearer the top. There is usually a search button near the box, which you click when you have finished typing in your search.

As an example, try typing in *who do you think you are bbc*. You don't have to use capital letters and you can use spaces. You can also usually choose whether to search the whole Web or restrict your search to the UK.

Click Search to get a page similar to the one shown in Figure 2.2. (Results can vary, as pages are constantly added, deleted and changed on the Web.)

The search has generated millions of results. Some of these are on BBC web pages as you would expect. Others are on websites that mention this programme. Fortunately, the particular magic of the search engine is that the information you want is usually towards the top of the list so you don't have to search through all the results.

Figure 2.2

Internet searching is developing into something of an art form: if you provide too little information, you get a mass of results that are impossible to evaluate; if you provide too much information, you may miss what you are looking for. As you do more online family history research, your Internet searching techniques will get more sophisticated. This applies both to search engines and to getting the best out of online and other databases.

Understanding the results page

Each result listed has three parts. The first is usually in blue and underlined. This is known as a 'link'. If you move your mouse cursor over this link, the pointer changes to a hand. When you click on the link, you are taken to the relevant web page. Think of the hand as pushing on an open door. Most web pages have dozens of links, either to other pages within the same site or to let you move to other sites.

Links on web pages may not always be in colour or be underlined. Sometimes a picture can be made into a link to another page. The BBC family history website is a good place to look for links like this. The technique is to move your mouse cursor around the page. Whenever the hand appears, this is a link to another web page.

The second part of the result shows you a little of what you will find on the web page. The web address at the end of each result shows you the website/page to which you are being taken.

If you ever want to return to your home page, click on the small icon that looks like a house on one of the menus near the top of your screen. If there is no house icon, look for the word 'Home'.

Marking useful web pages for future reference

When you have found a website that you think will be useful to you in the future, you can save it in a list called Favorites or Bookmarks. In Internet Explorer, look for a menu item called Favorites, or a yellow star and something called Favorites Center. The star opens a list of websites you have saved. If you have a lot of saved sites, you should create folders and organise the websites by category. Clicking on the saved link takes you straight to the website without the need for a search query.

To add a website to the list, you need to click the icon that shows a plus and the star. Other browsers may offer you these options from the Bookmarks menu. You may be asked for a title for the saved site. (Sometimes the title you are offered is too long or not meaningful.) You are also asked in which folder you want to save the site or whether you want to create a new folder.

> If you don't already use Favorites or Bookmarks, it may be worth exploring these now on your computer and setting up a folder ready for your family history websites.

Backing up your findings with a USB memory stick/flash drive

A memory stick, shown in Figure 2.3, is probably one of the most useful (and cheapest) pieces of computer equipment you will need in your research. These small, very portable sticks are 4cm to 8cm long and plug into USB sockets (Universal Serial Bus, for those with a desperate need to know). These sockets are now standard on all computers and can often be found on other pieces of equipment such as printers.

Figure 2.3

The memory stick acts as a detachable filing store. It can keep copies of your search results, your family tree data, scanned documents and photographs, draft copies of your novel, and sound and video files. You can use it to transfer data between computers and provide backups to the material on your main computer. Currently, a flash drive with 4GB (gigabytes) of memory can be bought for as little as £6. The capacity of these drives is getting higher and their cost is getting lower all the time.

These drives are very useful if you are working in an archive that has computer access and where you are allowed to save your search results. This is usually much quicker and cheaper than printing on site. Once you are home, you can transfer the material to your computer and print it as and when you need to. If you don't have a computer at home and want to make a printed copy in the archive, it still makes sense to store this material on a memory stick as well, for possible future use.

Gathering information with a digital camera

As with many things in the world of technology, the cost of digital photography is coming down all time, while the quality of what you can get for your money is going up. A digital camera can be used to take pictures of documents and images that relatives are reluctant to let out of their sight, or which may be too valuable or fragile to entrust to the post. Your research material can be supplemented with pictures of buildings and places that have significance to your family: where people were born, where they worked, even where they went on holiday. Sometimes these can be used for contrast with older photographs, particularly for showing places that have changed over the years.

In record offices and archives, you may be allowed to photograph documents and other materials. You need to check the rules operating in the archive, about whether you can use flash photography and how much material you can photograph. The rules are likely to be tighter for original and fragile material.

Photographing documents and material from books can produce disappointing results if the lighting and angle are not right. It is not always possible to do much about this. Tripods, which come in many different sizes, will give you the stability you need. They can be awkward to manipulate in confined spaces and an annoyance to other researchers. However, if you are planning to copy a large number of photographs or documents in a relative's home, then a tripod will be useful. If you don't have a tripod, try and borrow one (perhaps from someone you know in a U3A or local digital photography group).

The pictures you take with the digital camera are usually stored on a small electronic card. Compact flash, SD or XD are the main types. You can transfer pictures from your camera to your computer using a cable, supplied with the camera.

A less fiddly approach (and one that doesn't drain your camera's battery) is to treat the card like a memory stick and plug it directly into the computer. This requires a suitable slot on the computer. Many printers and computers now have these as standard. If yours doesn't, then for a few pounds you can buy a card reader that will plug into a USB slot and give you all the flexibility you need.

Using photo manipulation software

Most digital cameras come with software that allows you to transfer images to the computer and then catalogue, edit, print and view them. Editing images can involve cropping, rotating, improving contrast and colour and a range of other tasks. You can take pictures of the family today and produce a photograph with the same sepia tints as those of your relatives in the late nineteenth century. What and how much you do with the images you acquire will depend on your interest and the time you have available. Be warned, digital imaging can be as interesting and time-consuming a hobby in its own right as family history.

Using office software – word processing and spreadsheets

Your computer probably includes some form of word processing software, which allows you to create letters and other documents. More sophisticated programs let you include images and tables.

Spreadsheets are the electronic equivalent of bookkeeping/accountancy pages. Although many people think of them mainly for keeping track of finances and other figure-related work, they are excellent for recording your research results. You see how this works later in Chapter 9.

You can buy suites of office software if they are not already included in your computer package. You might want to investigate the free programs available at **www.openoffice.org.** These have most of the features you expect to see in the much more expensive commercial products available. More importantly, they are compatible with all these major products. This allows you to prepare and send documents to people who use other packages, and also to receive and open material that others send you.

29

Using family history software

This will be at the heart of your family research and is covered in detail in Chapter 10. Briefly, these programs allow you to enter information about individuals and link them to their parents and/or children, creating and growing your family tree. Information can be added, deleted or edited at any time. Their most important benefit is that the information needs to be added only once. A wide variety of reports can be produced almost instantly for inclusion in books, presentations and websites, and for sending to family members.

As with other software, there are both commercial and free programs available to download. Most of the programs now used are compatible with each other; that is, you can export the information from one program to another. This means that you don't have to re-key all your data if you decide that you want to upgrade to a program with more or different features and reports.

For more detailed information on choosing, installing and using hardware and software, you might want to look at *Computing for the Older and Wiser* by Adrian Arnold (2008, John Wiley & Sons Ltd, ISBN 9780470770993).

Summary

- Interview older relatives before doing anything else.

- Collect photos and family documents of all kinds.

- Minimum technology requirements: computer, multifunction printer, broadband Internet access and a USB memory stick/flash drive.

- Your local library can be a good starting point for both learning how to find your way round the Internet and accessing family history databases.

Brain Training

1. Which of the following is *not* an Internet browser?

a) Excel

b) Internet Explorer

c) Mozilla Firefox

d) Safari

2. Who provides you with Internet access on your home computer?

a) BBC

b) ISP

c) LDS

d) USB

3. Where can you save web pages for future reference?

a) Favorites

b) Search engine

c) Spreadsheet

d) Word processor

4. What is another name for a USB memory stick?

a) CD drive

b) DVD drive

c) Flash drive

d) Hard drive

5. What kind of office software is best for handling/presenting figures and research results?

a) Family history program

b) Photo manipulation software

c) Spreadsheet

d) Word processor

Answers

Q1 – a   **Q2** – b   **Q3** – a   **Q4** – c

Q5 – c

PART II
Basic Genealogy

It's the only photo I can find of my Great Uncle Bill.

The facts of life – birth, marriage and death

3

Equipment needed: Information about family births, marriages and deaths you wish to explore in more detail; computer and Internet access.

Skills needed: Searching a database so that you get neither too much nor too little information; thinking of alternative ways to search if initial results don't find your relatives.

The basic building blocks of family history are records of life events such as births, marriages and deaths. These are recorded locally and then data is collated into national records, which are available to search. Individuals are issued with a certificate of the event at the time it is recorded. Various projects now exist to make the certificate indexes available online.

Vital records in England and Wales

It is worth remembering that, in England and Wales, registration of our main life events – birth, marriage and death – by the civil authorities was only introduced in July 1837. Even then, it was not compulsory until 1874. Prior to 1837, these 'vital' records, as they are sometimes known, were kept by the church when baptisms, marriages and burials took place. Individual parishes kept their own records and searching can be difficult and time-consuming if you don't know where an ancestor was living at the time a particular life event occurred.

> The best way to find the information is to start as close to yourself as possible and work back in time.

Use what you already know to create the foundations of the tree. Set up your working hypothesis for each piece of information you are researching and then look at a variety of sources to confirm or reject your supposition. You may just require further evidence, of course. As each piece of the jigsaw begins to fall into place, you get a better idea of the bigger picture. There may always be some gaps. Your ancestors didn't know that you would want to do this research. If they didn't register a life event, there's no point in getting cross with them. Presumably they had their reasons.

You need to look briefly at what information you can expect to find in these records and then see what is available online to help your research. The original records, created locally at register offices, were compiled into national registers. Having a national system makes searching much easier since you don't need to know exactly where someone was born, married or died.

The indexes to these registers were compiled each quarter – March, June, September and December – for each year. If you find a reference to September 1894, it means the event probably took place at any time from 1 July until 30 September 1894. Marriages will be recorded very close to the event but there has always been some leeway with the registration of a birth so it may be wise to look in the following quarter as well. In some cases, this means looking in the next year. From 1984, entries are indexed by year and give the month in which the event was registered.

Up to December 1983, the index will show the following:

- the name of the person
- the district in which registration took place
- the volume and page numbers (which act as a reference).

You need all this information if you want to order certificates. From December 1983, there will be a register reference number.

Other information in the indexes can also help your research:

- From September 1911, the birth index shows the maiden name of the mother. This is very useful if you want to look up other children in the family born after 1911 as you now have two surnames to use in your search.

- From March 1912, the marriage index shows the surname of the new spouse. Prior to this, you have to know the spouse's name and search for both partners separately in the index, confirming that the district, page and volume numbers are the same. The alternative is to buy the certificate based on one name only and hope that it is the right marriage.

- Death indexes from March 1866 to 1969 show the deceased's age at death. From June 1969, the deceased's date of birth is shown.

> It is worth remembering that the person registering the death may not necessarily have known the age or date of birth of the deceased and might just have guessed.

This is the only information obtainable from the indexes. Anything else will require you to purchase the certificate. These can be ordered from the GRO (General Register Office) by post, telephone or online. If you can supply the index reference, the current cost of a certificate is £7. For information about how to buy certificates, go to the Directgov website at **www.direct.gov.uk/ en/Governmentcitizensandrights** and look at the section on Registering life events.

Using online resources

Online resources for birth, marriage and death records are of two kinds. Some sites have scanned copies of the index pages, which you can view to find your relatives. Other projects take the information in the index pages and create a searchable database. This is usually much more helpful for the researcher, particularly if you have only minimum information about the person you are researching and the dates of their life events.

Using FreeBMD

FreeBMD at **www.freebmd.org.uk** is a volunteer project that takes the information from the printed indexes of English and Welsh records and creates a searchable online database. Most of the records from the nineteenth and early twentieth centuries have been transcribed. More are being added all the time. Before you do your first searches, take some time to read the site's information page, which gives current statistics and coverage (see Figure 3.1).

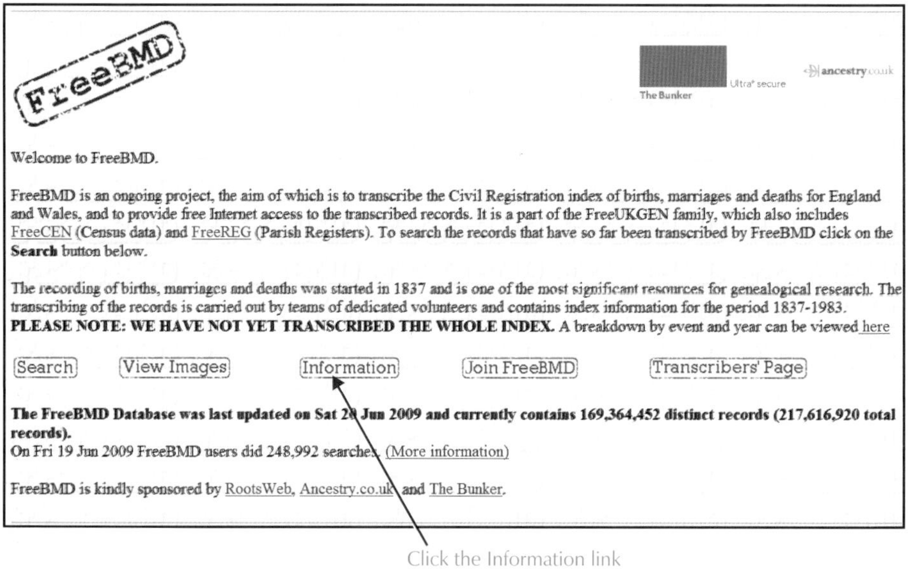

Click the Information link

Reproduced by permission of FreeBMD®

Figure 3.1

When you search using this and other databases, you need to think creatively if your search does not seem to bring up the results you were expecting. Worse still, it may find nothing. You saw earlier how important it is to construct a search (sometimes known as a query) that gives a balance between no results and millions of results.

The usual rule is that 'less is more'. If someone was given three forenames at birth, they may not necessarily use them all when getting married. The index may show initials instead of a middle name. The person may use a middle name in place of their original first name.

> ⚠ Spelling may not be as intended or as subsequently used. This may be an error on the part of the informant or the registrar.

You should therefore start with the minimum of information consistent with getting at least one result. If there are too many results, start adding one piece of information at a time to reduce the possibilities.

You have already extracted as much information as possible from the Fischer/ Smith 1890 marriage certificate. In practice, therefore, you wouldn't need to search for the reference on FreeBMD. However, since you have the data, it would make a good example to try out the search techniques (see Figure 3.2).

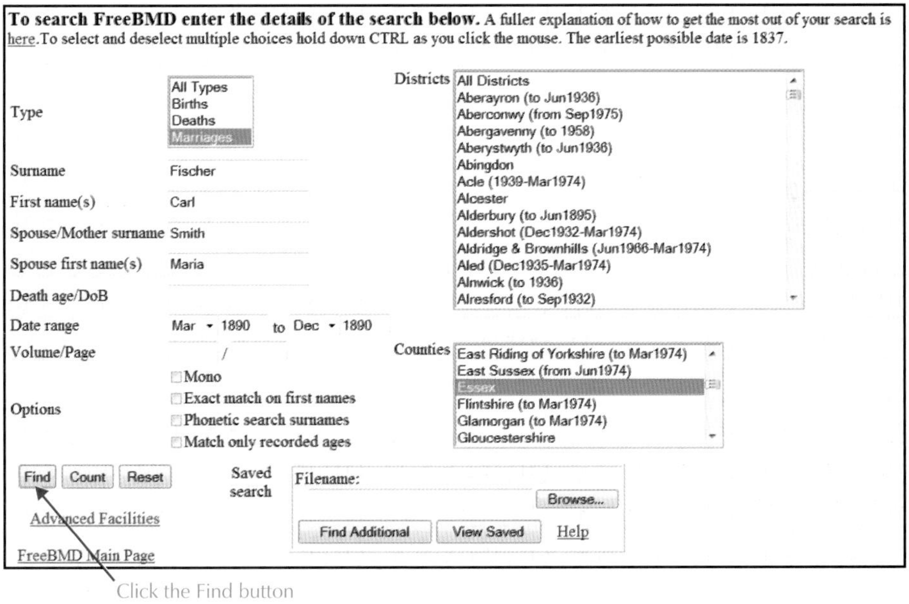

Click the Find button

Reproduced by permission of FreeBMD®

Figure 3.2

The search query shown in Figure 3.2 gives all the data you have on this couple and their marriage. In most cases, you won't be in such a fortunate position with your own family. Be careful to put the surname and first names in the correct boxes. It is easy to get these the wrong way round if you are thinking of the person's full name. The bride is Maria Smith but you have to remember to enter her as *Smith* and then *Maria*. (This will vary according to the website you are searching.) When you have entered the information you know, click Find. In this case, as shown in Figure 3.3, you only get one result – one you know will be correct.

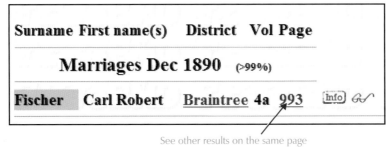

Surname	First name(s)	District	Vol	Page	
Marriages Dec 1890 (>99%)					
Fischer	Carl Robert	Braintree	4a	993	Info

See other results on the same page

Figure 3.3

Until the twentieth century, religious prohibitions prevented the marriage of people already related through marriage though not by blood, such as a father-in-law with his deceased son's wife or a woman with her deceased husband's brother.

This database is very useful in that it allows you to see other entries for that year and quarter with the same district, volume and page number. To see the others on the page, click on the page number link. This should give you the name of the spouse. In a large area, there may be several entries on the same page. You can eliminate those of the wrong gender, leaving yourself with a number of possibilities that you can then confirm through other sources, such as the next census following a marriage. You may already have some idea of the spouse's forename or surname and this will help you assess the results. The result will look like Figure 3.4.

Surname	First name(s)	District	Vol	Page		
Marriages Dec 1890 (>99%)						
Bishop	James	Braintree	4a	993	info	👓
Fischer	Carl Robert	Braintree	4a	993	info	👓
Smith	Maria	Braintree	4a	993	info	👓
Smith	Maria	Braintree	4a	993	info	👓
Taylor	Eliza Jane	Braintree	4a	993	info	👓
Tyler	Emma Eliza	Braintree	4a	993	info	👓

Reproduced by permission of FreeBMD®

Figure 3.4

You will see that Maria's name is entered twice. Sometimes this is because a name appeared twice in the register for some reason. It may also show that this entry has been keyed in by more than one volunteer. Click the pair of glasses at the end of each line to see entry information about the transcription. This gives a code for each volunteer transcriber. You can scroll (move) down the web page and find a link to an image of the original index page used for the transcription. If you are planning to buy a certificate, you may want to check this against the transcription, as it is possible for errors to occur.

What you will notice, if you look at the original, is what a boon it is to be able to search a database. Most people researching their family history before 2000 had to use microfilm/fiche of the registers or search through the bound volumes at the General Register Office. The amount of time that you can save thanks to these databases is incalculable.

If you go back to the original result page, you will see that the registration district is shown as Braintree. It is possible to click on the name of the district and get information about the places it includes. This is helpful where parish and registration boundaries have been redrawn over the years. If you follow up on the Braintree link, you can see that Feering was originally in the Witham registration district.

If you type the words *witham registration district* into a search engine such as Google, you should get a link to a list of townships and parishes close to Feering.

It can be important to know the names of these places when you are trying to establish whether someone could be a member of your family. You may find that John Smith was not born in Feering but, if Kelvedon or Great Braxted are shown as places where he was born or lived at some stage, you can add another tick to your list of confirming evidence.

Another facility on the FreeBMD site is the ability to save a search onto your computer and then retrieve it later. Carry out the search and then choose the Save Search option next to the Query buttons, as shown in Figure 3.5.

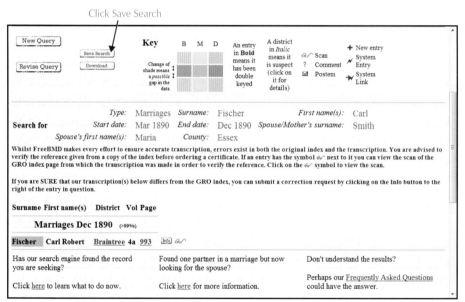

Reproduced by permission of FreeBMD®

Figure 3.5

The database will offer you a numeric file name. You might want to change this to something more intelligible to the average human, such as *Fischer_Smith 1890 marriage*. If your saved search contains many results, it can be loaded again using the Saved Search option at the bottom of the search page. You will need to use the Browse button to find the saved file in your folder/file system, as shown in Figure 3.6.

Date range	Mar ▾	to Dec ▾		
Volume/Page		/	Counties	All Counties

Reproduced by permission of FreeBMD®

Figure 3.6

As well as viewing the results of your original search, you can also revise the search.

> Another option is to find additional results based on your original criteria. This is useful when you know that the record dates from your first search have not yet been fully transcribed. Over time, as more records are indexed and added to the database, you can add them to your search and then resave the amended results for later use.

Using online resources: other BMD indexes

There are a number of other websites where birth, marriage and death records can be searched. Some of them make use of the work already done on the FreeBMD site. Others allow you to browse the index pages of the registers, often for a fee in the form of a subscription or credits that you can buy online. Typically you type in a surname and a year and you then get links to the pages in each quarter where the names might appear. Figure 3.7 shows an example of such results from the Ancestry website based on a marriage for Carl Fischer in 1890.

It is rather like searching in a telephone directory. Each page has an alphabetical listing showing the range from the first name to the last. The problem is that there is no guarantee that your relative will appear on that page. If you know the year but not the month of an event then you have to search through each of the four

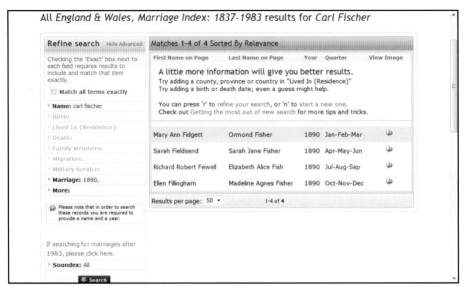

All England & Wales, Marriage Index: 1837-1983 results for Carl Fischer

Refine search Hide Advanced

Matches 1-4 of 4 Sorted By Relevance

Checking the 'Exact' box next to each field requires results to include and match that item exactly.

☐ Match all terms exactly

‣ **Name:** carl fischer
‣ Birth:
‣ Lived In (Residence):
‣ Death:
‣ Family Members:
‣ Migration:
‣ Military Service:
‣ **Marriage:** 1890,
‣ **More:**

Please note that in order to search these records you are required to provide a name and a year.

If searching for marriages after 1983, please click here.

‣ **Soundex:** All

⚡ Search

First Name on Page	Last Name on Page	Year	Quarter	View Image

A little more information will give you better results.
Try adding a county, province or country in "Lived In (Residence)"
Try adding a birth or death date; even a guess might help.

You can press 'r' to refine your search, or 'n' to start a new one.
Check out Getting the most out of new search for more tips and tricks.

First Name on Page	Last Name on Page	Year	Quarter	View Image
Mary Ann Fidgett	Ormond Fisher	1890	Jan-Feb-Mar	🔎
Sarah Fieldsend	Sarah Jane Fisher	1890	Apr-May-Jun	🔎
Richard Robert Fewell	Elizabeth Alice Fish	1890	Jul-Aug-Sep	🔎
Ellen Fillingham	Madeline Agnes Fisher	1890	Oct-Nov-Dec	🔎

Results per page: 50 ▾   1-4 of 4

Figure 3.7

quarters (with possibly one quarter from the following year in case the event was registered after 31 December).

If you don't know the exact year, you need to search through each quarter of each year, systematically. You can, of course, narrow down the search by trying to work out when an event took place, using other sources and guesswork. For example, if you had no way of looking at a single year for the birth of Carl Fischer, you would need to start in 1869 and work backwards. (If you remember, Carl must have been at least 21 in 1890 at the time of his marriage, which gives a possible last year for his birth of 1869.)

If you do have to use this method, it is important to keep track of the years and quarters you have searched, particularly if you are paying to view these pages. You can draw up a simple chart showing each year divided into four quarters like the one shown in Figure 3.8.

Many of the CDs that accompany genealogical magazines have a section with forms for such purposes, which you can print out and use. You can also make a table using a spreadsheet or a word processor.

REGISTRATION INDEX SEARCH SHEET

Name: | Event: Birth or Marriage or Death

YEAR
Mar | Jun
Sep | Dec

YEAR
Mar | Jun
Sep | Dec

YEAR
Mar | Jun
Sep | Dec

YEAR
Mar | Jun
Sep | Dec

YEAR
Mar | Jun
Sep | Dec

YEAR
Mar | Jun
Sep | Dec

YEAR
Mar | Jun
Sep | Dec

YEAR
Mar | Jun
Sep | Dec

YEAR
Mar | Jun
Sep | Dec

YEAR
Mar | Jun
Sep | Dec

YEAR
Mar | Jun
Sep | Dec

YEAR
Mar | Jun
Sep | Dec

YEAR
Mar | Jun
Sep | Dec

YEAR
Mar | Jun
Sep | Dec

YEAR
Mar | Jun
Sep | Dec

Search results:
    Name: _____

Registration district: _____
Vol: _____

Spouse/mother: _____

Page number: _____

Figure 3.8

For an overview and links to all the main sites providing access to transcriptions of birth, marriage and death records, look at **www.ukbmd.org.uk**. The home page, shown in Figure 3.9, explains what each site contains and outlines the methodology used to create the indexes.

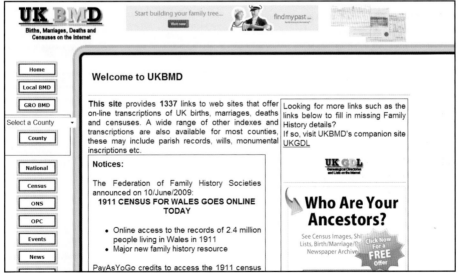

UKBMD is part of the British Genealogy Network Copyright and Database right Â © 2009 I. & S. Hartas

Figure 3.9

Obtaining Scottish records

Civil registration began in Scotland in 1855. As in England and Wales, events before this time can be found in parish records. Scottish records contain more information than those for England and Wales. The most important additional pieces of information for the family historian are:

- births: where and when the child's parents were married
- marriages: names of both sets of parents, including the mothers' maiden names
- deaths: names of the deceased's parents.

To search for your Scottish ancestors online, go to the ScotlandsPeople website at **www.scotlandspeople.gov.uk**, shown in Figure 3.10. You need to register to make full use of the site. Registration is free. You can then log in with your username and password to start searching.

Reproduced by permission of © Crown copyright and copyright brightsolid ltd

Figure 3.10

For births, marriages and deaths, you can enter details in a similar way to the FreeBMD site. You are then told how many results were found and how many index pages this covers. A page holds up to 25 results. You need to buy and use credits to view these pages. One credit costs 20p but you must purchase a minimum of 30 credits, which are valid for 90 consecutive days. If the index of names covers more than one page, you have to pay one credit to view each page. It therefore makes sense to try to narrow down your search at this stage, particularly if the surname is a common one.

Once you have narrowed down your search, you can pay five credits (£1) to download and view all the details from the register. This compares favourably with the cost of ordering certificates for events in England and Wales. You can save and print out the images. You can also return at any time to searches and images you have previously paid for.

In common with many such sites, there is a very comprehensive frequently asked questions (FAQ) section. This covers the cost of records, what you get for your payment and what information you can expect to find in these documents.

> Another site that allows researchers to exchange data extracted from primary (original) sources is Scotland BDM Exchange at **www.sctbdm.com.**

Obtaining Irish records

Full civil registration began in Ireland in 1864. Prior to this (from 1845), only non-Catholic marriages were registered.

The General Register Office in Dublin (**www.groireland.ie**) holds indexes and microfilm copies of the registers for all 32 counties up to 1921, and 26 counties from 1921. The website has comprehensive coverage of the history of civil registration, as well as information about how the records can be searched.

The General Register Office in Belfast (**www.groni.gov.uk**) has BMD indexes from 1864 (1845 in the case of non-Catholic marriages). It holds birth and death registers for this period and marriage records from 1922. It is possible to search the computerised indexes but not online. You would need to carry out a paid search in the public search room. For an additional fee, you can be assisted in your search by a member of staff. Details are available on the website.

If you wish to search the records yourself, this can also be done using the microfilms available through FamilySearch (**www.familysearch.org**). This source, which is shown in Figure 3.11, is covered in more detail in Chapter 5.

Title Details	FAMILY HISTORY LIBRARY CATALOG	THE CHURCH OF JESUS CHRIST OF LATTER-DAY SAINTS
		View Film Notes
Title	Marriage records, 1845-1870, with indexes to marriages, 1845-1921, in the General Registry Office of Ireland	
Authors	Ireland. General Register Office (Main Author)	
Notes	Microfilm of original records in Custom House, Dublin.	
Subjects	Ireland - Civil registration Ireland - Civil registration - Indexes	
Format	Manuscript (On Film)	
Language	English	
Publication	Salt Lake City, Utah : Filmed by the Genealogical Society of Utah, 1953	
Physical	334 microfilm reels ; 35 mm.	

For a printable version of this record click here then click your browser's **Print** button.

© 2002 Intellectual Reserve, Inc. All rights reserved.

FAMILYSEARCH   Home   Help

Figure 3.11

Local genealogical and family history groups may have produced indexes of records from their own particular area(s) of interest. Given that there is currently no equivalent of FreeBMD or ScotlandsPeople for records from Ireland, you should investigate such groups and see what they have available.

Research tasks: BMD for Fischer/Smith family

To complete this section on birth, marriage and death records, there are two tasks relating to the Fischer/Smith family that can be undertaken using the FreeBMD website. For each result that you find, give some thought to how sure you are that this is the correct person and what other information you might need to find to confirm your results.

continued

Maria Smith – birth

1. Either on your own computer or in your local library, go to the following website **www.freebmd.org.uk.**

2. Click the Search button.

3. Select a birth search. Enter *Maria Smith* in the correct boxes, put in a date range from Mar 1860 to Dec 1869 and choose Essex from the dropdown counties list. (You could put in a greater range of years but start from a position that she was married between the ages of 21 and 30. If this doesn't work, you can always widen the search.)

4. Click Count which is next to the Find button towards the bottom left of the window. This tells you how many records have been found that match your search criteria. If the number is too great, you may wish to refine your search.

5. In this case, there are not too many records so you can scan the list looking for the best match(es). Click Find to display the list.

6. Working back from the bottom of the list (ie the latest date), decide which Maria Smith might bear closer investigation (see the end of this chapter for possible answers).

7. You may decide to go back to the search page and save your results. If you eventually find that you have chosen the wrong Maria Smith, then you can review the list and start again.

Carl Robert Fischer – birth

1. Follow the same procedure for Carl as you did for Maria. You can skip the Count results as Fischer is much less common than Smith.

2. If you get no results with 'Carl Robert', try Carl on its own.

3. If you still get no results, try changing Essex to 'All Counties'. (There was a question earlier about whether Carl came from the same place as his bride.)

4. If this doesn't work, you'll need to widen the search. Remove his forename and just search for all Fischer births in that time period. (If you're lucky, you might even find some possible brothers or sisters.)

5. Once your search gives you a result list, review it and then save it.

6. Which entry is a strong candidate to be Carl Robert Fischer? What are the reasons for your choice?

Research tasks: BMD for your family

Taking the couple from your own family whose marriage certificate you looked at in Chapter 1, try to apply the same searching techniques. If the certificate is of a family who married in the mid to late twentieth century, their births may not yet be within the indexed range of FreeBMD. If so, try to find the marriage of your parents or grandparents. The chances are that you will know the maiden name of your mother and perhaps your grandmother. Work out a likely starting year for the search based on what you already know; for example, start working backwards from a possible birth date for the oldest child in the family. Record your assumptions and results.

Research tasks – Fischer/Smith suggested answers

Maria Smith (birth) – Dec 1867 Witham 4a 310. Witham was the district that was later incorporated into Braintree. If you find Maria in other records, such as censuses, with a birth year of 1867, then there is a strong possibility that this is the correct person.

Carl Robert Fischer (birth) – Mar 1866 Marylebone 1a 560. The index entry is for Karl R Fischer. There was a suggestion that the family could be of German origin and the alternative spelling of Karl might support this. The second initial is consistent and it explains why you found nothing when you included the name Robert in your search. There is an earlier record for a Friederich Carl Fischer in 1861, also in Marylebone. There was a possibility of a brother called Frederick who was a witness at the Feering marriage.

None of the above provides conclusive proof that you have found the birth records for this married couple. However, it shows how you can use the online resources to add to information you have extracted from other sources and begin to build up a convincing amount of evidence around the identity of family members. You'll review this evidence later.

Summary

- Birth, marriage and death records (BMD) are the building blocks of family history.

- Online record indexes exist and are growing.

- FreeBMD is creating searchable databases from the original paper indexes.

- It is not necessary to buy large quantities of certificates.

- Squeeze the maximum information from the data and documents you've got.

- Speculate and ask less obvious questions about the data.

Brain Training

1. If someone was born on 30 June 1884, in which quarter are you most likely to find their birth registered?

a) June 1884

b) September 1884

c) December 1884

d) March 1885

2. What additional piece of information is shown on the birth indexes from 1911?

a) Actual date of birth

b) Father's name

c) Mother's age

d) Mother's maiden name

3. In what year did civil registration begin in Scotland?

a) 1837

b) 1855

c) 1864

d) 1874

4. What do the letters GRO stand for?

a) General Record Office

b) General Register Office

c) Government Record Office

d) Government Register Office

5. When did the death indexes start to include the date of birth of the deceased?

a) 1874

b) 1912

c) 1969

d) 1983

Answers

Q1 – b   **Q2** – d   **Q3** – b   **Q4** – b

Q5 – c

Counting the people – census records

4

Equipment needed: Computer and Internet access to websites that have census data (Ancestry, FamilySearch, 1911census).

Skills needed: Relating earlier research on birth, marriage and death records to census returns to expand the information you hold on family members.

Census records provide a useful complement to your initial work on birth, marriage and death records. You are usually able to look at whole families instead of just individuals and it often helps you to push your research back a whole generation.

Once you have looked at these records, it is worth taking some time to review the information you have gathered from both BMD and census sources to look at how you can use it to ask further questions and keep your research active.

How the census can help family historians

While most family historians can find copies of birth, marriage and death records at home, none has similar direct access to the census returns filled in by their ancestors. The census has always been a tool by which governments assess the population for which they are responsible, a form of human stocktaking. Originally it was a means of working out who should pay tax and how much could be collected. It was also used to determine how big an army could be raised in times of emergency. In more recent times, it has allowed governments to plan future requirements for education, health and other services and to assess the success or otherwise of policies they have implemented.

For those researching family history, the census gives a much more complete record of families at a particular point in time. It can provide confirmation of research information gleaned from birth, marriage and death records. If you suspect, for example, that Frederick Fischer, in the case study family, has two sons, Frederick and Carl, then you may be able to confirm this from a census record, particularly if the ages appear to tally.

Other family members, such as grandparents, nieces or in-laws, may be living in the same house. This can sometimes provide additional surnames and the basis for research into other branches of the family tree. By working back through the census in the same way you have started to work back through civil registration records, you can combine two very powerful research tools.

What census records show

National censuses in England and Wales have been taken every ten years since 1801. During the Second World War (1941), only small areas were covered. For genealogists, the censuses before 1841 don't record personal information since the government was only concerned with counting the people. From 1841, more data was collected on individuals. Later censuses show not only the names of individuals and information about age, marital status, place of birth and occupation but also the relationship of an individual to the head of household.

The census usually took place in late March or early April (census night in 1841 was 6 June). The information was collected and recorded by enumerators who were given a district to cover. This might have been a number of streets in a large town or a whole village in a rural area. To find someone on the census, you need to know where they were living, since the records were recorded on a street by street, house by house, family by family basis.

Census information, as with many personal records, is subject to a 100-year closure period. When I first started my research in 1994, I couldn't understand why everyone was so excited about the 1891 census. On asking, I was told that this was the most recent one to be released (on 1 January 1992) and that the next wouldn't be available until 1 January 2002.

The censuses were gradually made available on microfilm and microfiche and many family history societies created indexes of the data for their area, which they then published in book, fiche or CD formats. These were of great help to other researchers, who did not need to trawl through all the records themselves in order to find a reference to their ancestors. It still required some knowledge of where a person was living, however, so that you could access the correct index. In urban areas, the problem was compounded by the large numbers involved and the reality that people often moved house as their family and financial circumstances changed.

What has made the census a more accessible and useable source is the creation of online indexes of names and sometimes streets. This has allowed the whole country to be searched at one time. This is helpful if you are unsure where an ancestor lived.

One of the first censuses to get this global coverage was the 1881 census, transcribed by the LDS and issued as a multi-part CD package. It is now available online, both on the LDS FamilySearch website and through sites such as Ancestry.

> The 1901 census was the first to be released from the beginning in an online form. Unfortunately, it coincided with a significant increase in computer ownership, broadband access, an interest in family history and the New Year bank holiday. The system was overwhelmed by the numbers trying to access it and promptly collapsed. No one had predicted how popular it would be to try to see where grandma and grandpa were living in 1901.

The most recent census to be made available for England and Wales is 1911, released early following a challenge under the Freedom of Information Act. Some sensitive information remains closed until 2012 but the material available is proving very helpful to researchers. The records are in the householder's handwriting, rather than the enumerator's, and the census shows how long a couple had been married. The number of children born and the number surviving were also recorded. This allows you to know if a child has died since the last census and how many children you should expect to find in this census (even if they are no longer living at home).

Detailed information on the data collected in each census can be found at the National Archives. Go to **www.nationalarchives.gov.uk** and click *Research guides A - Z*. Select C and scroll down to the guide to Census Returns.

Understanding transcriptions and original records

When researching online, it can be frustrating when you know that someone was living in a particular place or was born at a particular time and yet you still can't find them. There are various reasons for this, which you need to understand if you want to work round the problem and maximise your chance of success.

- **Using different names**: you saw this when trying to find a birth record for Carl Fischer. In a census, someone may give the name by which they are commonly known rather than the one they were given at birth.

- **Spelling mistakes can occur**: your ancestor may have a foreign name or one where there is more than one accepted spelling. If you think how often your own name is written incorrectly, then you have a better appreciation of how mistakes could occur in periods when levels of literacy were low.

- **Understanding the difference between primary and secondary sources:** an original document is created (which may or may not have errors in it). The data is copied for another purpose, for example, local registers sent to the national system. The national indexes for births, marriages and deaths are therefore not a primary source. To find this you need to go to the original local records. Whenever copying or transcribing takes place, there is the possibility that errors are introduced.

- **Large-scale transcription can result in errors:** the demand for online access has placed financial and time pressures on government agencies responsible for releasing data and also on the organisations partnering them. Although systems of checking are in place, errors can result where the transcriber is not familiar with local place names or where the handwriting is difficult to read. On the 1911 census, my family name of Fifer was transcribed in one instance as Tifer because a handwritten capital T looks similar to a handwritten F. In the same way, the middle f in another Fifer family was read as b giving Fiber.

There are a number of ways around this problem:

- The 'less is more' approach where you reduce the amount you include in a search and then build it up if you get too many results.

If you can't find surnames, try searching for first names together with a place of birth.

- In the census, use the name of another family member if you have other information about them, such as their age.
- Use wildcards in your searching if this is allowed. A wildcard lets you put a * to represent any number of missing letters. You can use a ? to represent a single missing letter.
- Some databases allow you to use Soundex searching, which gives you names that sound similar but may not be spelled in the same way.
- Other databases ask if you want variants of a name; this depends on how sophisticated the database is but it may, for example, give you Liz, Lizzie and Eliza for Elizabeth.

The 1881 census – free, online and comprehensive

The 1881 census is a good place to start an exploration of census resources as it is free, online and the transcription is well presented. Furthermore, you don't have to have a subscription or register for anything if you use the FamilySearch website.

You might think that it would be more logical to look at 1911, which is the most recently available census. Earlier advice did say that you should always work backwards in time. However, look at this trip around 1881 as dipping your toe into the water of census research, and you can investigate 1911 afterwards. This will give you points of comparison in terms of search strategies, which you can then apply to other censuses.

How to access the 1881 census

The following procedure lets you access the 1881 census at no charge.

1. Go to **www.familysearch.org**.
2. On the left of the page next to the Search button click Advanced Search.
3. In the panel on the left-hand side click 'Census'.
4. You are now offered a choice of three censuses: 1880 US, 1881 British Isles and 1881 Canada.
5. The census box shows All by default. Click on the small black arrow next to the word All (this is called a dropdown menu).
6. Select the 1881 British Isles census, as shown in Figure 4.1.

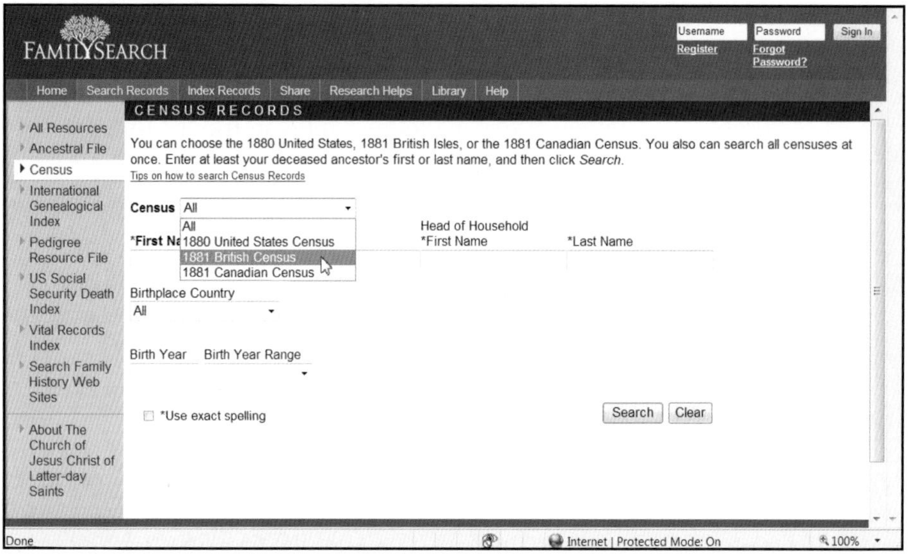

Reproduced by permission of © 2008 Intellectual Reserve, Inc.

Figure 4.1

Searching the 1881 census

This is where the fun starts. It's often a good idea to try out a census by searching first for someone famous. Of course, you may have famous (or even infamous) people in your family tree, in which case your research is going to be a whole lot easier than it is for the rest of us.

Try looking for Florence Nightingale on the census. You can easily find out her date and place of birth through an Internet search and this will give you information to put in the search query.

If you just enter *Florence Nightingale* and click Search, you get 129 results. The dates of birth of nearly all these Florences are after the Crimean War. From a research point of view, this would allow you to eliminate them as being too young. From the standpoint of the social historian, it is interesting to see how influential she was, to the point where girls with the surname Nightingale were being called Florence in her honour.

From the Internet, you find that she was born in May 1820 in Italy (hence her given name). If you now return to the search page, you can use the dropdown menu for Birthplace Country to select Italy and then click Search. As with the Fischer marriage search on FreeBMD, putting in the right data allows you to come up with what is very probably the correct result (see Figure 4.2).

Results for: Florence Nightingale, Birth, Italy
Census: 1881 British Census
Exact Spelling: Off

1881 British Census - 1

Select records to download - (50 maximum)

☐ **1.** Florence NIGHTINGALE - 1881 British Census / Middlesex
   Head   Gender: Female   Birth: <1821> British Subject, Italy

Figure 4.2

Before clicking on the name to take you to the individual record, check the data. The place of birth corresponds but the year of birth shows 1821 rather than 1820. This often happens in a census search and you need to understand why. In the census, individuals were asked for their age, not their date of birth. Florence was born in May 1820. On census night (3rd April 1881), she was 60 and wouldn't be 61 until May of that year (and why admit to being older than you really are). When censuses are transcribed, a year of birth is worked out by taking the given age away from the census year. In this case it makes the birth year 1821. If you do get a date that doesn't correspond exactly with a date you know from other sources, this may be the reason.

You can now find out more about Miss Nightingale's household by clicking her name and opening her transcribed census record, as shown in Figure 4.3.

FAMILYSEARCH

| Username | Password | Sign In |

Register   Forgot Password?

Home   Search Records   Index Records   Share   Research Helps   Library   Help

Individual Record   1881 British Census

Search results | Download   Next
                                                                         Individual

Florence NIGHTINGALE   Household
Female

Other Information:
Birth Year   <1821>
Birthplace   British Subject, Italy
Age   60
Occupation   Directress Of Nightingale Fund For Training Hospital Nurses
Marital Status   U <Unmarried>
Head of Household   Florence NIGHTINGALE
Relation   Head
Disability

Source Information:
Dwelling   10 South Street
Census Place   London, Middlesex, England
Family History Library Film 1341022
Public Records Office Reference RG11
Piece / Folio   0096 / 38
Page Number   29

Figure 4.3

All the information here confirms that this is the person you have been looking for. Her address is given, together with the reference, folio and page numbers that would allow you to look for the original census record, if you wanted to check it against this transcription. She is shown as the head of household and any other people in that same household will be designated by their relationship to her. This may be a family or servant relationship. Other 'relationships' in the census context may be 'visitor' or 'boarder.' You will find others in the course of your research.

On the right side of the screen, you have two possibilities. You can either look at the individual record for the next person listed or you can view the entire household. Click Household to view the record shown in Figure 4.4.

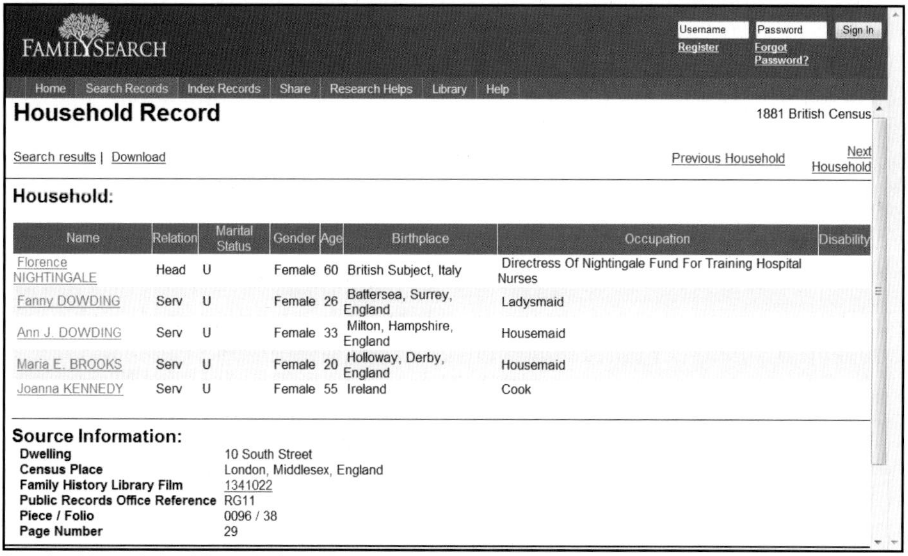

Figure 4.4

You can see that Miss Nightingale is living with four servants, two of whom have the same name, Dowding, and may be sisters or cousins. To see the individual record of any of the servants, click their names. (They are underlined, showing that they are likely to be links to other pages.)

As you are now viewing a household record, the database allows you to look at both the previous and next households in the census. This lets you see the kind of area in which the family or individual is living.

Next door to the Nightingale household, at 11 South Street, is the Secretary to the Speaker (presumably of the House of Commons). If you look at the following household, you will see that the Earl of Lucan is living at number 12. As you might expect, this is a prosperous area.

On this or other censuses, you may find a family where family members are missing. There could be a number of reasons:

- The person may have been visiting another household, in which case they will be recorded there. Remember, the census shows who was in a household on census night, not who lived there normally.

- A child may have been living with other relatives to allow parents to work. This is possible if the parent was in domestic service.

- A child might have been at a boarding school.

- A young person might have been in domestic service.

- A man could have been in the army or navy, either in the UK or serving overseas.

- Someone shown on a previous census may have died.

- The missing person may have been travelling abroad.

- A son or daughter may have got married and moved to their own household.

- The person may have been in hospital, in prison or in the workhouse.

Institutions, whether schools, workhouses, prisons, barracks or hospitals, will all have their own census entries.

Try looking for Benjamin Disraeli. I couldn't find him listed but I know he didn't die until two weeks after this census was taken. Wikipedia, the online encyclopaedia, reminded me that he was the Earl of Beaconsfield. I put Beaconsfield as the surname and Earl as the forename. A result! It looks from the household record as if he were living on his own but you might find it interesting to look at the records for the next two households, which show a large number of domestic staff, presumably his.

Why not go further afield and check out the 1880 US census? Look for Rutherford B Hayes with a birth date of 1823. You should get two results. Look at the one for the District of Columbia.

If your relatives were in any way in the public eye (whether for good or bad reasons), there may be biographical material available that can help your research. Most family historians will probably have to work harder than this to find their families but everyone understands the 'buzz' that comes from locating someone in the census or other records.

Forward to the past – the 1911 census

The early release of the 1911 census and the additional information it contains were outlined earlier. To transcribe the census, The National Archives (TNA) chose as a partner findmypast.com (previously known as 1837.com). There is a specific website for the 1911 census at **www.1911census.co.uk**.

Searching is free on the site. If you find records that you want to view in detail, you have two options, both of which you will need to pay for:

- view a transcription of the census data (the cheaper option)
- view the original census return, handwritten by someone in your family (the more expensive option).

Paying to view census images and data

The system is similar to that used on the ScotlandsPeople website (see Chapter 3). You buy a block of credits and then use 10 of them to view a transcription or 30 to view the original document. The minimum block you can purchase costs £6.95, which gives you 60 credits (12p per credit). Buying more can reduce the cost per credit to 8p.

This means that it currently costs between 83p and £1.16 to view the transcription. The original census image costs between £2.50 and £3.48 to view.

> Credits have a shelf-life of 90 days for the smaller packages and up to a year for larger blocks. When you buy additional credits, any unused credits in your account are 'reset' to the new expiry date.

Credits can also be used on the main findmypast.com website. A subscription service is now also available for the census website.

Once you have paid to view the images, they are saved and can be viewed and printed at any time without additional payment.

The costs associated with family history were considered earlier. The need to purchase credits and subscriptions to view data and images is likely to be a major cost in online research. To some extent, the costs are offset by the fact that you no longer need to travel to an archive to view the documents. There is also a time saving; someone else has done the initial work of trawling through the documents and put the results in a database. However, you may want to consider all the options before taking out a subscription or buying large numbers of credits. If the time you are going to be able to give to your research is limited, you may decide to restrict yourself to what is available free or through subscriptions at your library or family history society.

Searching the 1911 census

The home page of the site has a section that allows you to enter a simple search based on name, place of residence and year of birth. As a minimum, you are required to enter either a first name or a last name. If you want to enter more data, then you should choose Full person search or Search for a place before entering any details (see Figure 4.5).

Reproduced by permission of brightsolid ltd

Figure 4.5

Following the exercise with the 1881 census, you can try out this database by first searching for a well-known person. If you enter *Queen* in the surname box, you could expect to find Queen Mary as well as a number of people with the surname Queen.

If your original search brings up more than 1,000 results, you will be asked if you want to refine your query before you view the full list. The Queen search finds about 317 results. Scroll down the page to look at some of them. There are 25 results per page. To view more results, click the page numbers just above (or below) the results list, as shown in Figure 4.6.

		1 2 3 4 5 6 7 8 9 10 11 12 13							
Schedule type	Last names	First names	Sex	Birth year	Age in 1911	District / other	County / other	Transcript	Original page
INSTITUTION	H M QUEEN MARY	QUEEN MARY	F	1868	43	St George	London	View Transcript (10 CREDITS)	View Original P (30 CREDITS)
HOUSEHOLD	MC QUEEN	JAMES	M	1849	62	Berwick	Northumberland	View Transcript (10 CREDITS)	View Original P (30 CREDITS)
HOUSEHOLD	MR QUEEN	EMILY MARY	F	1865	46	Bishop's Stortford	Hertfordshire	View Transcript (10 CREDITS)	View Original P (30 CREDITS)
INSTITUTION	NC QUEEN	JAMES	M	1860	51	Shoreditch	London	View Transcript (10 CREDITS)	View Original P (30 CREDITS)
HOUSEHOLD	QUEEN	A ME	M	1851	60	Kingston	Surrey	View Transcript (10 CREDITS)	View Original P (30 CREDITS)
HOUSEHOLD	QUEEN	ADA	F	1883	28	Faversham	Kent	View Transcript (10 CREDITS)	View Original P (30 CREDITS)
HOUSEHOLD	QUEEN	ADA	F	1892	19	West Derby	Lancashire	View Transcript (10 CREDITS)	View Original P (30 CREDITS)
HOUSEHOLD	QUEEN	ADA	F	1871	40	Newcastle upon Tyne	Northumberland	View Transcript (10 CREDITS)	View Original P (30 CREDITS)
HOUSEHOLD	QUEEN	ADA	F	1883	28	Rothbury	Northumberland	View Transcript (10 CREDITS)	View Original P (30 CREDITS)
HOUSEHOLD	QUEEN	ADA E	F	1897	14	Steyning	Sussex	View Transcript (10 CREDITS)	View Original P (30 CREDITS)
INSTITUTION	QUEEN	AGNES M	F	1902	9	West Derby	Lancashire	View Transcript	View Original P

Reproduced by permission of brightsolid ltd

Figure 4.6

Look at how the results are presented and also what they show. Notice that the Queen is shown as 'H M Queen' and that the person below her is a 'James Mc Queen'. If you scroll through all 317 results, however, you will see that there are no other McQueens listed. This is surprising, as it is not an uncommon name. In fact, a search for McQueen from the home page yields over 900 results. So what happened when you instructed the database to search for Queen? Does this explain why you can't always find a person you know should be there?

The original search instructed the program to find every instance of a last name that contained the exact word Queen. The name could contain other words but the word Queen had to be distinct from these other letters. In the case of James, the handwriting has probably suggested to the transcriber that the name is made up of two parts: Mc + Queen. The program therefore treats them as quite separate words. Similarly, if you do a search for the single word McQueen (the more usual spelling), it will ignore the Mc + Queen result as not satisfying your criteria.

The third result on the first page shows a Mr Queen whose first names are Emily Mary. Might this also be a McQueen? How could you check without paying for the full census image? (The cheaper transcription option will only reproduce the same error.) Similarly, in the fourth entry, the M seems to have been misread, giving Nc + Queen.

If you find errors like this, you can report them, but only once you have paid to view a transcription or image. Consideration will then be given to making a change based on the original image. However, if the handwriting still causes doubt, it may not be changed. Understandably, the role of the transcriber is to write what is on the page, not what should have been there. Having been involved in transcribing and transliterating eastern European indexes, I can vouch for the fact that it is sometimes impossible to work out what has been written. The problem with the 1911 census is exacerbated because each household schedule has been written by a different person so there are millions of different handwriting styles to decipher.

Presenting the data in a different order

The 1911 census result list headed by Queen Mary that you accessed in the previous section is organised alphabetically by last name. If the last name is the same, then the alphabetical sorting moves to the first name. Unlike the 1881 census, you can re-sort the list yourself, simply by clicking the different heading titles at the top of the results list.

For example, clicking Sex sorts the list by gender. It first gives the results where no gender was noted on the census, then F for female and finally M for male. In computer sorting, numbers come before letters; spaces come before everything else. If you click again on the same heading, it reverses the sorting order so that all the males come at the top of the list.

You can use this technique of re-sorting by clicking a heading, to bring together all the people living in the same district or county. This can help to identify families, as they are likely (though not always) to be living in the same place. Sorting by age or date of birth can help distinguish between people with the same first name. Each time you click on the heading, the sort order is reversed. Try it out on the 'Queen' result list.

By the way, if you haven't come across this sorting technique before, it also works for file lists in the Documents folder on your computer, as well as on your email lists with their subject, sender and date headings.

Making your search results work harder

Before you spend your credits on transcriptions or census images, you should use all your creativity to ensure that you have found the correct family. Unlike the 1881 census, you cannot immediately see other members of the household. You might want to try another case study and see if it gives sufficient information to warrant paying to view.

The new search is for the children's author and illustrator, Beatrix Potter. Internet research shows her born in 1866 in Kensington. She married late in life (after 1911). You can therefore search on her maiden name. If you need additional information, you can use the fact that her father, Rupert Potter, was a barrister and alive in 1911 (always assuming that she was still living with her parents). You might want to work through this example to see how it is all presented on the screen.

1. Start with a simple search on the 1911 census home page for Beatrix Potter. This gives only one result, which is promising. When you look at the data, it shows her living in Kensington; another plus point. Unfortunately, she is called Ethel Beatrix and was born in 1883, which makes her much too young. Back to the drawing board.

2. You didn't specify a birth year in the original search. Might it help to enter it now? Probably not. All this would do is eliminate Ethel Beatrix, leaving no results.

3. The problem must lie elsewhere. Perhaps you need to look at an alternative spelling for Beatrix. Just above the person search results box there is an opportunity to search the records, as shown in Figure 4.7.

continued

4. Click the search the records link and it will take you to the first stage of the advanced search. Here you can enter more information drawn from other sources. This includes place of birth and names of other family members. If you tried entering her father Rupert, would this help?

5. Unfortunately, this won't work since the search is still going to look for the exact name Beatrix. In any case, you can't yet assume that she is living with her father or even that he is home on census night. So where next?

6. The solution lies in using the Show advanced fields button at the bottom of the search box. This will open up all the search fields and allow a wide variety of searching possibilities. You can leave the original spelling of Beatrix but change the search criteria to variants of name. You can also now put in her year of birth. There will probably be more results this time as you are widening the scope of the search.

You now have four results. There is no sign of Ethel Beatrix (who came up in our first search). Using a birth year has eliminated her. Of the new entries, the most likely is Helen Beatrice, born 1867 and living in Kensington. Further Internet searching shows that Beatrix Potter was indeed christened Helen Beatrice/Beatrix.

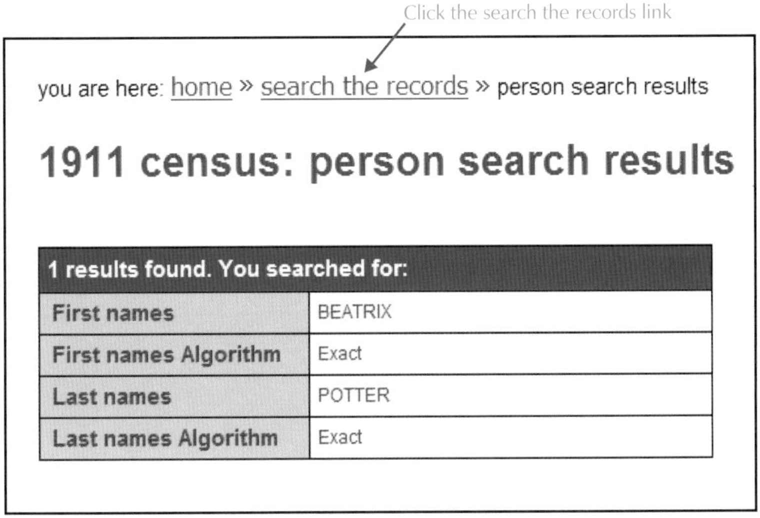

Click the search the records link

you are here: <u>home</u> » <u>search the records</u> » person search results

1911 census: person search results

1 results found. You searched for:	
First names	BEATRIX
First names Algorithm	Exact
Last names	POTTER
Last names Algorithm	Exact

Reproduced by permission of brightsolid ltd

Figure 4.7

The information you obtained here is probably enough to allow you to be confident that this is the right person. The process can appear slow and painstaking, although the speed with which the computer brings up any changed results makes this less painful. If you are going to alter something to enhance your results, change or include only one or, at most, two things each time. If you change everything and it still doesn't work, you can't focus on where the problem might be.

There is one more thing you can look at that would both provide extra confirmation and show other members of the family. To do this, you would need to search for members of the Potter family in Kensington living with someone called Helen Beatrice. The query looks like the one in Figure 4.8.

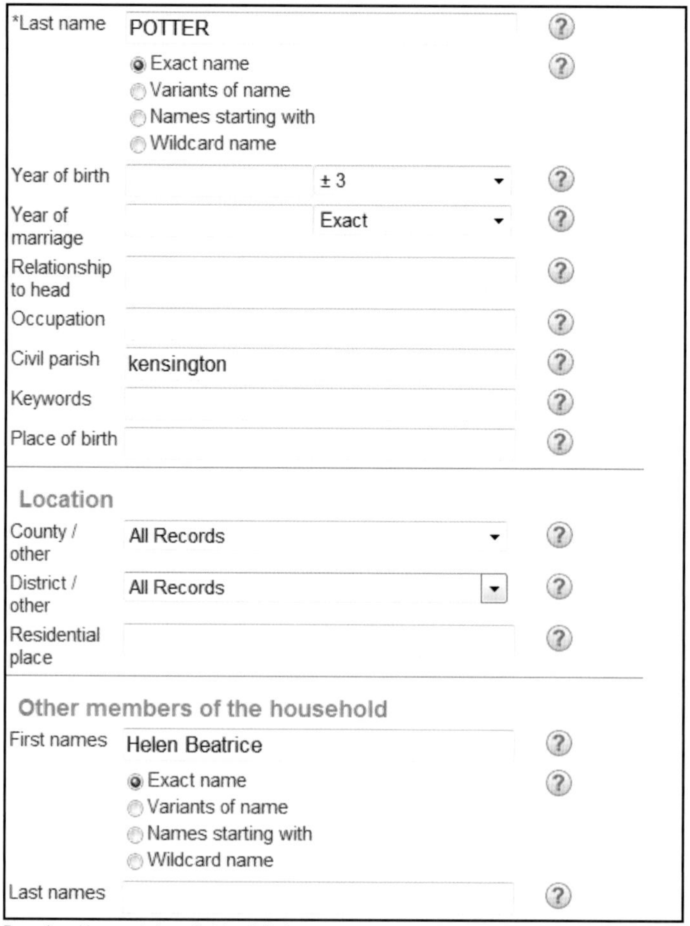

*Last name	POTTER	?
	◉ Exact name	?
	○ Variants of name	
	○ Names starting with	
	○ Wildcard name	
Year of birth	± 3 ▼	?
Year of marriage	Exact ▼	?
Relationship to head		?
Occupation		?
Civil parish	kensington	?
Keywords		?
Place of birth		?
Location		
County / other	All Records ▼	?
District / other	All Records ▼	?
Residential place		?
Other members of the household		
First names	Helen Beatrice	?
	◉ Exact name	?
	○ Variants of name	
	○ Names starting with	
	○ Wildcard name	
Last names		?

Figure 4.8

The first name at the top is removed, leaving only the surname Potter. The year of birth is also left blank. This produces a list of everyone with the surname Potter. Add the location of Kensington. In the box for other members of the household, put Helen Beatrice. (You now know this is how her name has been transcribed.)

The result of this search, shown here in Figure 4.9, is very satisfying, showing Rupert and Helen Potter, who are both the right age to be Beatrice's parents.

1911 census: person search results

2 results found. You searched for:	
Last names	POTTER
Last names Algorithm	Exact
Parish	KENSINGTON
Other person first names	HELEN BEATRICE
Other person first names Algorithm	Exact

Search again

Transcripts are 10 credits and original pages are 30 credits. You will not be charged for transcripts or original pages that you have already purchased and are in your "my records".

Schedule type	Last names	First names	Sex	Birth year	Age in 1911	District / other	County / other	Transcript	Original page
HOUSEHOLD	POTTER	HELEN	F	1840	71	Kensington	London	View Transcript (PAID)	View Original P (30 CREDITS)
HOUSEHOLD	POTTER	RUPERT	M	1833	78	Kensington	London	View Transcript (PAID)	View Original P (30 CREDITS)

Reproduced by permission of brightsolid ltd

Figure 4.9

Note that the result has not shown any servants in the household, since they are unlikely to have the surname of Potter. If you were to decide to pay for the full census transcription, everyone in the household would be listed.

I've decided to spend 10 credits and get a copy of the transcription (see Figure 4.10). Once I've paid, I can look at a screen view or a printer friendly view. In addition to the other members of the household, the record gives the exact address and the number of years the Potters have been married. The only piece of information not included, which would show up on the full census image, is the number of children born to the couple and the number still living.

Name:	Relationship to head:	Marital Status:	Years married:	Sex:	Age in 1911:	Occupation:	Where born:
QUARTERMAINE, DAISY	SERVANT	SINGLE		F	17	UNDER HOUSEMAID DOMESTIC	OXON GRADDINGTON
HOWARD, ADA	SERVANT	SINGLE		F	27	HOUSEMAID DOMESTIC	DERBYSHIRE BAKEWELL
HEDGER, ROSE	SERVANT	SINGLE		F	17	KITCHEN MAID DOMESTIC	OXON OXFORD
WILKINSON, HELEN	SERVANT	SINGLE		F	22	PARLOUR MAID DOMESTIC	LANCASHIRE ITALY BRIDGE
POTTER, HELEN	WIFE	MARRIED	47	F	71		CHESHIRE DUKINFIELD
POTTER, RUPERT	HEAD	MARRIED		M	78	BARRISTER AT LAW RETIRED	LANCASHIRE MANCHESTER
HARPER, ELIZABETH	SERVANT	SINGLE		F	65	COOK DOMESTIC	DERBYSHIRE BEARD
POTTER, HELEN BEATRICE	DAUGHTER	SINGLE		F	44	AUTHORESS	MIDDLESEX LONDON

POTTER HELEN (RG14PN124 RD2 SD1 ED37 SN387)			
Address	2 BOLTON GDN S KENSINGTON	County	London
District	Kensington	Subdistrict	Kensington South
Enumeration			

Reproduced by permission of brightsolid ltd

Figure 4.10

Searching Scottish census records

The census in Scotland was taken in the same years as in England and Wales and contains much of the same information.

 From 1891, the information in the Scottish census shows whether the person was a Gaelic speaker.

The best place to look for information about Scottish census records is on the ScotlandsPeople website **www.scotlandspeople.gov.uk**. At the bottom of the home page, as shown in Figure 4.11, there are links to groups of census years.

Statutory Registers	Old Parish Registers	Census Records	Other Records
» **Births 1855-2006** » **Marriages 1855-2006** » **Deaths 1855-2006**	» **Births & Baptisms** 1538-1854 » **Banns & Marriages** 1538-1854 » **Deaths & Burials** 1538-1854	» 1841 » 1871 » 1851 » 1881 » 1861 » 1891 » 1901 » 1881 (LDS)	» **Wills &** **Testaments Search** 1513-1901 (Free) » **Coats of Arms** **Search 1672-1907** (Free) » **Catholic Parish** **Registers 1703-1955**

Reproduced by permission of © Crown copyright and copyright brightsolid ltd

Figure 4.11

Clicking any link gives you detailed information about that census year. After each explanation, there is an opportunity to see in detail what each census contains and to look at a sample image.

On each of the explanation pages, there is a menu box on the left of the screen that allows you to go to any of the census years or to look at a more general overview of the census. For 1881, there are links and references to using the FamilySearch (LDS) website, which you have already looked at for English and Welsh records (**www.familysearch.org**).

Payment for viewing indexes and then images on the ScotlandsPeople site works in the same way as for birth, marriage and death records (see Chapter 3).

There are currently no plans to release the Scottish 1911 census ahead of the normal 100 year schedule.

Searching Irish census records

Researchers with Irish ancestry will find census research more difficult. Fire at the Records Office in 1922 destroyed the first four censuses (1821–1851). The returns for the next four (1861–1891) were destroyed by the government. This leaves only the 1901 and 1911 records available. The Mormons (LDS) have a microfilm of the 1901 census and this can be viewed at family history centres anywhere in the world. As with other LDS microfilms, if your local centre does not have a copy, one can be ordered at a very low cost for either temporary or permanent loan.

The 1911 returns for Ireland are held by the National Archives of Ireland **www.census. nationalarchives.ie**. The website, shown in Figure 4.12, provides information on the census, the project to digitise the records and a facility for searching.

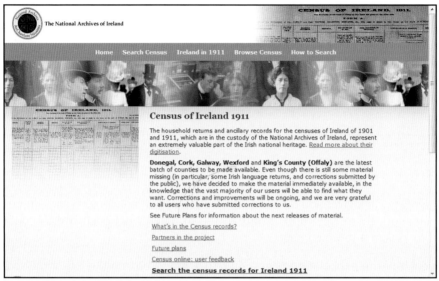

Reproduced by permission of The National Archives of Ireland

Figure 4.12

Because of the lack of census material for Ireland, you need to look at a range of possible sources. There is a useful website called Census Finder, which has a section on Irish records. Go to **www.censusfinder.com/ireland.htm** to see local census returns that may have been transcribed (see Figure 4.13).

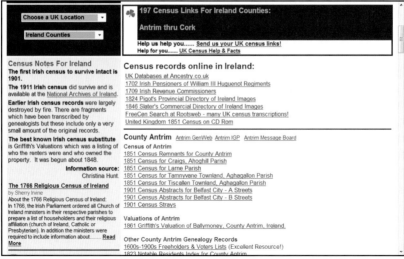

Reproduced by permission of www.censusfinder.com

Figure 4.13

This website also has pages with information about Scottish, Welsh and English records. There is a search box that allows you to choose a UK location and then counties.

You may come across references to Griffiths Valuation of Ireland, which took place from 1848 to 1864. These records show who owned and rented property in Ireland, and can therefore be considered as a proxy for the census. An Internet search for *griffiths valuation ireland* gives you access to information about these records: what they were, where copies are held and whether there are CD or online versions that can be searched.

Research tasks: Census for Fischer/Smith family

1881 Fischer family

The first task in this section is to find Carl Fischer's family in the 1881 census. Use the FamilySearch website we used for the Florence Nightingale demonstration. If you are successful, you should be able to add the following information to research notes for this family:

1. The name of Carl's mother
2. The places of birth of Carl's mother and father
3. His parents' ages and so possible birth years (Remember there may be a one-year difference in actual birth year from other sources depending on the date of birth in relation to the census date. Show this with c (circa=around) in front of the date.)
4. Name, age and place of birth of any siblings
5. Where the family was living

Hints: You already know his father's name and have a *possible* birth year for Carl from your earlier FreeBMD search. If you can't find the result you want, think around the problem. You have already seen the possibility that Carl might be Karl. What happens if you omit his first name but include his father as head of household?

continued

1881 Smith family

You should now try to find the Smith family in Feering in exactly the same way. The name is more common and first names may not have the benefit of more 'exotic' foreign spelling. You are looking for the following data:

1. The name of Maria's mother
2. The places of birth of her mother and father
3. Her parents' ages and possible birth years
4. Name, age and place of birth of any siblings
5. Where the family was living

Hints: Use the location options at the bottom of the search form to select England, Essex and then Feering to narrow down your results. If you don't find what you want, try leaving out the birth year first of all.

1911 Fischer

Looking forward in time to the 1911 census, you can now try to find Carl and Maria as a married couple. What can you find from the index alone without purchasing any census transcript? (You may want to save your credits for information about your own family.)

You know that, by 1911, Carl and Maria have been married for 21 years. They will probably have children, some of whom may be living at home; others may be living and working away. You are trying to find the following information:

1. What are the names of any children living at home?
2. How old are they and when were they born?
3. Are there any other family members living with the Fischers?
4. Do the ages shown for Carl and Maria match other dates you have found elsewhere?

Hints: Find Carl Fischer using his year of birth. Note the district where he was living. Do an advanced search looking for Fischer living in that district in the same household as someone called Carl Fischer. See if the ages are compatible with children born to this family.

> **Research tasks: Census for your family**
>
> Start with the 1911 census. Select the branch of the family about which you have the most information. Decide who you would expect to find and estimate how old they would be. Can you find them?
>
> Now take the family back to 1881 if possible. This may be prior to the couple's marriage, so you may have to search for people living with their parents. If you haven't already done so, you would first try to find the woman's maiden name through a FreeBMD marriage search. This would then let you search for her family.

Suggested answers to the census research tasks

If you took the time to work through the research tasks for the Fischer and Smith families, check your results with the answers given here.

The Fischer family

The 1881 Fischer family information should be as follows:

Carl/Karl is shown as Charles in this census. The other information you were looking for is:

1. Mother's name Sophie A Fischer (you don't yet have her maiden name).
2. Mother born in 'Adenburg', Germany. (A search for this town on the Internet suggests that this may be a transcription error.) Frederick was born in 'Stutgart' (not the accepted spelling but recognisable).
3. Sophie is 42 and so was born c1839; Frederick is 45 and born c1836.
4. Older brother Frederick, age 19. Born in Marylebone c1862.
5. Address is 164 Albany Street, London, Middlesex.

There are a number of things that make it reasonably certain that this is the case study family:

- Charles is a variation of Carl and Karl.

- The family comes from Germany, a possibility already considered.

- The father is a decorative house painter, an occupation seen on the original marriage certificate.

- There is a brother named after the father. (Note that decorating seems to be a family business.)

- If you investigated further on the Internet, you would find that Albany Street is in the same area as Harrington Street, the address on the original marriage certificate.

You now have a solid body of data to use in other searches and which will allow you to accept or reject the results of such searches with greater certainty. Each search opens up further questions. In this case, you should now be considering whether the parents were married in Germany or in England. Since the children were both born in England, a search of FreeBMD marriages before the birth of Frederick junior would be a good place to start.

From the 1911 Fischer family research, you may have come up with the following information:

1. The children are Doris and Freda.

2. Doris is five and was born c1906; Freda is 14 and was born c1897.

3. No family members called Fischer are living with the couple; insufficient evidence from the index search alone to know if any relatives with different surnames are living with them.

4. Carl is 45 and was born 1866. Maria is 43 and was born 1868. This confirms evidence from other sources.

The Smith family

The 1881 census should yield the following information about the Smith family:

1. Maria's mother is called Mary Ann.

2. Everyone in the family was born in Feering.

3. Both parents are 54 and were therefore born c1827.

4. There is a younger sister called Charlotte aged 7 and so born c1874.

5. The address is Feering Street, Feering.

Although there was another Maria Smith in a household with a John Smith in the first search results, she was too old to be 'your' Maria and she was already married. Don't be put off by the common names. The bonus you have in this case is the small size of Feering, which allows you some degree of confidence that you have the right result.

> It always helps to look for the 'bonus' factor in your research: a small or sparsely populated area, an unusual first name for one or more members of the family, an occupation that is not labourer, tailor or agricultural labourer (often referred to as AgLabs by genealogists).

Follow-up work on the Smith family would be to find Charlotte in the FreeBMD records and to look for the parents' marriage.

Reviewing the evidence collected so far

Don't worry if you have gaps. There are other censuses available for 1891 and 1901, which can be searched in different ways (either on microfilm or on other websites). These four censuses (1881–1911), your BMD searches and the information you are collecting from family documents should give you a good basis for your research.

Before moving on to search other major online sources, it probably makes sense to take stock of the information gathered so far on the 'adopted' family and then your own family. You have used FreeBMD, the 1881 census and the 1911 census. These sources usually gave you additional information, not only about the initial marrying couple, but also about their families. You can check out these other family members on FreeBMD and in other censuses where they may no longer be living in the parental home.

From birth, marriage and death records, you can often find supporting evidence back to 1837 (the beginning of civil registration in England and Wales). The earliest census useful to family historians is from a similar period (1841). You should try to create as complete a picture as possible of the family working back from yourself to the 1830s. You may start by working through your parents and grandparents. In each generation, not only do you double the number of your ancestors, you also double the number of potential names to research (unless marriages between cousins were common in your family).

Taking all these lines back, even to 1837, can be a big task. For many different reasons, some branches of your family may be elusive. What usually happens is that you focus on one family name for a while and then switch when you find that you are hitting a brick wall. Following up another family line can rekindle your enthusiasm and sometimes provides clues that help you with your original line of research. At each stage, you need to be clear about the focus of your search. By all means do a quick search on a number of lines when you first use a resource. However, the scattergun approach can be time-consuming and the results confusing if you don't have specific goals in mind.

There is also the problem of 'one-upmanship' that can creep into family research. Both genealogists and non-genealogists often ask you the same two questions: 'How far back have you got?' and 'How many people do you have on your family tree?' To some extent both questions are irrelevant. A family moving between several countries in the space of a few generations is much more difficult to track than one that has always lived, died and been registered in the same place.

> There is also the danger of 'trophy hunting', where you become convinced (on the slimmest of evidence) that one of your relatives is linked to someone famous. You then hook yourself into a well-documented family tree that goes back many generations and has hundreds, if not thousands, of individuals. If this is the case, you should be very thorough in finding the supporting evidence yourself.

As you get nearer in time to 1837, you will find that the births and marriages for people on your tree will have taken place earlier than this date. There will be records for you to search but they are likely to be local rather than national. You need to collect as much information about locations from the national records so that you can maintain your focus for your pre-1837 research.

What questions do you still need to ask?

You can add other censuses to your research to give as complete a picture as possible of the families you are researching. There are a number of websites that allow you to search these (usually for credits or a subscription). I have used Ancestry (which is now often available through local libraries). It is also possible to view microfilms of census records in various archives, though it's helpful if you have some indication of where a family was living at the time. This can sometimes come from the address on the birth certificate of the child born nearest in time to that particular census.

The research goals for the next stage of the Fischer/Smith research will be:

- to find the maiden name of Carl's mother and the date of her marriage to Frederick Fischer
- to find the same information for Maria's parents
- to work out a possible date/range of dates when the Fischers came to England from Germany (this would save you looking fruitlessly for them in earlier English parish records)
- to identify other siblings in the family
- to firm up on birth years by having evidence from a number of different sources
- to find any family deaths
- to find any family marriages.

Reviewing what you know

You can record the information that you find in a number of ways. Before you include any details in your family tree, you need to be reasonably confident that you have the correct person. Where a name is very common, you need more evidence. As you will be creating your family tree using a special computer program, you can alter and add details quite easily but it helps if you are reasonably sure of your facts before you begin.

I have been keeping a research log for the individuals in the adopted family and adding to it each time I use a new resource. I have used a spreadsheet to do this. Spreadsheets were mentioned briefly in Chapter 2 under Computing requirements. The spreadsheet is like a piece of graph or accounting paper, where you have rows and columns into which you can put information. Chapter 9 deals in more detail with how to set up a spreadsheet as a research log. For the moment, the focus is on the actual information collected, shown here in Figure 4.14.

Source	Year	Forenames	Surname	Spouse	Date	Age	DOB	Place of birth	Place/ District	Quar.	BMD ref
freeBMD marriage	1860	Ludwig Frederick	Fischer	Amelia Johanna Sophie Rubardt		24			Marylebone	Sep	1a 766
census	1871	Ludwik	Frischer	Sophie Frischer		35	1836	Stuttgart, Germany	St Pancras		
census	1881	Frederick	Fischer	Sophie A Fischer		45	1836	Stutgart Germany	St Pancras		
marriage certificate	1890	Frederick	Fischer		18/10/1890				Feering		
census	1891	Frederick	Fischer	Sophie J A Fischer		55	1836	Germany	St Pancras		
census	1901	Frederick	Fischer	widowed		65	1836	Germany	St Pancras		
freeBMD death	1908	Frederick	Fischer			72	1836		Tendring	Sep	4a 344

Items in RED are extrapolated from given data

Tabs: Frederick / Sophie / Carl / Maria / Lilian / Freda / Doris / Frederick C / Nellie

Figure 4.14

This spreadsheet shows the data on Frederick Fischer, the father of Carl. There is an entry from each of the censuses apart from 1861. There *is* a Frederick Fischer on the 1861 census but there are too many question marks against the data to include it here: marital status, age, location and occupation all differ from the evidence in other sources. There is sufficient information from elsewhere to make the 1861 census less critical for your research.

Initially, the family couldn't be found on the 1871 census. They were found when Frederick's first name and place of birth (Germany) were put in, the surname removed and Sophie entered as the spouse. This revealed that the transcription was for *Frischer*, not Fischer. The original census is quite faint but does show Fischer. It also shows Stuttgart and not Huttgart (which is how the transcriber read the place of birth). An alternative for the Frischer name has now been included in the database and so a search for Fischer will find the family.

The couple was married in England. There is no evidence of whether they came from Germany as adults or earlier with family members. Purchasing a marriage certificate, which is shown in Figure 4.15, would be justified in such a case as it would give the name and occupation of the fathers.

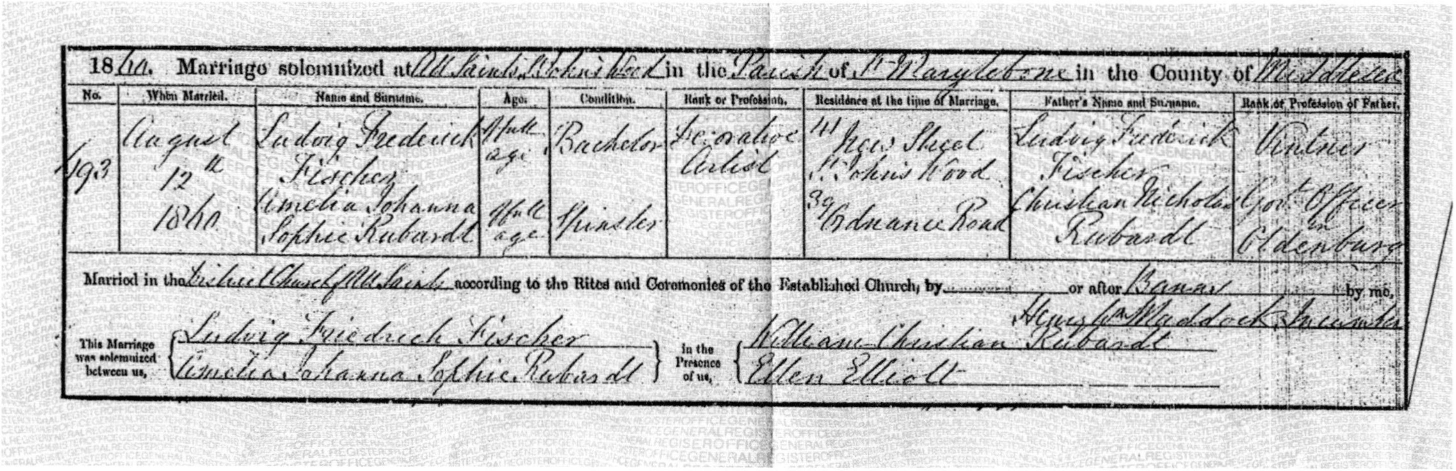

18*60*. Marriage solemnized at *All Saints St John's Wood* in the *Parish* of *St Marylebone* in the County of *Middlesex*

No.	When Married.	Name and Surname.	Age.	Condition.	Rank or Profession.	Residence at the time of Marriage.	Father's Name and Surname.	Rank or Profession of Father.
193	August 12th 1860	Ludwig Frederick Fischer	Full age	Bachelor	Decorative Artist	41 New Street St John's Wood	Ludwig Frederick Fischer	Vintner
		Amelia Johanna Sophie Rubardt	Full age	Spinster		39 Ordnance Road	Christian Nicholas Rubardt	Govt Officer in Oldenburg

Married in the *Parish Church of All Saints* according to the Rites and Ceremonies of the Established Church, by ________ or after *Banns* by me,
Henry Wm Maddock Incumbent

This Marriage was solemnized between us, { *Ludwig Friedrich Fischer* / *Amelia Johanna Sophie Rubardt* }
In the Presence of us, { *William Christian Rubardt* / *Ellen Elliott* }

Figure 4.15

You can see from this that Frederick shared both his first names with his father, who was a vintner. Sophie's father was a government official in Oldenburg named Christian Nicholas Rubardt. The witness was William Christian Rubardt (possibly Sophie's brother). Should you need to take your research back to German records, this information will be a very useful starting point.

In the 1901 census, Frederick is shown as a widower. This should encourage you to look for Sophie's death between 1891 and 1901.

Frederick could not be found on the 1911 census. A search on FreeBMD between 1901 and 1911 revealed that he died in 1908.

This should give you a flavour of how you can create the story of an individual's life from sources that are much more readily accessible to you now that they are online. There will still be resources and background information that can only be accessed in paper format or in record offices, though this situation is changing all the time. After a relatively short time researching, you are in a good position to put together an initial family tree and 'grow' it with further research.

Research tasks: Evidence so far for Fischer/Smith family

The task here is to create a similar sheet (written or in spreadsheet format) for John Smith, the father of Maria Smith. See how much you can find from the resources covered so far. If you have access to Ancestry, you can include material from other censuses.

Research tasks: Evidence so far for your family

Take an individual from your own research about whom you have found the most information. Record the data, either in spreadsheet or written format. Highlight or tick the evidence about which you feel confident. Make a list of other things to check or research as a result of reviewing this sheet.

John Smith suggested research answers

Figure 4.16 shows the information on John Smith that can be extracted from the sources you have examined so far.

	A	B	C	D	E	F	G	H	I	J	K	L	M
1	Items in RED are extrapolated from given data										Place of	Place/	I
2	Source	Year	Forenames	Surname	Spouse	Children	Date	Age	DOB	birth	District	Quar.	BMD ref
3	freeBMD marriage	1847	John	Smith	Mary Ann Cranmer		1847	19			Witham	Mar	12 367
4	census	1851	John	Smith	Mary	Jonah (2) James (1)	1851	23	1828	Feering	Feering		
5	census	1861	John	Smith	Maryann	John (12) James (11) Eligher (9) Maryann (6) Joseph (1mth)	1861	33	1828	Feering	Feering		
6	census	1871	John	Smith	Maryann	James (21) Elijah (19) Maria (3)	1871	43	1828	Feering	Feering		
7	census	1881	John	Smith	Maryann	Maria (13) Charlotte (7)	1881	54	1827	Feering	Feering		
8	marriage certificate	1890	John	Smith		marriage of Maria	18/10/1890				Feering		
9	census	1891	John	Smith	Mary A		1891	63	1828	Feering	Feering		
10	census	1901	John	Smith	Mary A.		1901	73	1828	Feering	Feering		
11	freeBMD death	1908	John	Smith			1908	80	1828		Braintree	Mar	4a 484
12	census	1911	Mary	Smith	widow		1911	deceased					
13													
14													
15													

John / Maria / Sheet3 /

Figure 4.16

Although the name John Smith is very common, there are few with that name living in the small town of Feering. The 1881 census was the first prior to Maria's marriage to show her living at home with her father, John Smith. This gave her mother's name as Mary A. Earlier censuses show John living with a spouse called Maryann or Mary. It is the information on the children and their names and ages across the census years that confirms that this is the same family. A marriage in 1847 is likely to be theirs since the names match and this ties in with when the first child was born. Where children 'disappear' from the census it means that they have died, that they are working away from home or that they have married and set up home themselves.

Coming forward after Carl and Maria's marriage, her parents are living alone in 1891 and 1901. In the 1911 census, Mary Smith is a widow. A search for a death for John Smith between 1901 and 1911 in the Braintree area gives his death in 1908.

Summary

- A Census is taken every 10 years. Records are usually closed for 100 years for privacy reasons.

- Census records allow you to see family groups.

- Information includes occupation, date and place of birth and relationship to head of household.

- They can provide confirmation of data from BMD records.

- Censuses from 1841 are the most useful for information about individuals.

- The most recent census available is 1911.

- Keep a research log as you go along and note down not only what you find but where you found it.

- Copy down what is there, not what you expect to be there.

- If you want to extrapolate information, eg a date of birth from a given age or a full name from a shortened version, record this in a different colour to show that it was not in the original document.

- Reviewing information on the same person from several sources allows you to see how data on an individual can differ.

Brain Training

1. How often is the national census taken in the UK?

a) Every 5 years

b) Every 10 years

c) Every 15 years

d) Every 20 years

2. In which of these years was a census first taken that provides coverage of individuals rather than just a headcount?

a) 1821

b) 1831

c) 1841

d) 1851

3. After how many years is the census data on individuals made available for searching?

a) 10

b) 50

c) 75

d) 100

4. In what month is the census *usually* taken?

a) April

b) June

c) August

d) September

5. What is the name of the person who records census information?

a) Clerk

b) Enumerator

c) Recorder

d) Registrar

Answers

Q1 – b   **Q2** – c   **Q3** – d   **Q4** – a

Q5 – b

PART III
Online Sources

Family history can be full of surprises. Most of my husband's ancestors turn out to be courageous, athletic and artistic...

FamilySearch

Equipment needed: Computer and Internet access to the FamilySearch website.

Skills needed: Searching databases, extracting information, refining search queries.

FamilySearch is the genealogical services website of the Church of Jesus Christ of Latter-Day Saints (LDS), also known as the Mormons. For religious and cultural reasons, genealogical research is very important to the LDS Church and its members, who devote to it considerable time and resources. The materials collected (usually microfilms of original records) are freely available to non-Church members. The FamilySearch website is at **www.familysearch.org**.

Sources on the FamilySearch website

The information from some records has been extracted to create searchable databases. The 1881 census you looked at in Chapter 4 is an example. If you wish to find the references for the images of the original documents after you have searched the database, then you can usually find these in the LDS Library Catalog. You will be referred to microfilm, microfiche or paper-based resources, which you can view at one of the many Family History Centers around the world.

Other database information is submitted by individuals who wish to share their genealogical research. This is from both LDS Church members and other family historians.

You can access most of the resources from the FamilySearch home page (see Figure 5.1).

Figure 5.1

You are offered the option to search for your ancestors, get research guidance and forms to use in your research, download free software to help you produce a family tree and search for the Family History Center nearest to your home. Menus at the top of the page let you search the records, access the Library Catalog and look at a wide variety of articles and guidance material.

Searching the site

When you put in the name of an ancestor, the following databases are searched:

- **Ancestral File:** Individual and family records submitted by LDS Church members. The data does not have to be corroborated and, therefore, there can be errors. You may find two submissions for the same person, with slightly different data. This occurs when different researchers have interpreted evidence or handwriting in different ways.

- **International Genealogical Index (IGI):** A vast resource created from names extracted from vital (BMD) records. In addition to the extractions organised by the LDS Church, there are personal submissions from individuals. In terms of accuracy, the personal submissions may have more errors.

- **Census records:** United States 1880; British Isles 1881; Canada 1881.

- **Pedigree Resource File:** Created from family pedigrees submitted in electronic format. As they are submitted they are included in the index and made available on CD-ROM. If the submitter subsequently updates information, this is resubmitted and appears on a new CD. You may find more than one entry for an individual if this person appears on more than one family tree.

- **US Social Security Death Index (SSDI):** A useful resource for those searching family who have emigrated to the US.

- **Vital Records Index:** Birth, christening and marriage records from selected countries.

Around 13% of the US population reported British ancestry (2000 US census) and a further 11% reported Irish origins.

For your first searches on this site, use the poet Percy Bysshe Shelley as your celebrity. His second name is very uncommon, so this helps your search. You can also use data from general Internet searching to give you more information to use in the search or to confirm any results.

If you enter Shelley's first names and surname in the search box on the FamilySearch home page, 95 results are shown as in Figure 5.2.

Matches: All Sources - 95

Ancestral File

1. Percy John Borlace SHELLEY - Ancestral File
Gender: M Birth/Christening: 1773

2. Percy Lee SHEALY - Ancestral File
Gender: M Birth/Christening: Abt 1902 , , Miss.

3. Percy Bysshe SHELLEY - Ancestral File
Gender: M Birth/Christening: 19 Dec 1895 Old Shoreham, Sussex, Eng.

4. Percy SHELLEY - Ancestral File
Gender: M Birth/Christening: Abt 1702 Of Bookham, Surrey, Eng

5. Percy Bishie SHELLEY - Ancestral File
Gender: M Birth/Christening: 12 Nov 1915 Schaffer, Mckenzie, Nd

6. Percy Bysshe SHELLEY - Ancestral File
Gender: M Birth/Christening: 4 Aug 1792 Of Fieldplace, Sussex, England

7. Percy SHELLY - Ancestral File
Gender: M Birth/Christening: Abt 1819

8. Percy SHELLEY - Ancestral File
Gender: M Birth/Christening: < 1891 <Denver, Denver, Co>

Matches: Ancestral File - 8

Census - 1880 US Census

9. Percy SHELLEY - 1880 United States Census / Missouri
Son   Gender: Male   Birth: <1856> MO

10. Percie SHELLEY - 1880 United States Census / Kansas
Wife   Gender: Female   Birth: <1860> KS

Figure 5.2

It's clear that these are not all for the poet Shelley. Since he died in 1822, you can obviously ignore all the census results, whether US, British or Canadian. Similarly, you can eliminate the seven US Social Security Death Index entries. How can you structure a query to return fewer results while making sure that you retain all the likely ones?

Given the bonus of Shelley's middle name, you could decide to ask the database for only exact matches with the full name. Unfortunately, this removes references to Percy B Shelley, for which there are two or three entries further down the original list.

A better solution is to put in his known birth year (1792). This reduces the list to 45 entries. If you change the search to show death year (1822), then this returns 42 results. The reason for this is that some of those submitting data may not have known his date of death or may have got it wrong or it may have been mis-keyed during a transcription. It may of course just refer to someone with a similar name born in the same year.

> If this problem occurs with someone well-known, you need to be even more cautious with entries that appear to relate to your family. There will certainly be fewer of them. This is good in that you can scan them more easily. The downside is that, if there are errors, you may not be in a position to decide which entry is correct. At least where there is a large number of results, you can use the laws of probability to decide which information is right.

This has perhaps painted a rather gloomy picture of the problems with search results. However, you shouldn't forget the advantage that these databases give you over painfully pursuing your own lonely research through the original records. These results at least point you in the direction of specific documents, years and names, which you can then add to your growing list of evidence for evaluation.

Understanding the information each database holds

The results from your search come from a number of different data sources. These include Ancestral File, the International Genealogical Index (IGI) and Pedigree Resource File.

Personal Ancestral File

Figure 5.3 shows the Ancestral File revised results list for Shelley. It contains only one entry that satisfies the search criteria.

```
Results for: Percy Shelley
              Birth/Christening, 1792, All Countries
              Exact Spelling: Off
Matches:      All Sources - 45
Ancestral File
1. Percy Bysshe SHELLEY - Ancestral File
Gender: M Birth/Christening: 4 Aug 1792 Of Fieldplace, Sussex, England
Matches: Ancestral File - 1
```

Reproduced by permission of © 2008 Intellectual Reserve, Inc.

Figure 5.3

The names in these result lists act as links to pages with more details about the individual. Click Shelley's name to find a record (Figure 5.4) which gives a lot more information.

Reproduced by permission of © 2008 Intellectual Reserve, Inc.

Figure 5.4

The Ancestral File Number (AFN) is a unique identifier assigned to each individual in the database. It is probably less confusing to ignore these numbers at this stage and focus on the data presented.

One recurring problem that you can see with data is where the spelling of a name is not as expected. Shelley's second wife was Mary Wollstonecraft Godwin, author of the novel *Frankenstein*. In this record, Mary is shown as Woolston Croft Godwin. You saw something similar with James Mc + Queen on the 1911 census search. In this case, you know what the name should be and it is sufficiently close for you to determine that this is the correct record.

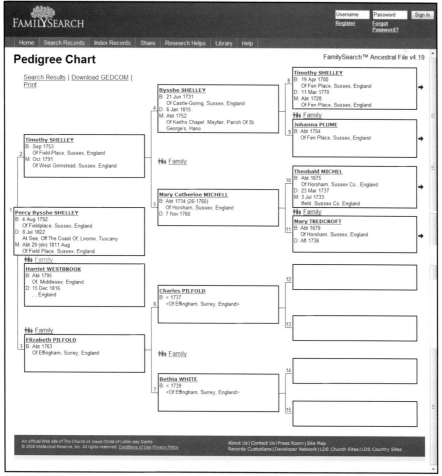

Figure 5.5

You are not yet at the end of the research trail. On the right side of the page you can look at Shelley's pedigree and his family group record. The pedigree is a chart showing parents, grandparents, great-grandparents and so on, as far back as the information submitter has researched. Figure 5.5 shows four generations, from Shelley to his great-grandparents.

What is even better is that, on the right, there are small arrows from some of these great-grandparents, which take you further back into their pedigrees. You can keep clicking such arrows until you run out of people. If you try this, sticking with the Shelley name, you end up at a William Shelley born about 1376 (Figure 5.6). Not bad for a few mouse clicks, is it?

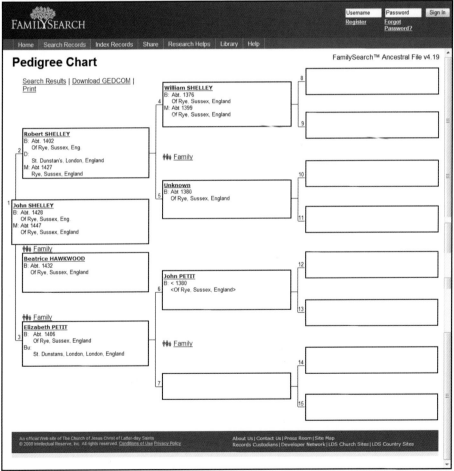

Reproduced by permission of © 2008 Intellectual Reserve, Inc.

Figure 5.6

The other option on the right of the individual record page (refer to Figure 5.4) is to look at a Family Record Sheet. In this case, there are several such links from different members of the family. If you follow the first of these from Shelley himself, you see a page showing his details, those of his wife and children and the names of his parents (see Figure 5.7). For each of these individuals, you can look at a pedigree, where one is available.

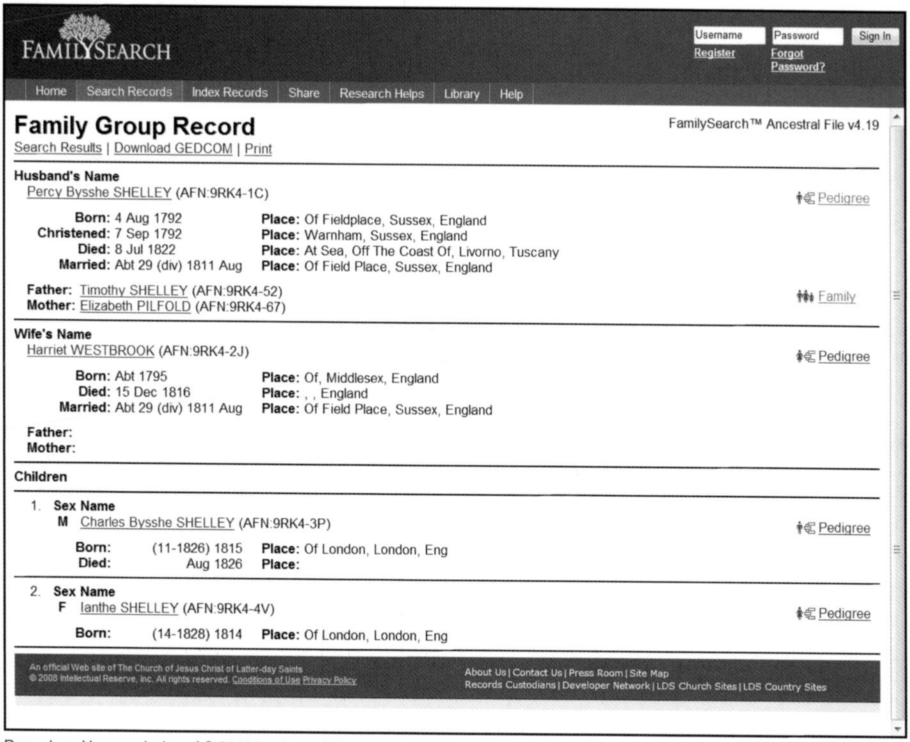

FAMILYSEARCH

Username | Password | Sign In

Register | Forgot Password?

Home | Search Records | Index Records | Share | Research Helps | Library | Help

Family Group Record

FamilySearch™ Ancestral File v4.19

Search Results | Download GEDCOM | Print

Husband's Name

Percy Bysshe SHELLEY (AFN:9RK4-1C) — Pedigree

Born: 4 Aug 1792 — **Place:** Of Fieldplace, Sussex, England
Christened: 7 Sep 1792 — **Place:** Warnham, Sussex, England
Died: 8 Jul 1822 — **Place:** At Sea, Off The Coast Of, Livorno, Tuscany
Married: Abt 29 (div) 1811 Aug — **Place:** Of Field Place, Sussex, England

Father: Timothy SHELLEY (AFN:9RK4-52) — Family
Mother: Elizabeth PILFOLD (AFN:9RK4-67)

Wife's Name

Harriet WESTBROOK (AFN:9RK4-2J) — Pedigree

Born: Abt 1795 — **Place:** Of, Middlesex, England
Died: 15 Dec 1816 — **Place:** , , England
Married: Abt 29 (div) 1811 Aug — **Place:** Of Field Place, Sussex, England

Father:
Mother:

Children

1. **Sex Name**
M Charles Bysshe SHELLEY (AFN:9RK4-3P) — Pedigree
Born: (11-1826) 1815 — **Place:** Of London, London, Eng
Died: Aug 1826 — **Place:**

2. **Sex Name**
F Ianthe SHELLEY (AFN:9RK4-4V) — Pedigree
Born: (14-1828) 1814 — **Place:** Of London, London, Eng

An official Web site of The Church of Jesus Christ of Latter-day Saints
© 2008 Intellectual Reserve, Inc. All rights reserved. Conditions of Use Privacy Policy

About Us | Contact Us | Press Room | Site Map
Records Custodians | Developer Network | LDS Church Sites | LDS Country Sites

Reproduced by permission of © 2008 Intellectual Reserve, Inc.

Figure 5.7

For your own research, the results are likely to be rather less spectacular. However, the principles for using the search function, both in Ancestral File and in most other databases, should encourage you, even if your initial search for a name seems less than promising.

Understanding the International Genealogical Index results

There were 19 International Genealogical Index (IGI) results for Shelley. Since these records were extracted from birth/baptism, marriage and death records, they tend to show the dates and individuals connected with particular events, rather than full-blown pedigrees or family groups. This also means that some show the parents of the person (because they came from birth records); others show the spouse (marriage records). In the case of Shelley, who was married twice, some records show his first wife, Harriet Westbrook; others show Mary Wollstonecraft Godwin.

Accessing the Pedigree Resource File

Your search for references to a birth year for Shelley gave 45 matches. However, a box on the right of the main results page (see Figure 5.8) indicates that there may be more.

This is because, although up to 200 results can be presented per page, no more than 25 from any one source are initially shown. This speeds up the downloading of results on the page. You can then select an individual resource from the list, should you wish to view more records.

There are 28 results listed in the category of Pedigree Resource File. Clicking a name takes you to an Individual Record page with links to pedigrees (see Figure 5.9). What the record also has is a submission number. All the records submitted by a researcher in a particular batch are given the same submission number. By clicking this number, you can search for the submission. This then gives you a listing of other people in that family whose data was entered at the same time (details of living individuals are not published in the online version). This is useful because it gives you other surnames to research. The details of the submitter may also be available to you.

Sources Searched Matches were found only in the sources listed below. Click on a source to see more matches for that source.

- Ancestral File - 1
- IGI/British Isles - 19
- Pedigree Resource File - over 25

Reproduced by permission of © 2008 Intellectual Reserve, Inc.

Figure 5.8

The CD reference and PIN number allow you to purchase the CD that contains this particular submission. The CDs contain more information than is available online.

```
┌─────────────────────────────────────────────────────────────────────────────┐
│ Individual Record                              FamilySearch™ Pedigree Resource File │
│                                                                               │
│ Search Results | Print                                                        │
│ ─────────────────────────────────────────────────────────────────────────── │
│ Percy Bysshe Shelley   Compact Disc #125   Pin #555194        ♰✞ Pedigree    │
│    Sex: M                                                                      │
│ ─────────────────────────────────────────────────────────────────────────── │
│ Event(s)                                                                       │
│    Birth: 4 Aug 1792                                                           │
│    Death: 8 Jul 1822                                                           │
│ ─────────────────────────────────────────────────────────────────────────── │
│ Parents                                                                        │
│    Father: Timothy Shelley      Disc #125     Pin #555192                     │
│    Mother: Elizabeth Pilford     Disc #125     Pin #555193                     │
│ ─────────────────────────────────────────────────────────────────────────── │
│ Marriage(s)                                                                    │
│    Spouse: Harriet Westbrook     Disc #125     Pin #555195                    │
│    Marriage:                                                                   │
│    Spouse: Mary Wollstonecraft   Disc #125     Pin #555196                    │
│    Marriage:                                                                   │
│ ─────────────────────────────────────────────────────────────────────────── │
│ Notes and Sources                                                              │
│    Notes: None                                                                 │
│    Sources: Available on CD-ROM Disc# 125                                      │
│ ─────────────────────────────────────────────────────────────────────────── │
│ Submitter                                                                      │
│    Ernest H GRUBB                                                              │
│    561 S. Sunnydale Way Hendersonville, NC 28792                               │
│ ─────────────────────────────────────────────────────────────────────────── │
│ Submission Search: 3273534-0913105070757                                       │
│              URL: http://worldconnect.rootsweb.com/cgi-bin/igm.cgi?db=101429  │
│          CD-ROM: Pedigree Resource File - Compact Disc #125                    │
│   CD-ROM Features: Pedigree View, Family View, Individual View, Reports, Downloadable GEDCOM files, Notes and │
│                    Sources.                                                     │
│   Order Pedigree Resource File CD-ROMS                                         │
└─────────────────────────────────────────────────────────────────────────────┘
```
Reproduced by permission of © 2008 Intellectual Reserve, Inc.

Figure 5.9

For further information on the Pedigree Resource File, you can click the Help menu near the top of the screen. These Help menus are context-sensitive so, if you select Help from any page, it will take you to the corresponding page in the Help file.

Using the Library Catalog

The main LDS Family History Library is in Salt Lake City. It has been described as a 'genealogical sweet shop'. Most of the microfilm and microfiche material is available on open shelves. The library holds nearly two and a half million rolls of microfilm, three-quarters of a million microfiche and over 350,000 books. If the film you require is in store, rather than on the shelves, this can be retrieved in a day or so. In addition there is a huge library of paper-based materials: family histories, 'how to' guides, language materials, maps, directories, gazetteers – almost every conceivable resource that the family historian might want.

Ordering information from Family History Centers

Most genealogists, sadly, have to remain content with the online databases (which continue to grow) and the microfilms and fiches of original records. These can be ordered at and sent to a Family History Center near you. You should also be able to access various online non-LDS subscription databases at these centres (1911 census or Ancestry, for example).

You can search on the FamilySearch home page for your local Family History Center. They are staffed mainly by volunteers and you may find that the opening hours are limited. If this is the case, make your first visit a reconnaissance, rather than a research visit. You can then find out what films they have available. Do they have only a paper list or is their list searchable on the Internet? How many computers and microfilm readers do they have and do these need to be booked in advance? What other materials are on site? In larger towns, there will probably be longer opening hours and more material held at the Family History Center.

Whatever Family History Center you plan to visit, you should have an idea of the films/fiche that you want to see or that you will need to order. The best way to do this is to search the catalogue online and make a note of the materials that you want to view, before you go. Some of the paper-based materials may only be available in Salt Lake City itself. Copies of almost all the microfilms can be sent anywhere in the world.

Searching the Library Catalog

The Library Catalog can be accessed from both the Search Records and Library tabs at the top of the FamilySearch home page.

Since many of the microfilms were of archival registers held in particular locations, searching for a place is probably the best starting point. You already have a number of possible locations for the Fischer/Smith families. Start with a search for Feering. As it is a small place, you probably won't be overwhelmed with information from this first catalogue search.

Click Place Search and then enter Feering. You have the option to include other information about the location. Many towns in the US have the same names as UK towns, so you may need to narrow your search. The search page provides some hints about how this works. In the case of Feering, you can probably be confident that a search will give Feering in Essex, England and nowhere else. This is indeed the case. Click the underlined place name link, to reach the catalogue page for this location.

It is worth noting that place names within the catalogue are usually listed with the country first, followed by the county/district and then the town/village. There are a number of standardised headings for record types and these are listed in alphabetical order. In this case the number of record types is quite small, reflecting the size of the location. If you had searched for Stuttgart, the birthplace of Frederick Fischer, there would be many more topics (and therefore records) for you to search.

Go back to the Feering list and select Church records. This takes you to a list with details of the selected topic. In this case, there are Bishop's Transcripts for 1801–1874.

Bishop's Transcripts are copies of parish registers made annually and sent to the Bishop. Some start as early as 1598.

If you click the underlined link, you are taken to a page giving details of the records held.

The details show the format of the resource (in this case 16mm microfilm), where it originated from, the language of the material and when it was filmed by the Genealogical Society of Utah. At the top right of the screen is a button that lets you look at the film notes. At the bottom of this screen (as in most screens in the catalogue), you can click to get a printable version of the page.

The film notes show in more detail what you can expect to find on the microfilm. You also see where there may be gaps in the records. The film number is the one you should note and request when visiting a Family History Center.

In this case, the film number is followed by the words 'Item 2'. You sometimes see references to item numbers in film details and you need to understand what this means, if you are to find the records on the film. If there is *no* reference to an item number, you can assume that all the records on the film relate to this catalogue entry. You can therefore start at the beginning and work your way through the film until you find what you are looking for. The records are usually in chronological order. If there are a lot of records, the years may be divided. There will be a film frame introducing the records (eg Start → Feering Baptisms 1801–1802) and then a similar frame when those records are finished (Feering Baptisms 1801–1802 → End). This allows you to locate where you are in the film.

Sometimes, the number of records in a register or in a location did not justify it having a complete microfilm. In this case, records from several different places were put on a single microfilm. You therefore need to wind on the film until you come to an introductory frame describing the records you want. In this case, this is the second set of records on the film, ie Item 2.

Be prepared for older records to be difficult to read. Some may be in Latin, some use a very ornate style and some are in bad handwriting. Reading the records does get easier the more you do it. Where documents are in a standard form, you learn to ignore the legal or religious jargon and focus instead on the important family data of names, dates and places.

Using family tree software

Because so many members of the LDS Church are researching their families, a computer program was developed to allow them to enter data in the same format. This program is called Personal Ancestral File, also known as PAF. The data can then be easily exchanged with other researchers without the problems of incompatibility that annoy users of many programs, from word processing to databases. In Chapter 10, you'll look at family history software in more detail. For now, take comfort from the fact that nearly all the programs available allow for this sharing and transfer of data.

PAF is downloadable free from the FamilySearch home page. It has various basic report features that let you show multiple generations. These can be enhanced by the use of another program called PAF Companion, which is also free but limits you to reports and charts showing three generations. The upgrade to PAF Companion offering reports for unlimited generations can be purchased for a few dollars.

Other software and databases can also be purchased, though you may decide to access the information, such as the census, from online sources rather than from CD.

Research guides

The FamilySearch website provides family historians with a variety of resources to support their research activities. These include information about researching in different countries, letter-writing guides and genealogical word lists for different languages.

Reading on screen or printing?

FamilySearch has a large number of articles and guides to help you with your research. Most of these can be read on screen. If you prefer to print them out for reading and reference purposes, some can be downloaded to your computer. It will say that they are available in 'PDF', which means Portable Document Format. PDF files can be read with a free program called Adobe Reader, which you have probably already got on your computer. If by any chance you haven't, use Google or another search engine to look for Adobe Reader and then go to the Adobe website. Before you download, you just need to check which version you need for the operating system on your computer (Windows XP, Windows Vista, Mac and so on). The Adobe site guides you through what to do.

> As always, if you don't yet feel confident enough to download and install a program yourself, there are bound to be family members and friends who can help.

One of the advantages of having Adobe Reader on your system is that you can read all kinds of documents, for family history and other purposes. The manuals for cameras, printers and computers are now often provided on disk in the form of PDFs. Although you have to pay for the ink and paper to print them out, it does mean that you need to print only the pages you want and not have a large unread manual clogging up your bookshelves. (You could be using that valuable space for family history books and papers instead.)

Articles and guidance

From the FamilySearch home page, select the Research Helps tab near the top. You have the choice of Articles or Guidance. Select Articles.

The list is sorted by place; you can find another location by clicking the alphabetical list near the top of the screen. Under the alphabet is a set of instructions telling you how to read on screen, download a PDF or order paper copies.

Viewing by place is probably the best way to look at what's available. The menu on the left, however, also lets you sort by title, subject or document type.

Click E in the alphabetical list and then scroll down past Ecuador and El Salvador to England. This takes you to a list of documents you can access to help with your English and Welsh research.

Now, from the Research Helps tab, select Guidance. Click E again in the alphabetical list. Choose England. This divides the guidance into vital records events (BMD) and by time period. For each event you can choose from the following:

- 1066–1537

- 1538–1837

- 1837–present.

Your strategy is to work backwards from the present, so choose Birth and then the 1837–present options, which leads to a suggested Search Strategy (Figure 5.10).

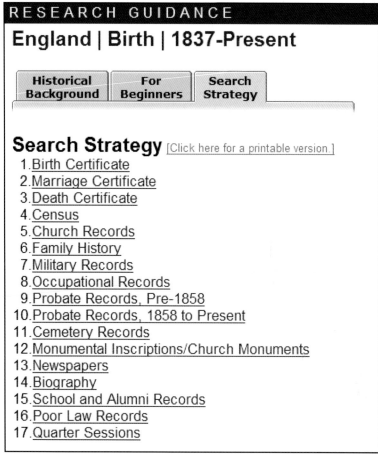

RESEARCH GUIDANCE

England | Birth | 1837-Present

| Historical Background | For Beginners | Search Strategy |

Search Strategy [Click here for a printable version.]
1. Birth Certificate
2. Marriage Certificate
3. Death Certificate
4. Census
5. Church Records
6. Family History
7. Military Records
8. Occupational Records
9. Probate Records, Pre-1858
10. Probate Records, 1858 to Present
11. Cemetery Records
12. Monumental Inscriptions/Church Monuments
13. Newspapers
14. Biography
15. School and Alumni Records
16. Poor Law Records
17. Quarter Sessions

Reproduced by permission of © 2008 Intellectual Reserve, Inc.

Figure 5.10

It starts with the obvious choice of a birth certificate and then suggests other sources to use if you can't find any records, if the information conflicts with things you know or that you have taken from other sources, or if you want to supplement the information you find. If you click the link from Birth Certificate, you are taken to a sheet on using civil registration records in England and Wales.

Document types

On the page you reached by selecting Articles from the Research Helps tab, there was an option on the left of the screen that allowed you to sort by Document Type. This groups the guidance as follows:

- **Forms:** Help you record your research.

- **Letter-writing Guides:** Useful if you need to write to foreign archives or government agencies.

- **Maps:** Often showing historical county boundaries.

- **Reference Documents:** For historical background on places.

- **Research Outlines:** The records available and the strategies for research are organised by location, and there are separate outlines for England, Wales, Scotland and Ireland.

- **Resource Guides:** Links to sources such as census indexes, handwriting, tracing your ancestors in England, Ireland Householders Index (Griffiths Valuation).

- **Step-by-step Guides:** Provide instructions on how to use the records and hints for searching.

- **Word Lists:** Provide English translations of foreign words. Can be of more immediate help than a standard dictionary because they focus particularly on words genealogists need.

Using the tutorials

The Family History Library in Salt Lake City runs courses, classes and lectures on a daily basis. Recognising that most family historians are not able to attend these workshops, there is now a series of video tutorials online (Figure 5.11 outlines the five videos), one of which covers beginning English research.

Go to the Library tab and select Education. Click Family History Research Series Online.

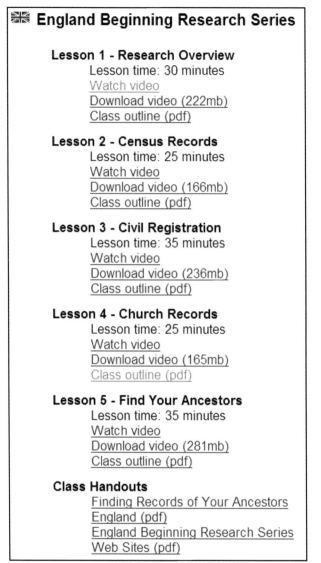

England Beginning Research Series

Lesson 1 - Research Overview
Lesson time: 30 minutes
Watch video
Download video (222mb)
Class outline (pdf)

Lesson 2 - Census Records
Lesson time: 25 minutes
Watch video
Download video (166mb)
Class outline (pdf)

Lesson 3 - Civil Registration
Lesson time: 35 minutes
Watch video
Download video (236mb)
Class outline (pdf)

Lesson 4 - Church Records
Lesson time: 25 minutes
Watch video
Download video (165mb)
Class outline (pdf)

Lesson 5 - Find Your Ancestors
Lesson time: 35 minutes
Watch video
Download video (281mb)
Class outline (pdf)

Class Handouts
Finding Records of Your Ancestors
England (pdf)
England Beginning Research Series
Web Sites (pdf)

Figure 5.11

There is also a detailed outline for each of the lessons. These are PDF files and so open in Adobe Reader. You can also download these lesson outlines to print out or to view at another time. The procedure for this is:

1. Position your mouse over the link on the web page.

2. Right-click.

> You may only have used the left mouse button before to highlight and open files. The right mouse button and its options can be a revelation. Try it from time to time in different contexts and see what it offers you.

3. Click Save Target As. You will be taken to your document filing system.

4. Find the folder in which you would like to save these files (or create a new one if necessary).

5. Click Save and the document will be saved as a PDF file.

You can then open the file in the same way as any other file on your system, by going to your filing system, finding the file and double-clicking.

Alternatively, open the appropriate program (Adobe Reader in this case) and use File → Open to find the document.

Using Record Search

There has been a sudden and significant increase in computer ownership and interest in family history. LDS Family History Centers (just like other libraries and archives) find their time and physical resources under pressure as more people want to view materials. Since so many researchers now have their own computers, the next logical step is to digitise the original documents. Individuals can then view these at home or in local libraries with Internet access. This opens up the materials and the possibilities for research to a much wider audience.

What is the Record Search project?

Until now, most of what you could view online at FamilySearch was transcribed material, collected into searchable databases. Where there are inconsistencies in transcriptions, you need to access original documents by ordering and then viewing microfilms and fiche at a Family History Center.

At the time of writing, the project to digitise material is still in its pilot stage but it is clear that its scope is potentially huge. Record indexes can be searched and then, where these are available, images of original documents viewed. In some cases, clicking to view these documents takes you to one of the subscription websites, where you may need to register and pay to view the material. Other records can be accessed directly through the Record Search site and payment is not required. These documents can then be saved, printed and incorporated into your research material.

How to access the Record Search site

To access the project, click the Search Records tab near the top of the FamilySearch home page. Select Record Search Pilot. From the front page of Record Search, you can search for an individual. The Advanced Search option allows you to add the names of parents or spouse.

Once you enter a name and get results, you can narrow down your search by using the menus at the top of the page. No doubt this project will continue to grow and the record numbers increase.

All the transcription work is undertaken by volunteers. The front page of the pilot site has a section inviting you to become an indexer. Click Find out more. You need to download some free software onto your computer. You then need to Register (sign up) or Start Indexing (sign in for registered volunteers).

To see a list of the indexing projects, click the Projects tab near the top of the page. If you click any projects, you see information about those records and usually some sample documents. This can be useful if you are likely to come across such documents in your own research as it gives you an idea of what you will need to tackle.

If you do have time, you might find it worthwhile to volunteer. Even if your own family research is not very advanced, your efforts can help such projects to progress much more quickly. It will also help to sharpen your skills in working with this material.

Research tasks: Using FamilySearch for the Fischer/Smith family

In this task, you use Record Search to find any members of Sophie's family living in England. Sophie was Carl's mother/Frederick's wife and her maiden name was Rubardt. You know from census research that both she and Frederick were from Germany, though they married in England. The name Rubardt will be uncommon in England, so it's worth investigating if other Rubardts have some family connection.

1. Go to the main FamilySearch page at **www.familysearch.org**.

2. From the Search Records tab, select Record Search pilot.

3. Enter the surname Rubardt and click Search.

4. At the top of the page, use the Filter option and select Place.

5. Tick the England box and click OK.

6. Of the results, some show individuals born in England but later living in the US. These may be family members and following up on them would be the subject of a separate research task. Use the Collections option to narrow the search to the 1861 census. (Note that to view the document you would need to go to another website.)

7. Click each name in turn and write down how old each person is. Work out a possible birth year for each.

8. Assuming this is a family, who are the parents?

9. Which children were born in England and which in Germany?

10. What does this tell you about where the parents were married and when they came to England?

11. Any ideas about how this family might be related to Sophie? (Hint – look back at the marriage certificate in Figure 4.15.)

Suggested answers to questions 8–11 can be found after the following research task.

Research tasks: Using FamilySearch for your family

Search for the family you used to do the task on the 1881 census in Chapter 4.

1. Do an advanced search on FamilySearch. Look at the results for Ancestral File, IGI and Pedigree Resource File separately. Note any new or confirming information you are given. If there are pedigrees to follow back, then follow them (as you did with Shelley).

2. If you know the name of the town where the family were living, you can search for this on the page of results (even if you are not given this option by the database). On your keyboard, hold down the CTRL key and press F once. This opens a Find box in which you can enter any word you want to find on that page. Click Next (or Previous) to find.

3. As a second task, go to the Record Search page from the Search Records tab. Try entering some family names and then narrowing down your research by date, place, name or collection. Remember that this is a work in progress, so it is worth coming back from time to time to see whether new records have been added.

Research tasks – Rubardt family Record Search suggested answers

-   The parents of the family are William and Maria.

-   Otto, William (Jr) and Louise were born in England. George was born in Germany.

-   The parents were probably married in Germany. They came to England between 1853 and 1856. This census (1861) will therefore be the first on which you will find the family.

-   William could be the witness to the marriage of Sophie and Frederick in 1860. He is likely to be a close relation of hers, either brother or cousin.

Follow-up work for this task would be to track the family through subsequent census records.

Summary

- The FamilySearch website has searchable databases extracted from parish records, some censuses and submitted family trees.

- Microfilms of original documents are viewable at Family History Centers.

- The online Library Catalog gives film numbers and details.

- Extensive research guidance is available on the site, including video tutorials.

- Most material is free, including Personal Ancestral File (PAF) family history software.

- Volunteering for the project to index and digitise original material can help develop your document research skills.

Brain Training

1. What does AFN stand for?

a) Ancestral Family Name

b) Ancestral Family Number

c) Ancestral File Name

d) Ancestral File Number

2. What is the family tree software developed by the LDS called?

a) Brother's Keeper

b) Family Tree Maker

c) Personal Ancestral File

d) Roots Magic

3. Which of these relatives would you expect to see on a pedigree sheet?

a) Brother

b) Cousin

c) Grandfather

d) Uncle

4. Which of the following records would you not expect to find in a Bishop's Transcript?

a) Baptisms

b) Burials

c) Marriages

d) Wills

5. Which of these censuses is not currently searchable on the main FamilySearch website?

a) British Isles 1861

b) British Isles 1881

c) Canada 1881

d) US 1880

Answers

Q1 – d   **Q2** – c   **Q3** – c   **Q4** – d

Q5 – a

Using the Ancestry website

6

Equipment needed: Computer and Internet access to the Ancestry website (check if your library has a paid subscription you can access).

Skills needed: Searching databases, extracting information, refining search queries.

Ancestry.com (or its UK equivalent, ancestry.co.uk) is one of a number of commercial websites that have collected in one place databases of interest to family historians. These databases cover the major genealogical resources such as censuses and birth, marriage and death. They also have hundreds of smaller databases. Everything is searchable, as individual databases, collections of related data or across all databases. Some material is free to search and access; other material requires a paid subscription.

What's on the Ancestry website?

The genealogy of family tree organisations is almost as complex as an individual's family history. A service or website starts up (birth) and sometimes closes down (death). More often, the activities are merged or taken over by another organisation (marriage). Updating my Favorites websites list recently was like going through an old address book. **1837.com** had become **FindMyPast.com**. The link to the software program, Family Tree Maker, now took me to a **Genealogy.com** website (where the program was still for sale). A search on the Ancestry site **www.ancestry.com** provides a 'family group sheet' of related organisations (see Figure 6.1).

Figure 6.1

Ancestry is best known for the millions of records it holds in searchable databases. Some come from links to other databases, such as FreeBMD; others were resourced or sponsored by Ancestry itself. There are links to a magazine and to one of the well-known family tree software programs.

In common with a number of such sites, you are able to create a family tree online. (You'll see how this can be done for the Fischer/Smith case study family in Chapter 13.) As a result of this, you can check your family data against that submitted by other researchers, view trees online (where the researcher has made the tree public) and contact other researchers. This gives you potentially millions more names to search and increases the chances of finding a match with someone who is researching one or more of the branches of your family tree. It's here, in particular, that the benefit of using a computer and being online is easy to appreciate.

Figure 6.1 also shows the international nature of the activity. The US site (**www. ancestry.com**) has the biggest collection of material, reflecting the organisation's origins in a large country with a population aware of its ancestral roots in many different parts of the world.

The UK site (**www.ancestry.co.uk**) also has a huge collection of material. This will be the focus of the examples and research tasks in this book and should be assumed whenever a reference to Ancestry is made (unless otherwise specified).

How to access the material on Ancestry

Ancestry is a subscription website. Initial searches are free but, should you wish to look at further details or digitised images from original documents, then you need to pay for an account. Some of the material on the Ancestry site is free.

> The easiest way to see which material is free is to go to another website called Cyndi's List **www.cyndislist.com/ancestry.htm** and click the Free Databases link.

There are a number of subscription options for Ancestry and you should try out the site before you hand over your credit card details. As always, you should investigate the free options first.

- Many libraries now have a subscription to Ancestry. You may need to book a computer session to use it. If you take a laptop to the library, you might be able to access it wirelessly on your machine. If Ancestry is available at your local library, you should check the following:

  - Does the subscription restrict the number of library users who can access Ancestry at any one time (this makes booking even more important)?

  - Can it be accessed in all local libraries or only in one (a central library and/or local studies centre)?

  - Is the coverage UK only or worldwide?

  - Does the package give all UK records including parish records pre-1837?

- LDS Family History Centers or organisations like the Society of Genealogists have Internet access in their libraries, which includes access to Ancestry and sometimes other subscription databases.

- You can sign up for a free Ancestry account. This allows you to search and access any of the free databases Ancestry holds.

- You can sign up for a 14-day free Ancestry trial. This requires you to give your credit card details. You have access to all the features of the site. If you don't cancel at the end of the trial, your subscription will be taken from your credit card.

- One-, three- or six-month (basic UK) access is included when you purchase Family Tree Maker.

If you do decide to purchase your own subscription, then you have three options, each of which is available on an annual or a monthly basis. As you would expect, annual subscriptions work out cheaper:

- **Essential**: All basic UK material back to 1837. No parish register records from earlier times or Irish records. (Current costs: £83.40 annual/£10.95 monthly.)

- **Premium**: As for Essential plus parish and Irish records. (Current costs: £107.40 annual/£12.95 monthly.)

- **Worldwide**: All UK and International records. (Current costs: £155.40 annual/£18.95 monthly).

> When your subscription is due for renewal, you will be informed. If you don't want to continue, you need actively to cancel the subscription.

There is also an option for pay-as-you-go, which currently costs £6.95 for 12 record views (credits last 14 days).

As with all such information, prices and pricing structures may change over time.

How to sign up for a free account

After you have done an initial search from the home page of the site, you will be offered the free account option. Don't confuse it with the 14-day free trial offer, which routinely pops up on your screen when you try to view details and images not accessible with the free account. Go to the Ancestry website **www.ancestry.co.uk**, which is shown in Figure 6.2. In the box, enter the name Carl Fischer. Tick the small box that restricts you to records from the UK and Ireland. Click Search.

Figure 6.2

In the page that appears, select Summarized by category in the View dropdown box. You'll see that more than 16,000 matches for the search have been found. Like Internet searches, some of these are unlikely to be what you want. Some show 'Carl Fischer'. Others may just show any Fischer, or even Fisher, since the search didn't require exact spelling.

Figure 6.3 shows the results page. On the left side is the box with the search requirements you entered. If you wish, you can refine your search, adding or taking away items, to improve the results you get. The results are summarised by category. Where there are more than five sub-categories (as in the census results), the others are not shown. To view them, you would need to click the See all 1361 results link (or some other figure). All initial searches work in this way on Ancestry.

While it's probably tempting at this stage to play around with the search options, you should do this after signing up. Scroll down the page until you come to the FreeBMD Marriage Index 1837–1915 (where you already know you will find Carl). Click the link. You will be taken to the Free Account page (Figure 6.4).

All Ancestry.co.uk images reproduced with the permission of Ancestry.com Operations Inc. All rights reserved

Figure 6.3

All Ancestry.co.uk images reproduced with the permission of Ancestry.com Operations Inc. All rights reserved

Figure 6.4

Put in your name and email.

> ⚠ If you don't want to receive any email from them, make sure the first three boxes below your email are unticked.

You need to tick the last box accepting Terms and Conditions. Click View Records.

You will be given a username and a password, with the option to change one or both of them if they are hard to remember. The password will probably be less than intuitive, so find something that works for you. You'll need these if you logout after a session and then want to login again. You can also request an email reminder if you forget your password.

Use the free account to practice entering a few searches. You could try the famous people you used for census and FamilySearch examples and see what comes up. You can also try entering some of your family members or members of the Fischer/Smith family. Some results may give you additional information to that which you already have. The 1881 census transcription data is available to you, as are the FreeBMD indexes; other census information and non-FreeBMD vital records are restricted.

The free account also lets you look at the Learning Centre. (Click the tab in the horizontal bar at the top of the screen. This is sometimes called the 'navigation' bar or menu, as it helps you navigate round the site.)

Now that you're in the site, with a licence to search, you can look at what records it holds, view some of them and learn how to find your way around. New sites are a bit like new cars; the basics are usually the same but the controls are often in a different place. Sometimes they have gadgets you haven't had before (like rear-view cameras to help you park and reverse). In doing research for this book, I realised that sites I'd used for years had features buried in them that I'd never investigated. Tutorials are a good example. Mostly I'd just played around with the site until I'd figured out how it worked (the 'caught, not taught' model of learning). Along the way, I often got frustrated with myself and the site for not doing what I wanted. As with many things in life, the solution was probably to read the manual but you don't always have time.

Another problem (the analogy, this time, is to supermarkets rearranging the shelves) is that sites often reinvent themselves. Generally, this is meant to improve the searching experience but, if you are already a regular user to the site and can search in autopilot mode, it's annoying if things aren't where they were yesterday.

Ancestry, like FamilySearch (and like the National Archives that you will be looking at in the next chapter), is a huge collection of material, databases and web pages and many of these are updated constantly. The numerical results shown, in the images in this book and the page layouts, may vary when you come to do your research tasks, but don't let this put you off. Where material is continually being added to a site, this is a bonus. It means that there are still opportunities for you to find that elusive relative or that missing piece of information, tomorrow if not today. FreeBMD is another example of an ever-changing and growing database that you should revisit from time to time.

Figure 6.5 shows the Ancestry home page as it currently looks when you login. Note that you may have to scroll down the page to view everything that is shown here, including the Search box.

The rest of the examples used in this chapter will be taken from the full Ancestry site, ie from a subscription account. This will show you what you can find when you go to a library or archive with access to Ancestry. It will also help you decide if a subscription is worthwhile for you.

Figure 6.5

Understanding what you can find on Ancestry

The key to successful searching of a website like Ancestry is to understand how the search options work, how the site is organised and how results are presented.

The Catalogue

Ancestry groups its records into these collections:

- census and voter lists
- birth, marriage and death
- military
- immigration and emigration
- directories and member lists
- newspapers and periodicals
- family trees
- stories, memories and histories
- pictures
- court, land, wills and financial
- dictionaries, encyclopaedias and reference.

When you first do a search, you have the opportunity to search all the records or to select a particular collection. It's useful to try a search of all Collections initially. Following your search plan, you would probably look at birth records, followed by census for the relevant years. If the timeframe is right, you could look at telephone directories. These enable you to track addresses over time.

For each of the Collections, you will use a celebrity and see what information Ancestry finds for you. This can be checked against other sources of known facts such as Wikipedia.

Another site with information on the great and the good is **www.nndb.com**, which has some 35,000 profiles from Oliver Cromwell to Oliver Reed.

There are usually several different ways to search. For these first searches, put your mouse cursor over the Search tab at the top of the home page (don't click – this is called hovering) and wait for the dropdown menu to appear. Move the cursor down to the relevant collection and then click.

Birth, marriage, death

Go to the Birth, Marriage and Death collection from the dropdown Search menu. Figure 6.6 shows how all these pages are structured.

At the top of the page is a brief definition of the records in this collection. You are also told why such records are important for the family historian.

In the panel on the left, you are shown the featured databases that comprise this collection. The most important ones are given first. You can search on the entire collection or select a particular title.

The right-hand panel has learning resources relevant to this collection. Selecting any of these questions gives you a brief dropdown tip on the same page. Clicking on the question closes it up again.

The central area allows you to search. There are many different search fields (categories). You can also select whether you want an exact search and whether to restrict your search to UK and Ireland records. When searching, remember the rule that 'less is more'.

Figure 6.6

Celebrity search – birth, marriage, and death

1. Enter the name of **Aubrey Beardsley**, born 1872.

2. In the results, look first at the FreeBMD Birth index.

3. The matching name and year (1872 Q. Sep) show you have the correct person. He was born in Brighton and his middle name was Vincent.

4. Click the Back Button arrow in the top left corner of the screen to go back to the original results page.

5. Select Christening Records 1530–1906.

6. Again, Beardsley comes at the top of the list.

7. Click View Record (using a paid personal/library subscription).

8. This gives his parents' names plus the date of Aubrey's christening.

Note that the christening gives more information about the parents than you get from just the BMD index. There were two results in the christening list. If you look at both, you will see that Aubrey's mother's name has been wrongly transcribed on one of them.

A tip for searching is: if you can't find a name spelled in the normal way, use a wildcard to replace some letters. This can sometimes overcome transcription errors, mistakes in the original documents or alternative names used (eg Rose/Rosie; Sophia/Sophie).

The current FreeBMD data on Ancestry goes up to 1915. The FreeBMD website itself has data up to the 1930s so, if you are looking for later years, use the FreeBMD site, until the information is updated on Ancestry.

If you want to view the original index pages from the registers, you can only do this with the subscription account. To view the pages free, use the FreeBMD site.

Until the seventeenth century, betrothals were considered almost as binding as marriages. This is why the baptism of the first child of a couple is sometimes recorded less than nine months after their wedding.

Census

You already have some experience of census searching and results from the 1881 records on the FamilySearch site and the 1911 website. Ancestry has the 1881 records and all other censuses back to 1841. What it doesn't have is the 1911 material.

Before your celebrity search, explore a little further the way the site is structured. Hover your mouse over the Search button in the navigation bar and select Census and Voter Lists. On the left is the Featured list. At the bottom of this list is the option to go to the Card Catalogue. Click this link. Figure 6.7 shows you the first page of the full Ancestry Card Catalogue. The results are ordered by popularity (the databases accessed most frequently by researchers). You won't be surprised that US census records head the list.

Sort by options

Ancestry Card Catalogue

Search Titles		Matches 1-25 of 28,887	Sort By Popularity ▾		1 2 ... 11 >
Title		**Title**	**Collection**	**Size**	**Activity**
Keyword(s)		1920 United States Federal Census	Census & Voter Lists	107,408,900	
		1930 United States Federal Census	Census & Voter Lists	124,450,859	
Search or Clear All		1900 United States Federal Census	Census & Voter Lists	77,277,541	
		1910 United States Federal Census	Census & Voter Lists	93,399,001	
Filter Titles		New York Passenger Lists, 1820-1957	Immigration & Emigration	82,905,466	
☐ Only records from the UK and Ireland		1880 United States Federal Census	Census & Voter Lists	50,475,325	
Reset all filters and start over		1870 United States Federal Census	Census & Voter Lists	40,325,362	
FILTER BY COLLECTION		Public Member Trees	Family Trees	585,730,026	
Census & Voter Lists	432	1841 England Census	Census & Voter Lists	14,726,532	
Birth, Marriage & Death	1000+	England & Wales, FreeBMD Marriage Index: 1837-1915	Birth, Marriage & Death	38,485,032	UPDATED
Military	941				
Immigration & Emigration	298	Social Security Death Index	Birth, Marriage & Death	84,571,388	UPDATED
Newspapers & Periodicals	1000+	England & Wales, Marriage Index: 1916-2005	Birth, Marriage & Death	96,512,216	UPDATED

Filter by Collection   Filter by Title

Figure 6.7

Filter the list by using the options on the left. First tick the box to show records from the UK and Ireland only. Then filter the collections, showing only Census and Voter Lists. The layout is still as in Figure 6.7 but the Catalogue has now been reduced to a much more manageable number of entries. As well as the more obvious national censuses, there are other less well known entries such as the Suffolk Returns from the Census of Religious Worship of 1851, and Ireland 1766 Religious Census. While your research may not yet be ready for these sources, it is useful to know they are here, if your detection trail leads you to these locations at these dates.

Each page of the Catalogue shows 25 results. Click the page numbers at the top or bottom of the list to view other pages. Clicking any individual Catalogue entry takes you to a search box just for that title. Information is also available on the database and its source.

Celebrity search – census

1. Use the Search button on the navigation bar to select Census and Voter Lists.

2. Scroll down the page to the bottom of the Search box. Make sure the box for UK and Ireland records only is ticked.

3. At the top of the search box, enter the name of **Emmeline Pankhurst**, born 1857. Click Search.

4. Make sure the results are sorted by relevance.

5. The first three results are for the same person, in three censuses (1881, 1891 and 1901).

6. Hover your mouse (don't click) over the census date at the left of each result. You will be given a preview of the information contained in the transcribed record.

7. Click the View Image link for the 1881 result (using a paid personal/ library subscription). This will take you to the original image of the census (see Figure 6.8) rather than a transcribed version. If this is the first time you have viewed an image, the site may ask if you want to install an enhanced viewer. It should work on most systems (though unfortunately not with Mac computers and with Netscape browsers). If you wish, you can stick with the basic viewer.

8. Find the printer icon towards the left, just above the census image (see Figure 6.8) and try printing a copy of the information. You will be offered a choice of options (image only; image with source; customized print). By default, your printer is probably set to portrait printing. You will need to set it to landscape each time, which is better suited to the census layout.

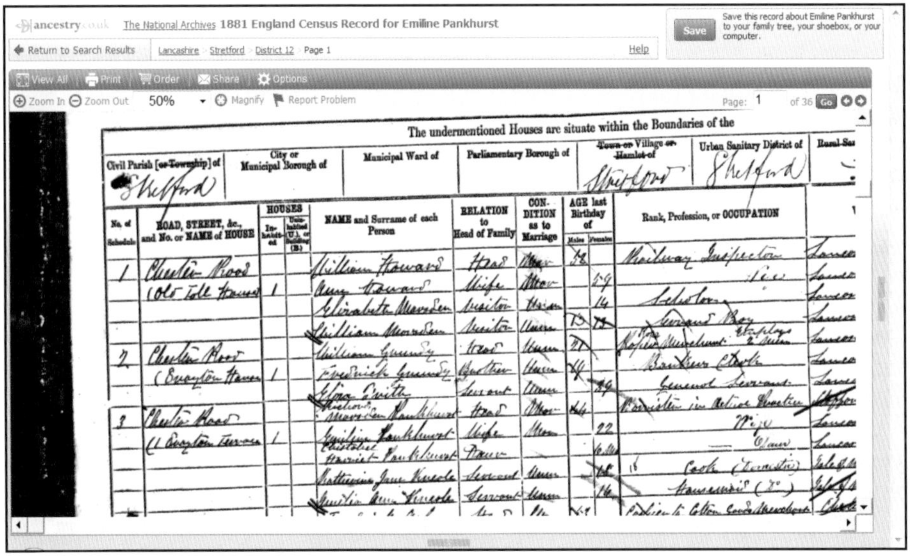

Figure 6.8

Note that the results of your search will only give you records where Mrs Pankhurst is shown by her married name. It is under this name that she is best known. Her maiden name was Goulden and you would need to use this for any birth search or if you were looking for census records prior to her marriage. When you record your family history, the custom is for women to be recorded under their maiden names (presumably on the basis that you can be married more than once but only have one birth).

It is useful to look at the various tool options you are offered for viewing images. Figure 6.8 shows you some of these, though, like many toolbar icons, they can seem rather small. You can zoom in and out using the icons which have + and − on them. There is a magnifier option which transforms your cursor into a magnifying glass, enlarging the area under your cursor as you click and move the mouse.

By default, the cursor when you open the image is in the shape of a hand rather than the normal arrow head. This lets you click a part of the image and drag it to bring up another area in the main window. This is very useful if you want to keep the image at a reasonable magnification but then can't see the whole picture at once. You might want to play around with this to see how it works.

This 'click and drag' function can be found in a number of programs where you are working with graphics.

You can select the size by percentage. If you click the black dropdown arrow next to the percentage box, you will see a number of options such as Fit Image (on screen), Fit Width and Fit Height.

When you print, you have the option to choose Entire Image or Current View (that is, whatever is currently visible on screen). Experiment with the settings so that you get something that is reasonably legible but that also contains all the information you need. A whole page may not be necessary.

There is also a button at the top right for saving the record. This can be done in three ways:

- Starting an online family tree with this person (or saving to an existing tree if you have already started one).

- Putting the record in an electronic 'shoebox' on the Ancestry site. This allows you to retrieve it without going through the search process. It is useful if you are not yet sure where someone fits in but want to keep the details. The shoebox and its saved contents can be found at the bottom of the home page.

- Saving to your computer (this would include saving to a memory stick). You may want to have a new folder on your computer ready for anything you save. It could be subdivided for different families. The file you save will be in JPEG format (the same format that a digital camera uses when it takes photos).

Census records were often recorded in enumerator books. This image, therefore, is only one of a series. In this case, it's page 1 of 36 and these numbers are also shown in the toolbar. You can put in any number in the box and click Go. You can also use the arrows to move forwards and backwards through the whole set of pages. There are several reasons why you might want to do so:

- The family is large (or starts at the bottom of the page) and the household continues on the next sheet.

- You want an idea of who else was living in the district: did they come from the same place, did they have similar occupations and were they wealthy or very poor?

- Family members often lived in the same area, so you may find other relatives just by looking in nearby streets.

> If you have trouble finding someone in the census and all your searching skills have been exhausted, try looking in the previous and subsequent censuses to the one that is giving you grief. There may be information in those records that you didn't have before and that could enhance your original search.

Military records

If you are researching family in the UK at the beginning of the twentieth century, it is likely that one or more members of your family served in the armed forces during the First World War. You may have their service medals and formal photographs of them in uniform. Other family members may have been in the regular army or have served in other conflicts.

Using the same technique as for the census records on Ancestry, take a look at the Card Catalogue and filter it by UK/Ireland and then by Military. This will show you the databases you can access. You will see that there are separate databases for Service Records and the Medal Rolls Index. You might expect that there would be one record for each serving soldier, matched by a service medal reference (these are service medals, rather than medals for gallantry). As you can see, however, there are nearly four times as many medal records as there are service records.

The reason for this discrepancy is that about 60% of the service records for non-commissioned officers and other ranks who served between 1914 and 1920, were destroyed in a fire during the Second World War. This means that you only have a four in ten chance of finding the record for your ancestor. The remaining records are called the Burnt Documents. They were microfilmed and are accessible at The National Archives and through Ancestry. Officers' records were held separately and most of them have survived.

If there is a pension record, then this may provide some of the information from the missing records. The medal cards don't give much information beyond name and number.

Celebrity search – Military

1. Use the Search button on the navigation bar to select Military.

2. In the search box, enter the name of **Victor Silvester**, born 1900 (though he claimed to be 20 when he enlisted in 1916).

3. Select the Medal Rolls Index link.

4. He had the unusual middle name of Marlborough. The first entry on the list is therefore likely to be the right person.

5. Click View Record and then View Original Image (using a paid personal/library subscription).

6. Return to the results list using the Back button (you will need to click more than once).

7. Select British Army Pension Records. The first entry is the correct person. Hover the mouse cursor over View Record to get a preview of the details.

8. Click the magnifying glass icon on the right of the entry to go directly to View Image (this is one of several ways in the results to get to the document images).

Note that the ordinary soldier's record for Victor Silvester did not appear in the results. You should therefore assume that it was one of the destroyed records. In this case, fortunately, there was a pension record that can act as a proxy.

In the Image Viewer, you can move between the pages of the record by using the Next and Previous arrows just above the image. At some point, you will come to the record of the next person with the surname Silvester.

England had no regular standing army until the Civil War in 1642.

If you want to go back to the original search results list, it can be tedious to keep clicking on the Previous arrow or on the Back arrow at the top left of the Internet Explorer page. As shown in Figure 6.9, if you click the small black arrow next to the Back and Forward buttons, it gives you a list of the most recent pages viewed.

Figure 6.9

Using this, you could now skip all the Pension pages and click Victor Silvester –
Ancestry.co.uk. This would take you straight back to the search results page.

Using the Back and Forward buttons works for all Internet searching, not
just on Ancestry. It's very useful if you have viewed dozens of pages and
don't want to go back through them page by page.

Immigration and emigration

Immigration and emigration records start to point you in the direction of resources
outside the UK and Ireland. If you need to undertake significant research in
places like the US, Australia and Europe, you may need to consider whether
a worldwide subscription to Ancestry is worth the additional £50 for you. For
the moment, keep the focus on the UK and extract the maximum information
available from these records. (You could always make a list of international
resources to search and then initially access Ancestry at a library or archive to see
how useful it might be.)

Free settlers always outnumbered transported convicts in Australia.

If someone can't be found on a census and there's no obvious death record in the period since the previous census, one conclusion to draw is that the individual has left the UK permanently. What would help confirm or reject this theory?

● First check in a subsequent census to make sure that the person hasn't just been misnamed or eluded the census taker.

● If it's a woman, check that she hasn't got married and is now reported under another name. Remember that she may have been living with someone (not just a modern phenomenon) and taken his name to be 'respectable' without an official marriage ever taking place.

● If you are looking for a child, how likely is it that he/she would have emigrated alone? If the rest of the family is still around, who would have taken the child? One possibility is that a child from a large family was informally adopted by a smaller family or by a childless couple. The adopting family may or may not have been relatives.

● Given that a large number of people went to the US, one useful free resource that you can check is Ellis Island **www.ellisisland.org**. You have to register to search this site but registration is free. You can also view digital images of ships' passenger lists, which contain information about country of origin, relatives left behind (usually a parent, brother or uncle) and with whom the person intended to stay (often a relative who had come over earlier). Not all migrants went through Ellis Island but it is a good place to start.

There are few sources of information about people coming to the UK until well into the twentieth century. There is no equivalent of Ellis Island and its records. There are online arrivals and departure records but these only cover travel to and from places outside Europe and the Mediterranean. Ancestry has some of these records. This topic will come up again in your tour of The National Archives online holdings in Chapter 7.

Start your search of the Ancestry records by going once again to the Card Catalogue. Go straight there from the Search tab (not an absolute requirement but it highlights the number of different entry points you have on the site). The Card Catalogue is the last item on the Search tab list.

You might be interested to look first at the full listing of immigration and emigration sources before filtering for UK and Ireland records. On the left of the page, untick the box for UK records (assuming it is ticked). Select Immigration & Emigration and browse the list to see what's on offer. Then filter by United Kingdom. You can see that the most extensive listing, and one of the most popular, is UK Incoming Passenger Lists 1878–1960. Because this shows recent records (well, recent in genealogical terms), you can sometimes find relatives who were holidaying or travelling on business. The records show the individual's date of birth and where they were living.

Celebrity search – immigration and emigration

1. Use the Search button on the navigation bar to select Immigration and Emigration.

2. In the Search box enter the name of **David Niven**, born 1910.

3. All results are from the Incoming Passengers List. Click the link.

4. There are a lot of results for David Niven born 1910. If you know that his full name was James David Graham Niven, then this opens up even more possibilities.

5. On your keyboard, the comma and full stop keys have left and right pointing arrow heads. Try using these keys to scroll up and down the results list.

6. If you want to preview the results while using these arrow keys, press P once. This gives the preview for the current record. As you move through the list with the arrow keys, a preview will pop up for each record, removing the need to use the mouse.

7. *Hot key* is the computer term for using the keyboard rather than the mouse to make something happen. In these search activities, P and the arrow heads are hot keys. Two more you can use: R is the hot key for Refine Search; N is the hot key for New Search.

8. Select the first entry on the David Niven list. Click the magnifying glass icon on the right (using a paid personal/library subscription) to view the image.

9. Use the hand icon to drag the image around until you can see the entries. These are alphabetical by surname.

Note that these lists can be a useful way of identifying families if they are travelling together. The ship details are at the top of the page. This was the Normandie, travelling from New York to Southampton, with an arrival date of 21 June 1937. The column headings tell you about age, occupation, address in London, country of last permanent residence and intended future permanent residence.

Niven is a young actor and is travelling cabin class. If you go back to the search results and view the image for 9 March 1950, you will see that he is now travelling first class on the Queen Mary, accompanied by his second wife Hjordis. They are permanently resident in the US and will be staying at Claridges Hotel in London.

You might want to try a few searches for your own family names using this resource. Even if you are convinced that no one emigrated, it may reveal family travel of which you were not aware.

Accessing records from Scotland, Wales and Ireland

Records for relatives from Scotland, Wales and Ireland may be included with other results. You have already seen that BMD and census records cover England and Wales. If you search for Scottish census results, you will see that Ancestry does not currently have permission to include access to the census images and so has transcribed these censuses itself. Scottish BMD records seem also to be restricted to parish records. If you are researching extensively in Scotland, start with the Ancestry census transcriptions and use the data to find BMD on the ScotlandsPeople website **www.scotlandspeople.gov.uk**.

You might want to look at the Card Catalogue and see what records are available both specifically and more generally for these places.

1. From the Search tab near the top of the Ancestry home page, find and click the Card Catalogue.

2. Scroll down the screen until you find Filter by Location on the left-hand side.

3. Click United Kingdom. This opens more possibilities for filtering by location within the UK.

4. Select Scotland from the Filter Location list. The results are broad in coverage (Medal Rolls) or specific to Scotland (Scotland Census).

5. It is possible to 'drill down' a further level and view results by county.

6. If you want to look at records higher up the 'filter chain' you can close filters by clicking the X next to each one, as shown in Figure 6.10. You also have an option here to Reset all filters and start over.

Note that the options shown within the UK do not include Ireland, only Northern Ireland. To look at records from Ireland, restart the filtering process and select Europe, rather than United Kingdom. Ireland will then appear as a separate category within which you can filter further by county.

Figure 6.10

You can see that the filtering option will work for English counties as well. If you are researching other countries, then you may wish to restrict your research to a particular state or region, if these options are available. Filtering by language is also a possibility for some international records.

Searching other collections

You have now looked at the major collections important to anyone starting their family history. As a summary, it might be interesting to take another well-known figure, Sir Arthur Conan Doyle, and do a general search. This should show him in the major collections and may bring up some others, such as pictures or obituaries. As he was born in Scotland, the results should, therefore, include Scottish resources.

Searching other collections

1. Go to the Ancestry home page.

2. Scroll down to the Search box. Enter Arthur Conan as first names, Doyle as a last name and a birth year of 1859. (Note that most Internet searches don't require you to use capital letters, even for names or places. Upper and lower case distinctions are usually only important in things like passwords.)

3. Make sure UK/Ireland records are selected. Click Search.

Search results can be presented in different ways. If you look at the top of the results box (Figure 6.11), it will tell you how many matches there were and whether they are sorted by Category or by Relevance.

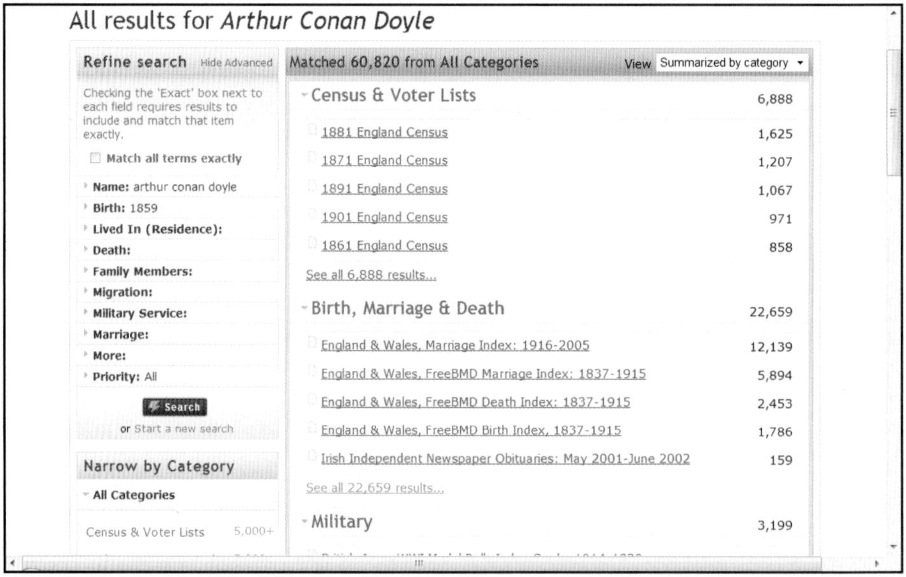

Figure 6.11

● Category means that all the census results are shown together, as are BMD results and so on. This is useful to get an overview, or where you are mainly interested in the results from one collection.

● Relevance will give you individual records from all collections, putting the most likely ones (according to your search criteria) at the top of the list.

On the right, there is a box marked View with a small black dropdown arrow. This lets you change options. If you click the arrow, you will see both options. Choose Relevance if it is not already selected.

Whichever option you select will be used for all subsequent searches, even when you shut down the computer and then turn it on again. Ancestry assumes that this is how you want the default view to be. Changing it back is simply a matter of clicking on the dropdown arrow again and altering the option.

Figure 6.12 shows the results sorted by Relevance. The first has an apparent transcription error. On its own, this would have caused the search function to put this result much further down the list. However, there is a small icon (a pencil) next to the name. If you hover the cursor over this icon, a correction to the entry comes up. Once a correction has been added, both possibilities are included in the search.

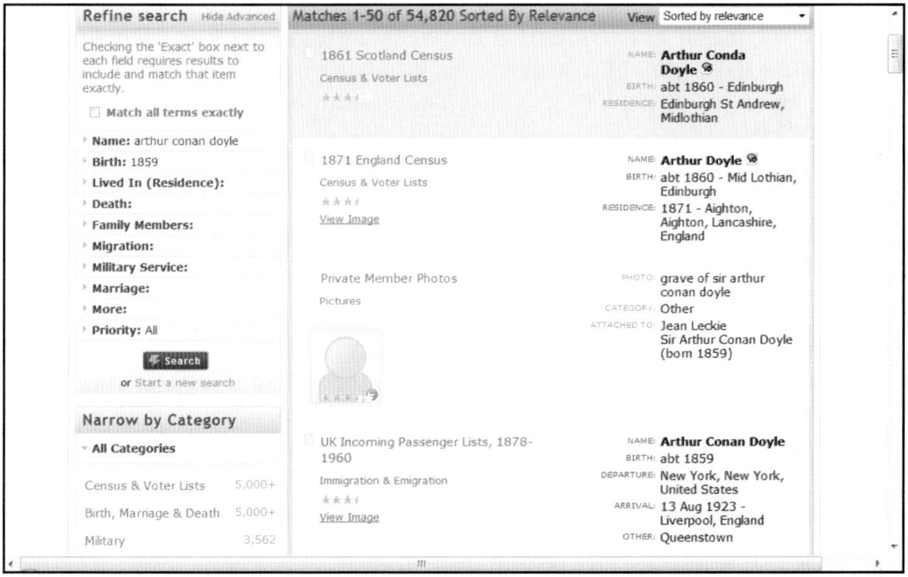

Figure 6.12

The first eight results are all for the correct person and include items from the pictures collection. Some of these are available for everyone to see; others, like the third result, are marked private. If you want further information, you can email the data holder directly.

The next set of results seems a bit more problematic for the search engine. It's possible to make a more intelligent guess than the computer. The first two are correct, as the known place of birth matches, even if the year and the name are not as expected. (This is a bit unfair to the computer, since it hasn't yet been given the birthplace.) Later results from Incoming Passenger Lists could be confirmed through viewing the image for data such as occupation and possible family travelling companions.

Go back and resort the list by Category. Scroll down to see some of the material that you could search. At the bottom of the list is a section on family trees. Click the Public Member Trees link. This shows trees submitted by subscribers to Ancestry. Like the pictures, such trees can be public or private. If they are private, then you will need to contact the tree owner if you want more information.

The results list shows many trees that include Conan Doyle. You can be confident that you have the right person, as the parents' names on the right-hand side match information you can find elsewhere (Internet and census, for example). What you don't yet have a feel for is the accuracy of the information in any of these individual trees. It is tempting to assume that the information must be accurate because it is the same in a number of different trees. However, it is possible that one tree owner shared data with other tree owners. This would make their trees look very similar, if not identical. If the original tree creator had errors in the data, these would be passed to other researchers and perpetuated in their trees.

> Because it is so easy to share data and because in-depth research requires time and persistence, it is tempting to accept that the other person has made all the necessary checks and enquiries and that the data is accurate. Sharing takes seconds; corroborating evidence by going back to primary sources is a much longer task.

Click on the name of the tree in one of the results (using a paid personal/library subscription) and explore the way the data is presented. It works in a similar way to the pedigree data in FamilySearch, where you used the poet Shelley as an example.

If the tree owner has researched back a long way, then you can follow that trail in the Family Tree view and click on any arrows on the right of the page to view earlier generations. You might even want to do the search again with Shelley to see if the long pedigree has been posted on this site.

Alternatives to Ancestry

By now, your Internet searches have probably shown you that there are hundreds of genealogy websites, many of which include or deal exclusively with UK/Ireland records. The services they offer fall into four broad categories:

- Create a family tree online. Search the trees of other researchers and contact them. Your data can be viewed by your family and other researchers if you wish.

- Access general or specialised research information and guidance, which will include links to other sites of genealogical interest.

- Join discussion groups and share ideas or ask questions of more experienced researchers.

- Search public records such as census and BMD. There may be transcriptions of such records or access to digitised images of the originals as well.

As a general rule, creating a family tree is free. After all, the more names on a site, the more attractive it is to researchers. Research information and guidance websites are also free. Some of these sites are part of the government agencies' information network or have been created by family history societies to help their members. Online discussion groups usually require some form of registration. This may be free or may be included in a subscription membership package.

Genealogists have shown they are prepared to pay for access to indexes and digitised images of records. The following list may help you decide whether it is worthwhile to sign up to a site:

- Is there free registration and what will this give you access to? (Free is good, so you've nothing to lose. Make sure you tick all the privacy options and un-tick email/information updates unless you really want them. You can always change your mind later.)

- Does this site give you any *significant* additional resources to those where you already have a subscription or access (for example through a library)?

- How many online family trees do you want to maintain? Every time you make a change, you would need to update each of the sites you are using.

- If the site offers free searching, how easy is it to scan the results and how much information are you given? You may decide that a free search, on a particular site, is better for this purpose than some others. You can then use the information in a more focused way on a site where you are signed up to pay for a transcription or image view.

- If there is a discussion group, is it moderated? This means that offensive posts or off-topic discussions are prevented or removed by a team that manages the site. This prevents abuse (known as 'flaming') by quick-tempered members who have forgotten what it was like to be a beginner. Family history groups are usually more helpful in this respect than some other Internet discussions groups.

- How many records does the site hold and how does this compare with major sites you have viewed? Do most of the records come from submitted family trees or from public documents?

- If you are taking out a subscription, make sure that the site doesn't operate an automatic renewal system. You can usually change the options in My Account once you are logged in.

- If buying credits, ensure you have enough time to make full use of them, as many have a 'use by' date. If you think you will want to look at a lot of records, credits can be an expensive way to research.

Part of the pleasure of travelling is putting away the guide book, wandering off by yourself and finding some undiscovered gem hidden in a backstreet. The same is true of web resources. Many of the major ones are well documented but you will always find others that may just give you the help and records you need. The bonuses will come from wherever these sites and your own searches lead you.

Research tasks: Using Ancestry for the Fischer/Smith family

Lilian Alice Fischer was the oldest child of Carl and Maria. Using Ancestry as your source, what information can you find about her?

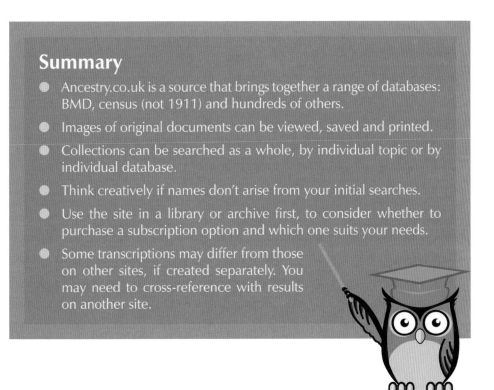

👉 **Research tasks: Using Ancestry for your family**

Take one relative for whom you have some information from other searches, and look them up in each of the main Ancestry data sources. Add any new information to your research log.

Research task – Fischer/Smith suggested answers

It is likely that your search yielded these results.

1. Born 1892, Pancras, (registered Dec qu.) Ref:1b 26

2. 1901 census, Pancras, age eight, daughter of Carl and Maria

3. Died 1901 age eight (registered Sep qu.) Pancras Ref:1b 35

Summary

- Ancestry.co.uk is a source that brings together a range of databases: BMD, census (not 1911) and hundreds of others.

- Images of original documents can be viewed, saved and printed.

- Collections can be searched as a whole, by individual topic or by individual database.

- Think creatively if names don't arise from your initial searches.

- Use the site in a library or archive first, to consider whether to purchase a subscription option and which one suits your needs.

- Some transcriptions may differ from those on other sites, if created separately. You may need to cross-reference with results on another site.

Brain Training

1. Which major UK census is not currently available through the Ancestry website?

a) 1841

b) 1881

c) 1901

d) 1911

2. What are the Burnt Records?

a) Census records

b) Officers' records

c) WW1 records for NCO and other ranks

d) WW2 records for NCO and other ranks

3. What records can you find at the Ellis Island website?

a) Arrival records

b) Birth, marriage and death records

c) Census records

d) Departure records

4. If the mouse cursor over an image changes to a hand, what are you able to do?

a) Copy the image

b) Delete the image

c) Drag the image across the screen

d) Reduce the image

5. From which of these countries would you not find arrivals on the UK Incoming Passenger Lists?

a) Australia

b) France

c) South Africa

d) USA

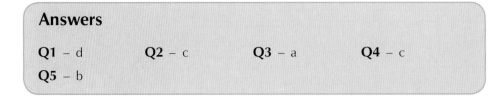

Answers

Q1 – d   **Q2** – c   **Q3** – a   **Q4** – c

Q5 – b

Using the National Archives

7

Equipment needed: Computer and Internet access to The National Archives website.

Skills needed: Searching databases, extracting information, and refining search queries.

The National Archives (TNA) is different from other major resources that you have looked at so far. TNA has a legal responsibility to hold and preserve original documents. It is the government archive, and its purpose is broader than just family history research, unlike Ancestry or FamilySearch. It is required to conserve documents and make them accessible, subject to privacy and security legislation.

What is TNA?

TNA has been in existence for hundreds of years in one form or another. Catalogues and indexing systems were introduced as appropriate for their times. Each development of the system required it to be applied to previous (legacy) systems. This process has been repeated many times. Current developments focus on computerisation, digitisation and making material available in new forms, including online access.

If you go to Kew, where TNA is located, access to resources, whether paper-based, microfilm/fiche or online is free. You will be charged for any printing or photocopying but you would expect the same in any library or archive. Searching the website at **www.nationalarchives.gov.uk** is also free.

What researchers sometimes query is why online access to documents requires payment. After all, the organisation is funded through taxpayers' money and you are, in effect, paying for something twice. There are two main reasons why payment is required. First, like all government agencies, TNA is required to be cost-effective. If some of its operating costs can be offset by income from publications and charges for viewing documents online, then this makes its continuing operation more viable and allows it to justify further investment in conservation and digitisation activities.

The second reason relates to the costs involved in undertaking large-scale indexing and digitisation projects, such as releasing an entire census online. TNA now works in partnership with commercial organisations to achieve this. The development and running costs are borne by the partners who, naturally enough, wish to recoup their costs and make a return on their investment. TNA also profits from this activity through licensing agreements.

What is available in TNA?

Because of the size and scope of the materials held by TNA, this chapter will focus on topics that are of particular interest if you are starting out in family history. The website holds a lot of material and can appear confusing for the beginner, but there are specific sections designed to help genealogists and these are a good place to start. The Catalogue describes the materials held. Not all are available online. Large collections, such as censuses, have been made available in various ways and access to these was discussed in Chapter 4. There are guides to a wide variety of topics. These are worth reading even if, as with census and BMD records, you have already explored these in some depth elsewhere.

Figure 7.1 shows the home page of the website. Access to the information you need is through the Records site in the middle of the screen or via the Records tab in the menu bar.

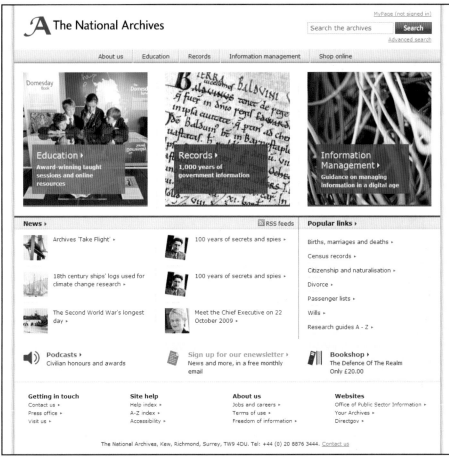

Reproduced by permission of The National Archives

Figure 7.1

Understanding how the records are organised

As soon as you start looking at the Catalogue or reading one of the subject guides, you will come across the referencing system used by TNA. It can seem quite intimidating but you are likely to need only a few major references. The references are needed to access records at Kew, and come up when you search online.

Each document in the archives has a reference number. The documents are in various formats such as printed books, parchment volumes, diaries or letters. The basic reference number consists of letters and numbers that describe the document by Department, Series and Piece:

● **Department**: There are nearly 400 collections relating to the work of government departments, the courts and the armed services. Each department has a code of up to four letters. Examples of these codes and some of the responsibilities of the departments are:

   ● **ADM**: Admiralty (Navy and Marines)

   ● **AIR:** Air Ministry (RAF)

   ● **BT:** Board of Trade (shipping)

   ● **CRIM:** Central Criminal Court

   ● **FO:** Foreign Office

   ● **HO:** Home Office (naturalisation)

   ● **MEPO:** Metropolitan Police

   ● **RG:** Registrar General (census)

   ● **T:** Treasury

   ● **WO:** War Office (Army)

● **Series**: Each department has various series of records arranged by topic or record type. In total, there are about 15,000 Series. Examples are:

   ● **BT 27:** Outward Passenger Lists 1890–1960

   ● **HO 1:** Naturalisation papers 1789–1871

   ● **HO 334:** Duplicate nationality certificates 1870–1982

   ● **RG 12:** 1891 census

   ● **RG 13:** 1901 census

   ● **RG 14:** 1911 census

- **Piece**: This is the box, volume or file that contains the document(s). The individual contents of the Piece are known as *items*. There are millions of Pieces in the archive. An example:

  - **RG 13/1724:** 1901 census: Essex, Braintree, Coggeshall registration sub-district including the parish of Feering.

For the census, you would also need to know the page or folio numbers to find the place in the document that you need (in this case, the household of John Smith, the father of Maria Smith). This is where census indexes are so useful, since you don't have to work your way through the whole of this Piece to find the record you want.

Finding family history records

A good place for you to start is by selecting the Records tab in the menu bar at the top of the home page. (You might want to save this in your Favorites list, so you can return here straight away.)

The Records page (Figure 7.2) tells you how to look for a person, a subject or a place. You can also access the Catalogue from here and find tutorials on the archives and different aspects of research.

To make the best use of TNA and the website, it is worth investing some time in understanding how it can help you achieve your research goals. Over the last few years, the amount and quality of guidance has increased significantly. The advantage of accessing such material from the website is that it is likely to be up to date, and will let you know about current and possible future developments.

Reproduced by permission of The National Archives

Figure 7.2

What you can find in the records

Depending on how far along you are with your research, you will probably want to start by finding out about individuals, then move to looking at particular subject areas then places.

- **Looking for a person:** This covers life events, military service and civilian life. Within each category there are more specialised references, such as Marriages of British Nationals at Sea or Abroad; British Army Nurses; Railway Workers. Each of the reference pages has a section covering the following topics:

  - What do I need to know before I start?

  - What records can I see online?

  - What records can I find in The National Archives at Kew?

  - What records can I find in other archives and organisations?

  - What other resources will help me find information?

  - In-depth research guides

  - Did you know?

  - Related brief guides to records

  - Understand the archives videos

- **Looking for a subject**: This takes you to a list of research signposts laid out like the Looking for a person guides, which are a great place to start. If you need more in-depth guidance, this page also takes you to the extensive list of research guides. These are organised alphabetically. If there is something here that looks like it might be of interest, for example Internees First and Second World Wars, or Education, Teachers' Records, then you can click the document link and read the guidance on screen. It can also be printed for future reference.

- **Understand the archives**: This includes a series of short videos that act as an introduction to the archives. Looking at these is well worth your while. They explain how the documents are arranged, how to use the Catalogue and how to order documents (either to view at the archives or to have paid access to digitised records). There are also videos on how to prepare for your research and recording your results.

Within the section on understanding the archives, there is also information about reading old documents. The language of old documents, particularly legal or church records, may be in Latin. Legal language has its own peculiarities, even when in English. Finally, your problems may be compounded by flowery scripts that are no longer commonly used or just by bad handwriting. This guide has sections on Latin (basic and advanced) and on palaeography (the study of old handwriting). There is also advice on caring for your own records.

The Records page also has video clips and podcasts (audio broadcasts you can hear on your computer) and updates on TNA developments.

You should remember that, as with all websites, the content and look may change over time to reflect additions to the material held or improvements to the layout. However, since the archives have been around for so long, it is safe to assume that the materials you need as a family historian are going to be preserved and available to you in a growing variety of formats (that is, after all, the primary purpose of TNA).

Searching the Catalogue

Access to the Catalogue is from the Catalogue and online records link in the Records page. There are two main ways to use the Catalogue: Browse and Search. Browse lets you look through the Series lists of all the Departments, so you get a feel for the type of documents they hold. Search allows you type in a query for a name or a place.

Browsing the Catalogue

Towards the top right of the Catalogue page, there is a section with various options (Figure 7.3). Select Browse.

Reproduced by permission of The National Archives

Figure 7.3

You are initially presented with the Catalogue in alphabetical order by Department, starting with A: Records of the Alienation Office (apparently to do with the transfer of feudal lands without a government licence) and ending with ZWEB: Regularly Archived Government Websites. I suspect that some of the letters between these two extremes will be of more interest to most family historians.

It is possible to click a tab at the top of the list and sort it by Title rather than by Department Reference. This is not as helpful as it sounds. Large numbers of the entries start with the word Records and are all, therefore, indexed under R.

Each page displays about 15 entries and you can move back and forwards between pages or go from the first to the last. If you know the Department Code, you can enter it in the Browse from Reference box.

As you have some experience of dealing with census records, you might want to see how the Catalogue deals with them. Enter RG (for Registrar General) in the Browse from Reference box. Click Go.

Each reference code has a small folder icon next to it. If there is a + next to the folder, this means that you can click to open it and see what it contains. When it is open, there is a − (minus) next to it. If you click this, the folder and its contents close. Figure 7.4 shows how this looks in the Catalogue.

Browse from reference:	Go>			
Reference Hierarchy				
	Title/Scope and content	Covering dates	Last Piece Ref.	
RG	Records of the General Register Office, Government Social Survey Department, and Office of Populatio ...	1567-2003		
RG 13	General Register Office: 1901 Census Returns	1901 March 31	5338	
		Previous | Next		
Subseries within RG 13	London	1901		
Subsubseries within RG 13	Registration District: ST. PANCRAS	1901		
RG 13/131	Registration Sub-District: Regent's Park Civil Parish, Township or Place: St Pancras (part)	1901		
RG 13/132	Registration Sub-District: Regent's Park Civil Parish, Township or Place: Chalk Farm (part) St P ...	1901		
RG 13/133	Registration Sub-District: Regent's Park Civil Parish, Township or Place: St Pancras (part)	1901		
RG 13/134	Registration Sub-District: Regent's Park Civil Parish, Township or Place: Chalk Farm (part) Have ...	1901		
RG 13/135	Registration Sub-District: Regent's Park Civil Parish,	1901		

Reproduced by permission of The National Archives

Figure 7.4

153

The document filing system on your computer uses this + and – feature in the same way. It means you can look at the contents of an open folder without needing to scroll down dozens of other open folders.

The folders are organised rather like a family tree. Folder RG is the 'parent' folder of RG 1, RG 2 and, in this case, RG 13. The offspring of these folders are in the subfolders RG 13/131, RG 13/132 and so on. You can see that, each time you click a folder, you are drilling down to a more detailed level of information.

- **RG:** records of the General Register Office
- **RG 13:** 1901 census returns
- **RG 13/1 to RG 13/5338:** registration sub-districts. The first of these is St Mary, Paddington, London; the last is Dalton, Dalton in Furness, Ulverston, Lancashire. In the terminology of the Catalogue, these are the Piece numbers.

Each of the Registration districts has a group of sub-districts. Paddington is RG 13/1 to RG 13/18; Kensington is RG 13/19 to RG 13/38. In Figure 7.4, the registration district is St Pancras. The subseries RG 13/131 is of interest because this was the reference which appeared on the 1901 census entry for Carl and Maria Fischer.

If you click the RG 13/131 entry, it gives you more information about that particular Piece (Figure 7.5).

Piece details RG 13/131

Quick reference   Full details   Browse from here >   (Request this >)

Context   ?Help : **quick reference**

RG_ Records of the General Register Office, Government Social Survey Department, and Office of Population Censuses and Surveys

    RG 13_ General Register Office: 1901 Census Returns

        Subseries within RG 13_ London

           Subsubseries within RG 13_ Registration District: ST. PANCRAS

Record Summary

Scope and content	Registration Sub-District: Regent's Park Civil Parish, Township or Place: St Pancras (part)
Covering dates	1901
Availability	Open Document, Open Description, Closed For 100 years
Held by	The National Archives, Kew

Q̇ Add further information to this Catalogue entry on Your Archives or see what other users may have written

Go to Your Archives >

Reproduced by permission of The National Archives

Figure 7.5

Just above the detailed results, on the right, click the Request This box, to open a new window (Figure 7.6) where you are offered a number of options to view the actual record.

Reproduced by permission of The National Archives

Figure 7.6

The link to a digital record takes you to the census links page from where you are directed to the 1901censusonline website.

The link to a printed or digital copy (PDF) leads to an order form page. There will be a large number of census pages for this district so the cost of making copies could be prohibitive. It might be better to limit the number of pages by including relevant details. One possibility could be to include the household schedule number. This could be seen on the Ancestry census transcription.

The final link refers to viewing the records at Kew. The information is generic, about how to plan a visit to Kew and how to access the documents you want to see.

Searching the Catalogue

Constructing a search in the Catalogue is like searching the Internet more generally. You are offered a basic search, which you can then refine using more advanced options. As always, you need to start with minimal search criteria and then build up your query. It also helps to understand how the search engine processes your query and how to get it to understand what you really want. The problem is that, although the computer is very fast at scanning and retrieving information, it is a very literal servant and will do exactly what you have asked, even if this wasn't quite what you meant.

From TNA Records page, open the Catalogue. Figure 7.7 shows you a basic search window where you can enter keywords and (optionally) a date range. If your main research is currently focused on nineteenth and twentieth century records, it might make sense to eliminate medieval, Tudor and other early records at this stage.

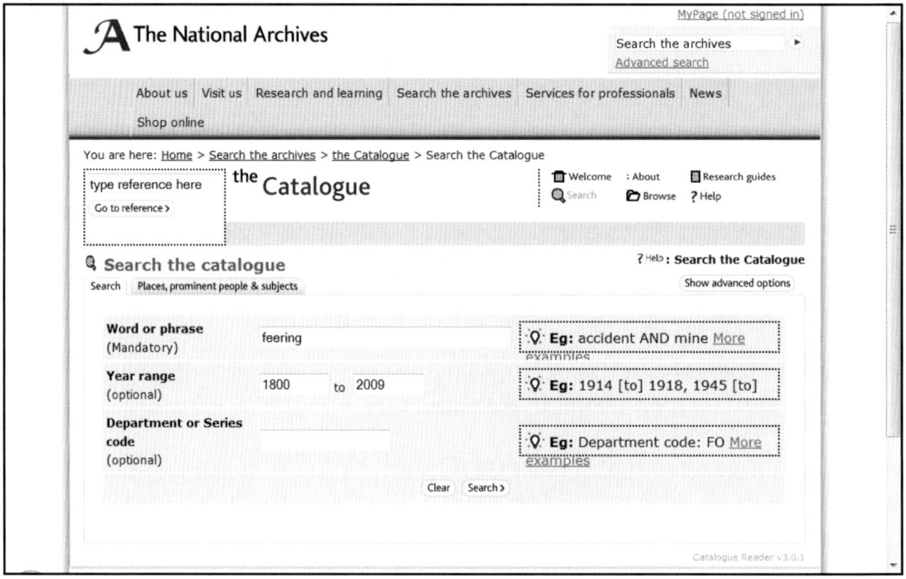

The National Archives catalogue search screen is reproduced here, showing the "Search the catalogue" form with fields for "Word or phrase (Mandatory)" containing "feering", "Year range (optional)" from 1800 to 2009, and "Department or Series code (optional)".

Reproduced by permission of The National Archives

Figure 7.7

The designers of sophisticated search engines and databases have tried to overcome the rather literal and simplistic tendencies of the computer by allowing you to insert some sneaky upper case commands in the middle of your search. If any IT person ever talks to you about 'Boolean operators', this is what they mean. (You might think they deserve a quick slap as well but every profession and hobby has its jargon. Even family historians are not immune.) In a nutshell, this is how it works:

- **maria smith:** This finds all the results (also known as 'hits') that contain these two words one after the other. The problem with this is that, in many records, surnames are presented first (ie Smith, Maria).

- **maria AND smith:** This finds results containing these two words, even if not in this order. (Note that you don't need capital letters on the names when searching but the 'Boolean' bits must be in upper case.)

- **maria OR smith:** This finds results that contain any of the terms.

- **maria NOT smith:** This finds all results that contain the word Maria but eliminates any that contain the word Smith.

> I have had to use this last option in family research for the name Milstone. Because search engines sometimes look for alternative spellings, it may bring up Milston (a spelling used by some of the family). Unfortunately, there is a place in Wiltshire of this name; a place with no connections to my family. If I use **milstone NOT milston** as my search, I lose any alternative surname spellings. The solution is to use **milstone NOT wiltshire**. This removes most of the place name results, since the town is usually described with the county name (like Feering, Essex). If there are a few Milston town results still left, this doesn't matter. I have reduced the list to a more manageable size but have not risked losing family names.

- **"milstone" (with inverted commas round a name or keyword):** This searches for the exact spelling and returns no alternatives.

- **fischer AND (carl OR frederick OR ludwig OR robert):** It is also possible to combine search options, as in this example. All results must have Fischer plus one or more of the names in brackets. This would let you search for more than one member of a family at a time.

In the Catalogue, you are only allowed 3,000 results. This is not such a bad thing as it would take some time to look through a list this long. You are therefore encouraged to refine your search if too many results are found.

Using the Catalogue to do some sleuthing

Figure 7.8 shows the initial results of a Catalogue search for Feering, grouped by department.

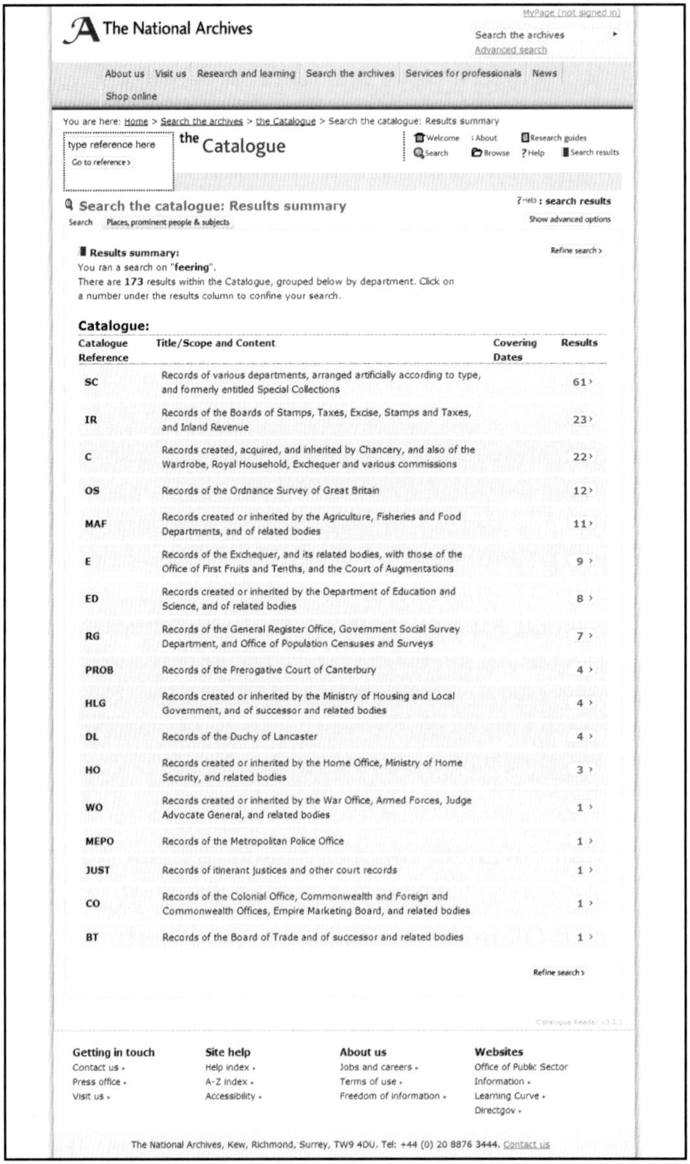

Reproduced by permission of The National Archives

Figure 7.8

There is a single entry for MEPO (Metropolitan Police). Following it up gives the intriguing result shown in Figure 7.9.

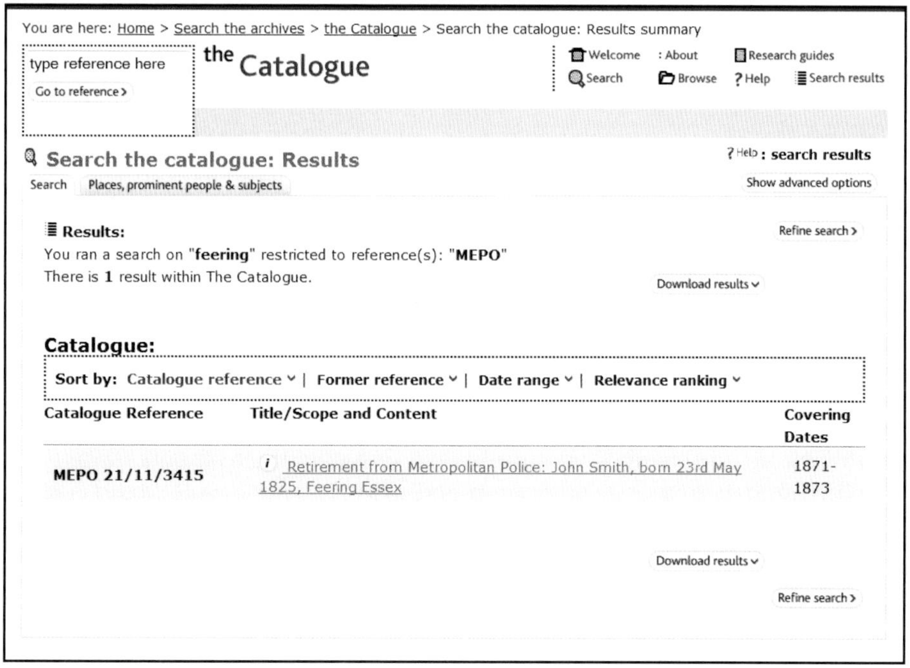

Figure 7.9

There is now another John Smith, born in Feering in the mid-1820s. The view that the town was too small to have more than one John Smith of the right age will have to be re-examined. As with all the best detective stories, the only way to deal with it is to review the evidence.

- This John Smith is a policeman; Maria's father was an agricultural labourer.

- The policeman was born in 1825; all the evidence collected for the original John Smith (Chapter 4, Figure 4.16) pointed to a birth year of 1828. However, a difference of two or three years either way is not always conclusive.

- Is there anything in other records such as census? 1861 gives John Smith, a policeman, living in Hoxton New Town, Shoreditch. By the kind of strange coincidence you find all the time in family history, his wife is also called Mary Ann (albeit mistranscribed). At the same time, the John Smith of the case study family and his wife, Mary Ann, are still living in Feering, where they were both born. The policeman's wife was born on the Isle of Sheppey.

- In the 1851 census, John Smith, a police constable, is living in Sewardstone, Waltham Holy Cross, in Essex with his wife, Mary Ann, and two year old daughter, Esther. (Easy to miss with a search on Feering as the transcription is Ferring.)

It's clear, therefore, that you are dealing with two families and there is enough evidence to let you distinguish between them, particularly later in life as their work and places of residence diverge. So, does it make any difference if you are trying to reconstruct the case study family? Well, it might.

- Both men were born before 1837. Their births would probably not be registered but their baptisms might be. However, a baptism doesn't necessarily occur within a set time after a birth. How could you be sure that the baptism of a John Smith in the mid- to late-1820s is the right one?

- It might be a problem if you are trying to identify their parents. When both John Smiths are young, unmarried and living at home, you would hope to find them listed with their parents on the census. The 1841 census shows only one John Smith in Feering. The age would make it Maria's father but what might confirm this?

There are two ways to try to find additional evidence. The first would be to get the marriage certificates of both couples and see who their fathers were. (If you were really unlucky, both fathers would have the same name.)

The second (and perhaps more interesting possibility) would be to look at the MEPO 21/11/3415 record. The Catalogue says that MEPO 21 has registers of Metropolitan Police officers granted pensions after retiring or resigning from the force. This particular series covers 1872–73. What is useful is that the record has personal information, including the names of parents and next of kin. This might help you check the policeman's parents from sources such as International Genealogical Index (IGI) christenings and confirm if the family on the 1841 census is Maria's father's family. Finding the names of both parents provides additional confirmatory information, whereas the marriage certificates would give only the names of the fathers.

I've decided to invest in getting this record. By clicking on the result, I am taken again to a page where, on the right, there is a Request This box. There will be different options depending on whether the record has already been digitised or whether a copy needs to be made. In the latter case, an assessment will need to be made based on the size and relative condition of the document. You may therefore have to pay both for the assessment and the subsequent copying of the record but you will be notified of this in advance.

In the case of my MEPO document, I will receive an electronic copy of up to 10 pages from the document. I can give information to narrow down the search and ensure that I get what I'm looking for. To avoid paying this, I could go down to Kew to look at the records. This may not always be cost-effective for you to do for your own family records, if you live a long way from Kew.

What TNA records provide, therefore, are additional pieces of the puzzle. Pension records for government or civic employees are very useful for this purpose. Not all TNA documents have the same level of personal information so important to family historians. The detectives have had a lucky break.

Understanding the difference between the Catalogue and the archives

The searches so far have focused on the Catalogue, which describes the records held by TNA. The website also acts as a gateway to other sites that hold transcribed and indexed census material. It also hosts a number of smaller databases and has links to a range of documents held in local and private archives.

It is important to understand that, while TNA can point you in the direction of these other archives, you may need to contact them or visit their websites to get more direct access to the records. Each archive has its own structure for organising its holdings and providing access for researchers.

From the TNA Records page, click the Catalogues and Online records link. This time you will be looking at the whole range of archives, rather than just the TNA Catalogue.

You are shown a list of databases that are available to search. Any of these can be accessed and searched separately. The main search page has a brief description of each source. Clicking a link takes you to a search and/or information page. To understand each source, find the FAQ section (Frequently Asked Questions) or a button that says About. If a collection has a * by its name, it means that the contents will be included if you do a global search. Sources currently available are divided into three groups.

- Records held by TNA
  - TNA Catalogue*
  - Cabinet papers*
  - DocumentsOnline*
  - Electronic Records Online*
  - Equity Pleadings
  - National Digital Archive of Datasets (NDAD)
  - Library Catalogue*
  - Taxation records
  - Trafalgar Ancestors database
  - UK Government Web Archive
  - Your Archives*
- Records held on partner websites
  - Census records
  - First World War soldier records
  - Non-parochial records
  - Passenger lists
- Records in other archives
  - Accessions to Repositories*
  - Access to Archives*
  - Archive contact details (ARCHON)*
  - Hospital records
  - Manorial Documents Register
  - National Register of Archives*

You can see how vast a resource is available to researchers and why it can sometimes appear overpowering (to experienced, as well as new, researchers). Not all resources are necessarily of immediate interest to those focused on constructing a family tree. However, there may come a point in your research where the material held can provide clues about the way your ancestors lived their lives and how they interacted with government and other authorities.

There are some differences between this search function and the one described for the Catalogue. The Advanced Search gives you a number of possibilities.

If you enter **feering essex** in the search box, you get the same number of results as if you enter **essex feering**. The only difference seems to be the order in which they are presented. As with search engines like Google, it gives you first of all those results closest to your original request and then moves on to others that contain the two words somewhere (a case perhaps of playing the right notes but not necessarily in the right order!). What this means is that it finds a first name and a surname if they are both in the database, no matter how the name is set down. If you want to exclude a term, then use NOT. A search for **milstone** returns about 330 hits (including milston). A search for **milstone NOT Wiltshire** returns 58 hits.

Use **feering** as a search term to view how the results are presented and what categories of documents are available. Figure 7.10 shows the start of the results list, which has about 479 entries.

Reproduced by permission of The National Archives

Figure 7.10

Like an Internet search, each result has three parts: a link to more information about the source; some details of what the source contains; and an indication of where the information is held. In the case of the first two results, you can see that the source is Access to Archives (a topic you'll look at in more detail later in this chapter). You are reminded that this material is not held at TNA.

On the right, the results are shown in categories, with the top five first. It's probably no surprise that Tax, Money & Finance account for about a quarter of the results. You can click at the bottom of the list if you want to see the categories for all results. Family & Personal Papers are likely to be of most interest.

 One thing to be careful of in results is where a surname may also be an occupation or a town name. This may require some creative search queries.

Using DocumentsOnline

You have seen that TNA website hosts various databases. The three largest are the Catalogue, DocumentsOnline and Access to Archives (A2A). The Catalogue has always been around in one form or another, to enable researchers and officials to find archived documents. DocumentsOnline is a response to increasing demand, from researchers and others worldwide, for access to images of the documents held, without the requirement to be physically at Kew. This has benefits both for researchers and for the archives. If a document is scanned and the image made available, it means that the document is no longer handled by large numbers of people. This increases its longevity and makes the conservation role of TNA much easier. There is also an issue of the physical size of any archive and how many researchers it can comfortably accommodate at any one time. Due to the size of the holdings, it will take a great deal of time and money to digitise all the major record collections.

DocumentsOnline can be reached from the Catalogue and online records link on the TNA Records page. Figure 7.11 gives an overview of the most popular content and various featured items of interest.

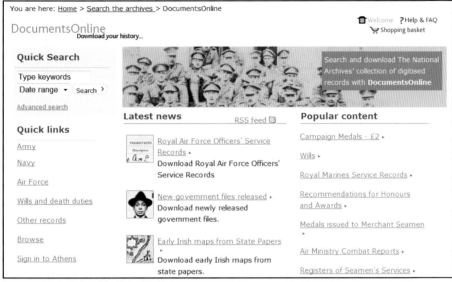

Reproduced by permission of The National Archives

Figure 7.11

Check this page regularly to see what has been added to the material available.

As in previous practice searches, enter *feering* in the search box and browse the results. Most of the records available appear to be for family history purposes, reflecting, no doubt, the service requirements of the majority of TNA users. There are references to Feering in the Domesday Book and you might be interested to look at the information contained in the database entry. It gives a list of names (which naturally makes it easier for you to decipher the record, should you decide to purchase it).

You may find, in fact, that this indexing is as useful a feature as the possibility of viewing a digitised copy of the original document. Click Advanced Search in the Quick Search box. This lets you refine your search by name, place, dates and collection types. Enter the name of the place where you were born or where you are currently living and see what documents are available.

When you find a document of interest, you can get further details. This also includes the cost. Most documents cost £3.50. Some documents are available free, usually where their production has been sponsored by another organisation. This is shown in the records.

If you want to buy a record, you need to be in the details page where there is a link enabling you to add this item to your shopping basket (see Figure 7.12).

Reproduced by permission of The National Archives

Figure 7.12

If you have done any Internet shopping before, you will be familiar with the shopping basket concept. If not, just think of supermarket systems.

1. Put an item in your basket (click the Add to shopping button).

2. Continue shopping if required. You can review the contents of your basket and remove items as necessary. The basket can contain up to 15 items.

3. Go to Checkout.

4. If the items are free, click Proceed to Download and you are able to download the document onto your machine.

5. If you require paid documents, you are taken to a secure payment system (the ones on large well-known sites such as this are reliable).

6. You need to give your credit card details and your email address.

7. An email is sent to you confirming the transaction and giving you instructions about how to download the document. You have a certain number of days to download the material and save it to your computer.

8. If you have concerns about buying and paying for things over the Internet, one suggestion is to have a credit card with a low limit that is only used for this purpose.

Some of the documents may be very large. These can take a long time to download and can use a lot of memory on your computer. If you have many such documents, you might want to consider archiving them on a CD once you have used them for your research.

Access to Archives (A2A)

Access to Archives allows you to search centrally in the catalogues of a number of private and public archives. It is estimated that it contains about one third of the archival collections in England and Wales. New collections are not being added to A2A, though existing ones will be updated. You cannot access digital images through A2A. The archive owners may, of course, have digitised some of their records or plan to do so. You need to look at their websites to see how their materials are organised and catalogued and how they can be viewed.

As with other collections, A2A can be accessed from the Catalogues and online records links on the TNA Records page. Select Advanced search. To get some idea of the range of archives available, click the dropdown arrow in the Select Repository search box, to access a dropdown list. Browse the list for the town or area where you live or where your ancestors lived. If there were particular interests and occupations within the family, this can also be the basis for your research.

If you are able to access records, either online or by visiting the archives, don't be disappointed if the material does not immediately provide you with personal data to fill in gaps in your family tree. Archives reflect the needs and interests of the organisations from which they originated. They may be more focused on buildings, artefacts and systems than on the people who worked in or with them. Once you start delving into these records, you are moving your research to a different level. It will require more digging on your part but can provide the fine-tuning of your research and a much greater insight into the fabric of your ancestors' lives.

The College of Arms in London keeps records of those entitled to have a coat of arms. The officers of the college are known as heralds.

Finding Welsh records

Most of the major record sources looked at so far have been for both England and Wales. Some problems for researchers with Welsh ancestors arise because surnames were adopted relatively late and the same surnames recur frequently. There are a number of websites that give you an overview of the Welsh system of patronymics (naming after the father rather than with a fixed family surname).

Two sites that you should visit if you have Welsh ancestry are the National Library of Wales **www.llgc.org.uk** and Archives Wales **www.archiveswales.org.uk**.

The National Library of Wales has catalogues and electronic resources that can be searched, as well as material held on site at Aberystwyth. The home page of the site has a link to a family history section with details about research preparation and a variety of resources available for searching. These include: the Church in Wales and Non-conformist records; Wills and maps; and Pedigree books.

Archives Wales performs a similar function to TNA's Access to Archives. It allows you to search over 7,000 collections created by different bodies and individuals.

Scotland – National Archives

Archives in Scotland are held or made available to researchers through a number of agencies.

● **ScotlandsPeople**: **www.scotlandspeople.gov.uk** You will have seen references to this site earlier, in connection particularly with BMD and census material.

● **National Archives of Scotland** (NAS): **www.nas.gov.uk**. This operates in a similar way to TNA. The Catalogue will be your first stop in searching the archives. Figure 7.13 shows the NAS home page. An item on one of the menu bars at the top of the page is for Catalogues and indexes. This will take you a page describing what is available and with a link to the NAS Catalogue. The Search the NAS Catalogue link is in the middle of the page. This then takes you to a page with a Search facility at the top.

Reproduced by permission of The National Archives of Scotland

Figure 7.13

If you are researching family in Scotland, then Scottish archives are an obvious place to start. However, it is possible to find records relating to other places. From the Search facility, entering *feering* brings up a single reference. Display the results and click on the reference number. Looking at the details (Figure 7.14) explains why this record is here.

Reference	Title	Date
GD281	Records of the Carnegie United Kingdom Trust	c 1890-2007
GD281/132	Carnegie United Kingdom Trust: Village Hall Grants	1990-2006

Country code	GB
Repository code	234
Repository	National Archives of Scotland
Reference	GD281/132/210
Title	**Feering** Village Hall, County Essex
Dates	1992-1994
Access status	Open
Access conditions	No publication without owner's permission: consult NAS staff
Level	File

Reproduced by permission of The National Archives of Scotland

Figure 7.14

The NAS holds the records of the Carnegie UK Trust, which apparently made/ considered a grant towards Feering Village Hall in the 1990s. In the same way, it is possible for records of Scottish places and individuals to be found in TNA. Searching in both archives is a useful strategy.

● **National Register of Archives for Scotland** (NRAS): NAS has the remit to encourage private organisations to catalogue and preserve their records as part of the national heritage. Over 4,000 collections are included in the Register. As always, follow the links from the NAS home page and read about the Register to make your research time and effort more profitable.

● **Scottish Archive Network** (SCAN): **www.scan.org.uk**. A project to provide online access to Scotland's history. There is an Online Catalogue covering the holdings of over 50 archives. The Directory will give you information about how these archives can be contacted. There is also a FAQ and research guide section.

Ireland – National Archives

The National Archives of Ireland has already been mentioned in connection with census research. On the home page of the site, **www.nationalarchives.ie**, there is a Genealogy link which takes you to information about records held in the archives that are of interest to family historians. There are also links to county-based genealogical centres which hold parish records for their area. The links also cover Northern Ireland.

The Public Records Office Northern Ireland (PRONI) **www.proni.gov.uk** holds public records, many dating back to the early nineteenth century. As with Scottish records, you are very likely to find ancestors and the places in which they lived in TNA, so searching on both sites is highly recommended.

Research tasks: Using The National Archives for the Fischer/Smith family

The Police Pension record for John Smith (Figure 7.9) ordered from TNA has arrived. It shows his father as Samuel Smith and his mother as Mary Smith. How could you use this information to confirm the parents of the John Smith in the case study family?

Research tasks: Using The National Archives for your family

Make a list of names and places that keep coming up in your research. Check to see if there are references to these people and places in The National Archives. Practise different search techniques, adding or excluding search terms as necessary.

Research task: Fischer/Smith suggested answers

1. The 1841 census for Feering shows a John Smith born c1826 to William and Frances Smith. This is therefore not the John Smith who later became a policeman.

2. In the International Genealogical Index (IGI), a search for births/christenings around 1826 (+/− two years) in Essex gives 31 results. Narrowing the search by including the father's name (William) gives two results, both from Feering. The mother's name is Frances Lewsey. Searching for a John Smith whose father is Samuel yields no results (though this may be because this entry hasn't been transcribed).

The evidence is still not conclusive. The chances of Maria's father being the son of William and Frances is stronger now that the policeman (son of Samuel) has been taken out of the equation. There is always the possibility of yet another John Smith who is the son of these parents. The next step would be to get the marriage certificate of John and Mary Ann to confirm that his father was William.

Summary

- The National Archives includes a collection of materials created for a wide range of government purposes.

- Digitised images for downloading (most for a small fee) are increasingly available.

- Search the Catalogue for materials held by TNA itself.

- Search the Archives for documents held both by TNA and other archives (Access to Archives – A2A).

- There are partnership projects with other organisations (eg Ancestry) to make records available online.

- Be persistent and creative in your searching.

- Understanding the document referencing system can help you make more sense of your search results.

Brain Training

1. What is the study of old handwriting called?

a) Palaeography

b) Palaeontology

c) Transcription

d) Transliteration

2. What records would you expect to find in the collection ADM?

a) Criminal

b) Naturalisation

c) Navy

d) Treasury

3. In which collection would you find census records?

a) HO

b) MEPO

c) RG

d) WO

4. Which of these is not a 'Boolean' search term?

a) AND

b) FIND

c) NOT

d) OR

5. What does A2A stand for?

a) Access to Ancestry

b) Access to Archives

c) Add to Archives

d) Aids to Archives

Answers

Q1 – a   **Q2** – c   **Q3** – c   **Q4** – b

Q5 – b

Accessing information from wills, newspapers, directories and other sources

8

You've now had a chance to examine in some detail three major resources for family history research. This chapter looks at some other sources, including wills, newspapers, historical directories and maps. As you develop more specialised interests, you may want to contact other researchers and join family history societies focused on similar topics. As you've probably realised by now, there's a vast amount of genealogical material and resources out there, much of which can be explored online.

Equipment needed: Computer and Internet access; copies of wills, newspaper articles and old address books from your personal family research collection.

Skills needed: Understanding wills; making assumptions and connections to test theories about family names, occupations, dates and locations.

Wills

Wills can be a good source of information for the family historian. They mention a number of specific family members and their genealogical relationship to the deceased; just as interesting can be what they tell you about social and economic relationships within the family. You may well have seen films or read books where an individual is mentioned in a will but all he/she is left is the deceased's 'good wishes'.

Some wills can be fairly short and factual and have no surprises for you, and probably not for the original legatees. Others may raise certain questions in your mind, which will only be answered with documentation from other sources. An example from my own research is a will of a distant relation killed on active service during the First World War. Not long married, he had no children but did have four nieces (children of his sister). He left money to these young girls, to his mother, his wife and even to someone I suspect was a cousin. It always seemed odd that he hadn't mentioned his sister at all, even though her husband was the executor of the will. It was only when reading some correspondence between my own grandparents, from the time when they were courting, that I realised that his sister had pre-deceased him. Since she was a relatively young woman, it hadn't occurred to me to look for her death before his. I hope I remember to do this the next time I come across a similar problem.

As with birth, marriage and death records, there is a dividing date before which wills were dealt with regionally or locally by the church authorities. After 1858, records from wills handled locally were sent to a Principal Probate Registry, rather like BMD records and the General Register Office.

The following key terms crop up when you are researching wills:

- **Probate:** the process by which a court examines a will and decides that the deceased's wishes can be carried out (and by whom).

- **Proving a will:** convincing the probate court that the document is the deceased's will.

- **Executor:** the person named in the will to carry out the deceased's wishes.

- **Intestate:** dying without leaving a will.

- **Letter of administration:** instructions by the probate court relating to a deceased's estate where there is no will or where there is no executor. This is often referred to as 'admon' in various documents. Since there are no instructions from the deceased to the contrary, the distribution of assets is carried out according to a series of established legal precedents.

- **Administrator:** person nominated by the court to distribute the estate according to the details in the letter of administration. This person can be a family member.

A witness to a will or the spouse of a witness cannot benefit from the will. If a witness is a beneficiary (or the married partner or civil partner of a beneficiary), the will remains valid but the beneficiary will not be able to inherit under the will.

Finding a will

Your initial focus will be to trace wills back in time. This corresponds to your research plan for BMD and census records. You are more likely to know about death dates for family members who died more recently. The will may also contain enough information about other family members for you to expand your research.

There are two processes involved in finding a will: searching the index and then buying a copy. The first involves searching for an index entry in the National Probate Calendar, which covers the period from 1858. The good news is that these entries give the name, address and occupation of the deceased and the date and place of death. The value of the estate is shown, as is the place and date of probate or administration being granted. Executors or administrators are named and there may be information about their relationship (if any) to the deceased.

The bad news is that the National Probate Calendar is not currently available to search online. Microfiche and microfilm copies can be seen at The National Archives, the Society of Genealogists and the Guildhall Library. It is worth checking with any local family history groups or local history archives to see what indexes are available where you live.

Bound copies of the National Probate Calendar can be seen at the Probate Search Room in High Holborn, London. Information about probate and family history can be found at **www.hmcourts-service.gov.uk/cms/1183.htm**. For each year there are several volumes organised alphabetically. Bear in mind that complex wills and estates may have taken some time (occasionally years) to sort out. The entry you are looking for may not be in the same year as the death. For once, you should start with the known date of death and work forwards.

Since 1996, the indexes have been held on computers that you can search in the Probate Search Room but not online. Once you have found the will you are looking for, you can order a copy of the grant and, if there was one, the will (currently £5).

This is usually sent by post or you can collect it yourself. It is also possible to ask for a search to be carried out for you. There is information on the Probate Registry website (**www.hmcourts-service.gov.uk/cms/1183.htm**) that tells you how you can do this, together with forms with which you can request a search.

Gleaning information from National Probate Calendar entries

It might be useful to look at an entry in the National Probate Calendar for the case study family and see what information could be used.

> **FISCHER** Frederick of 8 Harrington St, Hampstead Road, Middlesex died 22 Sep 1908 at sea. Probate London 15 Oct to Frederick Charles Fischer and Carl Robert Fischer painters. Effects £1053 10s 9d [Folio 1456]
>
> *National Probate Calendar, 1908 Vol D-G*

Things to note:

- The exact date of death is given. Usually you would have to buy the death certificate to get this, so you now have this information free.

- Although it doesn't specifically tell you that Frederick Charles and Carl Robert are siblings and the sons of the deceased, this would be a reasonable assumption to check out, if this were the first time that you had come across their names. In this case, it confirms evidence that you already have from BMD and census returns.

- The family is still in the painting business. It must be reasonably successful as Frederick has left over £1,000. If you want to see how much this would be today, you can check on The National Archives website. Go to **www.nationalarchives.gov.uk/currency/**. In today's money, Frederick's estate would be worth £60,000. On this site you can also see what could be bought with this money at the time. It would pay for over 3,000 days of craft labour in the building trade.

- Frederick died at sea. This may have been in an accident or on a boat trip. If it was an accident, it may have been reported in a newspaper, either local or national, depending on the scale of the incident.

- The folio number was added for London probate entries between 1858 and 1930. You need this if buying a copy of the will.

Wills in Scotland

The ScotlandsPeople website at **www.scotlandspeople.gov.uk** is again the place to search for information about wills. You can search (free) for wills between 1513 and 1901. The wills have been digitised. You need to be registered and then login to search.

For wills after this period, visit the National Archives of Scotland at **www.nas. gov.uk/guides/wills.asp**. The indexes here are called Calendars of Confirmation. They are in a printed format from 1901 to 1959 and on microfiche from 1960. From 1985 to 1996 there is a computerised index searchable in the National Archives search room.

Wills in Ireland

The Public Record Office (PRO) in Northern Ireland at **www.proni.gov.uk** has access from the home page to an online search of will calendars. There is information about plans for digitising wills and creating links between the indexes and the copy wills.

The National Archives of Ireland has a genealogical sources page with a link to information about wills and probate: **www.nationalarchives.ie/genealogy/ sources.html**.

Newspaper archives

Newspapers can be a wonderful resource for family historians. Even if you think your ancestors weren't noteworthy enough to appear in the national press, there is always a chance that they gained their 15 minutes of fame in a local journal, perhaps as a result of involvement in some illegal activity or an accident. The reporting may be lurid and less than complimentary about your ancestor but, if it provides you with details about their name, age, occupation, marital status and residence, then this must be of help to you in your research.

Of course, it will not necessarily be the seamier side of life that is reported, though sleazy bits do tend to creep in. Families themselves put notices in the paper to mark births, deaths and marriages; but also sometimes to disclaim responsibility for a spouse's or child's debts. Family businesses may advertise for years in the same newspaper, often in the same place on the same page, trying, no doubt, to imprint themselves in the minds of the reader of what is essentially an ephemeral document.

Family scrapbooks may have newspaper cuttings. If something was particularly noteworthy it may be worthwhile searching in other publications of the time for the same story.

What information can you find?

As with family resources in your home, you can find almost anything in newspaper archives. The following list should give some idea of the scope but your research is bound to find other possibilities if you spend time using newspapers as a resource:

- Birth, engagement, marriage, death announcements and obituaries
- Legal notices involving things such as business partnerships starting or ending, bankruptcies, executors searching for creditors or those with other claims on a deceased's estate, name changes and naturalisations
- Club membership, posts of responsibility, academic and sporting awards
- Missing relatives notices (particularly common after the turmoil of the two world wars)
- Seaside towns and tourist resorts used to list the names of guests staying at local hotels
- Advertisements for family businesses
- Photographs from local or national events such as flower and agricultural shows, theatrical events and local outings
- Correspondence to the editor, raising a particular point or arguing with views expressed in earlier editions (such exchanges could go on for a while, usually until the editor intervened and deemed the discussion closed)
- Reports from inquests, criminal trials and civil matters such as divorce. Some of these can also be reported in more than one edition of the paper.

Finding out what newspapers are available

If you are using newspapers as a resource, you need to find out the titles that were available for the timeframe in which you are searching. Major newspapers, such as *The Times*, have been around for a long time. Other newspapers may have changed their name at different times as a result of mergers. For example, the *Daily Chronicle* was founded in 1872 and merged with the *Daily News* in 1930 to become the *News Chronicle*. This paper and its evening partner, *The Star*, closed in 1960. There is a website for educational use which has information about journalists and the history of various newspapers: **www.spartacus.schoolnet.co.uk/journalists.htm**.

A comprehensive list of local and national newspapers can be found at **www.onlinenewspapers.com**. This site also covers international news media. On the home page, select United Kingdom and use the dropdown arrow to select English, Scottish or Welsh papers. Irish newspapers can be found in the Europe menu. Each of the newspaper names on the list is a link to that paper's website. Once you have found newspapers of interest, you need to search the site to see if there is an archive and whether it is available online. The list covers newspapers currently operating. Where older newspapers have merged with others, the archives may cover earlier incarnations of the paper.

British Library newspapers

The British Library, located at St Pancras, has millions of items in its collections: books, manuscripts, maps and printed music – all types of printed material. Newspapers form a significant part of the collection and have their own separate location at Colindale, in north London.

Like The National Archives, the British Library has an integrated catalogue for its holdings. If you have an ancestor who published a book or a pamphlet, there is a good chance that the British Library has a copy. One member of the Barnet U3A family history group found that an ancestor had published a large number of books on handwriting. He was able to view these books (dating from the early 1800s) and found one with a line drawing of this ancestor at the front, a really wonderful discovery.

Just as the newspaper library is housed in a separate building, so it has its own catalogue, which is a subset of the main catalogue. It has a long web address, so it is probably easier to do an Internet search for *british library newspapers catalogue*. Make sure that the search result you use gives you newspapers rather than the catalogue as a whole.

On the website, you are offered a basic or an advanced search. By default, you are shown the basic search. Put in the name of a place. Then, against Search by, dropdown menus let you choose whether the word you are looking for is in the newspaper title, a place name in the description of the paper or any word in the description. There are other search possibilities (such as Shelfmark, the reference number used to indicate the location of a document in a library or archive).

If the place you are looking for is small and no results are found, try entering a nearby, larger town. For example, *Feering* produces no results but *Witham*, *Braintree* and *Colchester* do have newspapers associated with them.

The advanced search lets you combine several search terms and produces both individual and combined result totals. Once you have a title in which you are interested, you can click it to give more information about the publication, including reference numbers. You need these if you want to order materials at the British Library.

Digitising newspapers

Searching through a newspaper for information relating to your family can be a slow process, if you are physically reading the newspaper in an archive or on a microfilm/fiche. Newsprint is, by its nature, not a long-lasting medium. Many of the original papers are bound in volumes but are extremely fragile. As with many such documents, the priority now is to digitise the material so that the originals no longer need to be handled, while the images can be viewed online by any researchers who need to access them.

There are a number of possibilities. One is to scan the page and then present it as an image file (JPG). This means that you need to view it at a large enough magnification to be legible on screen or when it is printed. The other possibility for printed material is to use a scanning process that allows the computer to 'read' the letters. This is known as Optical Character Recognition (OCR). The benefit of OCR is that, since the letters (and therefore words) can be read, the document can be indexed and searched in a way that would not be possible if it were in an image format.

There are some particular problems with newsprint, again relating to the medium. It is quite absorbent and, in old papers particularly, the letters seem to 'bleed'.

This can make it difficult for the software to recognise the letter. I spent some time looking for a family in Muswell Hill; the problem was that the letter M was fuzzy and was misread by the software as H. There was no way that I could have anticipated that I should search for Huswell rather than Muswell. A wildcard search was eventually the answer to the problem but it took a while.

Many newspaper archives are now available in a digitised format. These are searchable and the results often highlight the search term entered, which can be very helpful when you are trying to find a word in a large page of newsprint.

The British Library has now begun to put newspapers online. The website at **http://newspapers.bl.uk/blcs/** has digitised versions of nearly 50 newspapers from the nineteenth century. Some of the content is free to view; other material can be viewed with a 24-hour or seven-day pass, enabling you to view and print 100 or 200 articles respectively. Academic libraries and some public libraries may have subscriptions to this site, so it is worth checking with your local library before taking out a subscription yourself.

From the basic search page, you can browse the publications on offer if you wish to restrict your search. Further refinements are possible using the date options. You will be presented with both paid for and free search results unless you indicate otherwise.

The Times online archive

It is possible to search and view 200 years' worth of material from *The Times* newspaper (1785–1985). The website is at **http://archive.timesonline.co.uk/tol/archive/**. Searching the archive is free but you need a subscription to view the articles. Subscriptions are available on a daily, monthly or annual basis and provide unlimited access to the archive. Many public libraries have subscriptions to the archive as part of their digital services to readers.

While you are investigating whether your library has newspaper archives on offer, you should also look at the other facilities available digitally, many of which can be accessed on your home computer using your library card number. These could include Encyclopaedia Britannica, the Oxford Dictionary of National Biography and Who's Who, all of which may contain information on people, places and topics that will be useful in your research.

The London, Edinburgh and Belfast Gazettes

These are available at **www.gazettes-online.co.uk**. As it states on each home page (Figure 8.1), the Gazettes are 'Published By Authority. Official Newspaper of Record for the UK . . . to disseminate and record official, regulatory and legal information'. Originally in print form, this remit now extends to online and electronic formats.

Reproduced under the terms of the Click-Use Licence. PSI Licence number C2009002412

Figure 8.1

The Gazettes publish a range of information, which includes:

- New Year and Queen's Birthday Honours
- Medals awarded
- Official notification of changes in postal rates
- Judicial, military and ecclesiastical appointments
- Civil service appointments
- Unclaimed Premium Bond prizes
- Corporate and personal insolvency notices
- Formal changes of name
- Naturalisation certificates granted

- Business partnerships
- Gas and electricity licensing arrangements

> A deed poll is a legal document involving only one person and used, for example, to change a surname. It is not illegal to change your name without a deed poll, providing the intention is not to defraud.

The web address for the London Gazette is **www.london-gazette.co.uk**/. You can click links at the top left of the home page to change the edition; you can also substitute Edinburgh or Belfast for the word London in the web address.

If you are a first time user of the site, there is a button near the top of the page that explains more about the Gazettes, how to search the archives and the benefits of registering (which is free).

As with similar sites, you can chose a simple or advanced search and restrict results in various ways, including search terms and dates. When you have a result that you wish to view, clicking the link opens the Gazette at the relevant page. You can print or save the page and, should you wish, you can go to different pages. The original results lists has the date, issue number and page number where the item is located. Searches can be saved and retrieved later.

Figure 8.2 is a formal notice about the estate of William Henry Theodore Rubardt, dated 27 August 1901. William was the nephew of Sophie Fischer (nee Rubardt).

Re William Henry Theodore Rubardt.
Under a Deed of Assignment.

NOTICE is hereby given, that all persons having claims against the estate of William Henry Theodore Rubardt, of 2, Wells-road, Regent's Park, and 1A, Woronzow-road, and St. John's Wood-terrace, in the county of London, Builder, and who have not already forwarded particulars of their claims, are required to do so to Robert James Ward, of 2, Clement's-inn, in the county of London, Chartered Accountant, the Trustee under Deed of Assignment, dated 16th day of May, 1901, on or before the 10th day of September, 1901, otherwise they will be excluded from participation in the Dividend about to be declared.—Dated this 24th day of August, 1901.

TRASS and ENEVER, 25, Coleman-street, E.C., Solicitors to the Trustee.

Figure 8.2

If you try further searches on the name Rubardt, you will see earlier notices about bankruptcy and the dissolution of a business partnership. The dates and addresses in such notices, together with information about the nature of the business, allow you to track an individual in parallel with census information. Not all your relatives will be the subject of such notices but, as with all sources, it may be worth revisiting as you acquire more information about your family.

Other newspaper sources

Ancestry has collections of both UK and international newspapers that can be searched. *The Times* is available from 1788 to 1833. To see other sources, go to the Ancestry Card Catalogue (found on the Search Tab), filter by Collection (Newspapers and Periodicals) and then filter by UK.

Historical directories, maps and gazetteers

Long before most people had telephones, there was a recognised need to have collections of names and addresses for business purposes. The growth of large towns and increased industrialisation heralded the decline of many small communities where tradespeople and customers alike knew one another by name and had few local alternatives to sell or purchase goods. Choice was now possible and those offering goods or services began to understand the need to advertise in a crowded market.

Directories were developed for both urban and county-wide communities. In London, the Post Office Directory eventually became the most important, though there was always strong competition from Kelly's and a number of others.

The first London Directory of city merchants was published in 1677.

Early directories had both advertisements and single line entries. There would often be a description of the locality. The entries were then presented in a variety of ways, so that the name of an individual might come up several times. Street names were given, together with the names, addresses and occupations of those engaged in business. These streets might be ordered alphabetically or might follow a route, rather like that of the census enumerator. There was an alphabetical list of tradespeople, most of whom used their own names rather than inventing business names. This was then followed by an alphabetical listing of types of business, each with its own practitioners, whether artists, builders, grocers or tailors.

There was also sometimes what was called a 'court section', which recorded the names and addresses of the middle and upper classes in an area. The purpose of this was presumably twofold: tradespeople had a place to check addresses for the delivery and invoicing of goods and services; and the more affluent social classes perhaps saw it as a membership list of those with whom it would be respectable to engage in social activities. Later directories saw an expansion of the numbers of names included.

Printed copies of some directories can be found in local study archives. A large collection of online directories for England and Wales can be found at: **www.historicaldirectories.org/hd/index.asp**. The directories are free to search and the results can be saved as an image or printed out.

It is possible to search by location, by time period or by keywords (which can include names). As with any site that is new to you, it may be helpful to look first at any advice given about the databases on the site and how you can get the best results from your searches.

Sometimes the directories may help you to speculate about individuals without giving definite proof. As always, what you need to do is weigh up the balance of probabilities and see if you can cross-reference with other evidence.

As an example, Kelly's Directory of Essex, Herts and Middlesex for 1894 gives a Charles Fischer, artist, living in Bushey, Herts and a Mrs Maria Fischer running a confectioner and tobacconist in the same area. How much of the evidence points to this being the case study family?

- Charles is the anglicised forename of both Carl Robert and Frederick Carl, the sons of Frederick Fischer.

- Charles is an artist, an occupation shared with his brother and his father.

- Both brothers have wives called Mary/Maria.

- Frederick Arthur Fischer, the son of Frederick Carl, was born in Barnet, Hertfordshire in 1895.

- Mary Ann, the wife of Frederick Carl died in 1896 (death registered in St Pancras).

To follow this up, it would be necessary to see if Charles Fischer appeared in the Hertfordshire directories after 1896. The birth certificate for Frederick Arthur should provide an address in Hertfordshire. If this is the same as the directory address, then you know that there is a family match.

Telephone directories

The Internet is full of information about individuals. There is something of a paradox that, while people are prepared to reveal all sorts of things about themselves on social and networking sites, they have a fear about making personal data available, whether in printed or electronic formats. Large numbers of people are now ex-directory, so the possibility of contacting relatives that you discover through your research is more difficult. Telephone directories now seem more like the trade directories of past times, full of businesses but with much more limited private contacts. The growth of mobile phones has added to this problem.

Ancestry has a section with a range of directories and membership lists, both for the UK and elsewhere. Figure 8.3 shows the most popular items in their collections, which include 100 years of British phone books. The list includes things that you might not expect to find in this collection, such as Parish and Probate Records. However, since you can search the entire collection at one time, this does not involve you in multiple searches and may reveal sources that you might not otherwise have considered. You can further filter the list by type of directory, for example, Professional and Organisational Directories.

Many people remember that 192 was originally the dialled number for directory enquiries. This was before such services were opened up to competition and found their way onto the Internet as well as in printed and dialled directory enquiries. The website **www.192.com** brings together a range of resources that allows you to search for individuals and businesses. Initial searching is free. If you want to see detailed records, you need to purchase (time-limited) credits. The site is useful if you want to search for people in the current electoral roll

Matches 1-25 of 164	Sort By Popularity ▾		1 2 >
Search entire "Directories & Member Lists" Category			
Title	**Collection**	**Size**	**Activity**
British Phone Books, 1880-1984	Directories & Member Lists	278,407,920	
U.K., City and County Directories, 1600s-1900s	Directories & Member Lists	19,148,350	
London, England, Poor Law Records, 1834-1940	Directories & Member Lists	1,135,782	UPDATED
England (General): Parish and Probate Records	Directories & Member Lists	1,383,080	
Pallot's Baptism Index for England: 1780 - 1837	Directories & Member Lists	605,931	
Yorkshire, England: Parish and Probate Records	Directories & Member Lists	1,989,224	
Yorkshire, England: Parish Records	Directories & Member Lists	720,750	
UK Medical Registers, 1859-1959	Directories & Member Lists	625,022	
U.K. and U.S. Directories, 1680-1830	Directories & Member Lists	2,518,462	
Lancashire, England: Parish and Probate Records	Directories & Member Lists	1,244,262	

Figure 8.3

(assuming they have not signed to opt out of their personal information being used in this way). Electoral rolls from 2002–2008 are also available. BMD is also included in the credits system but this only gives you access to the indexes, despite a reference to 'the records'. If you are using Ancestry with a personal subscription or in a library, you already have this available to you.

Gazetteers and maps

Gazetteers are alphabetical listings of place names in a locality. They can be useful if a census or other record gives you a place name that has changed or vanished over time. When used with historical maps and the place information in many directories, you can pinpoint more accurately the district in which someone lived. This may help you to find the local parish and therefore search the appropriate parish records.

The information included in a gazetteer will vary, but they provide fascinating snapshots of even quite small places. The *Imperial Gazetteer* of 1872 shows Feering in the Witham district of Essex with a population of 804. There are 166 houses and a note that the property is 'much subdivided'. The value of the property is given, as is the value of the 'living' of the vicarage. Architectural features of note are also given. Larger places may show famous people who were born or lived there. There may also be records of the numbers of births, marriages and deaths in a given year.

Most of the monthly genealogical magazines that are published in the UK have a CD on the cover. These often include either full or extracted material from gazetteers and directories. A quick trawl through a selection of these found the following resources:

- 1851 Post Office Directory, Surrey
- 1851 Kentish Strays (people from Kent living elsewhere at the time of the census)
- 1891 Guide to Carlisle
- 1934 Almanack and Directory of Nantwich
- 1924 Guide to Durham
- 1900 Inhabitants of County Down Towns
- 1868 Directory of Monmouthshire
- 1904 Llandudno Illustrated
- 1904/1908 Guide to North Wales

At family history fairs, you can often see such CDs available at very little cost. They have usually been donated by family history society members who are not researching in the areas covered but who are reluctant to throw them away. If you are a member of a family history society yourself, it may be useful to maintain a library of such CDs (minimal shelf space) and create an index to the gazetteers and directories they contain.

If you do find information about the place(s) that your ancestors came from, you might wish to include this in presentations about your family tree. This will be dealt with in more detail in Chapter 12.

GENUKI

This site (**www.genuki.org.uk**) acts as an online reference source for genealogical information covering England, Ireland, Scotland, Wales, the Channel Islands and the Isle of Man. The resources are provided by volunteers and members of family history societies. There are other web sources dealing primarily with names, (for example, the RootsWeb surname list at **http://rsl.rootsweb.ancestry.com**). In contrast, GENUKI focuses on historical material. Figure 8.4 shows the scope of the topics covered. Some links may be to websites of specialist interest, such as the Jewish Genealogical Society of Great Britain. Others may link to leaflets about the topic or databases compiled by interested researchers.

INFORMATION RELATED TO ALL OF THE UNITED KINGDOM AND IRELAND

- Archives and Libraries (Separate page)
- Bibliography (Separate page)
- Biography
- Cemeteries
- Census (Separate page)
- Chronology
- Church History
- Church Records (Separate page)
- Civil Registration
- Colonization
- Correctional Institutions
- Court Records
- Description and Travel
- Directories (Separate page)
- Dwellings
- Emigration and Immigration (Separate page)
- Gazetteers (Separate page)
- Genealogy (Separate page)
- Handwriting
- Heraldry
- Historical Geography
- History (Separate page)
- Jewish Records
- Land and Property

- Language and Languages
- Manors
- Maps (Separate page)
- Medical Records (Separate page)
- Merchant Marine (Separate page)
- Military History (Separate page)
- Military Records (Separate page)
- Names, Geographical
- Names, Personal (Separate page)
- Newspapers (Separate page)
- Nobility
- Occupations (Separate page)
- Periodicals (Separate page)
- Politics and Government
- Poorhouses, Poor Law, etc
- Population
- Postal and Shipping Guides
- Probate Records
- Religion and Religious Life
- Schools
- Social Life and Customs
- Societies (Separate page)
- Taxation

Reproduced by permission of Genuki

Figure 8.4

As you explore the list, you will see some reference to resources that you have already used. You should also come across materials that are not so common and this site allows you to benefit from the expertise and efforts of a range of other researchers.

Family history societies

The best place to start looking for a group which will help you develop your interests is the website of the Federation of Family History Societies (FFHS) at **www.ffhs.org.uk**. They currently have more than 160 members and the list can be searched in the following ways:

- Alphabetically
- England
- Wales
- Ireland
- Overseas (mainly Australia)
- One-name studies (where people interested in a particular surname collect all instances of the name, not just those to whom they are related)
- Other, which includes religious or ethnic focused groups (Catholic, Quaker, Jewish, Romany and Traveller); geographical interests (Anglo-German, Anglo-Italian, Families in British India); and subject specific groups (Railway Ancestors)

Scotland has its own Association of Scottish Family History Societies, which can be found at **www.safhs.org.uk**.

Most of these groups have their own websites which give information about membership, meetings, publications, databases and projects. Many of them have stalls at various family history events around the country and, if you can attend any of the larger shows, this will give you the chance to check them out and see whether they can provide the specialist support you need. It is certainly a good idea to be a member of a society, perhaps one that focuses geographically or ethnically on your main area of interest. Many researchers have been involved in family history for a long time and they are generally more than happy to help newcomers, providing that you too, contribute in your turn, as you become more experienced. Such contributions usually involve taking part in indexing projects, whether of registers, cemeteries, memorial inscriptions or local records.

There is often an overlap between the work of local history societies and groups researching their family history, so you may also decide to visit your local history centre and see what talks and projects are on offer.

Mailing lists

Mailing lists offer a way to contact other researchers with the same areas of interest. People post messages, queries and advice. Some lists are moderated to prevent arguments and off-topic postings. There are a number of things to consider before joining a list (which is usually free).

- Join the list and 'lurk' for a week or so to find out the tone of the group, how questions are put and the etiquette the group adopts (eg which things require a public answer because they are likely to be of interest to a lot of people; which require a private answer because they are very specific to your family).

- If the group has a FAQ, then read it before posting queries.

- Subject lines in postings need to be brief and specific. If possible, give a surname, a location and a date or date range. Many people scan the subject listings to decide whether a posting is worth reading. A subject such as 'Looking for my Watson family' will not attract them, particularly if the name is common.

- The convention is to put surnames in upper case throughout the heading and the posting. This lets others focus on the names more easily.

- Many mailing lists have hundreds of postings each day. You can opt to receive these as individual emails but I would suggest that, if there is a 'digest' option, which bundles a lot of these together, you should use it. If not, you can get overwhelmed by the amount of email coming in.

- Try not to give an entire potted history of your family in each posting. Sadly, your family history and its intricate web of relationships is really only of interest to yourself and your immediate relatives. Be concise about what you want to find out (the same advice applies to going to archives and libraries).

- If you are replying to a message, particularly publicly, learn how to cut bits from the original message when you reply. It is frustrating for others to read an entire message that they have already seen, followed by your contribution saying, 'Yes, I agree'.

- Where people have expertise and have offered help such as reading foreign or old documents, don't abuse this help. If you are likely to be using many such documents, then teach yourself how to read them. There are many guides available to help you. It will take some time, but this is how these experts gained their expertise. I have just seen a posting on a mailing list where someone wanted a translation of six birth and marriage records from a foreign language. What was more, she asked for a full translation and not just an extraction of the basic family information. From the posting, it was clear that this wasn't the first occasion on which help had been requested. I'm sure I wasn't alone in thinking, 'Isn't it about time you learned how to do this yourself, if only so you could free up other people's time? Perhaps you could then offer your services to those starting out as a way of giving something back for the help you've received.' Who knows, perhaps someone emailed her privately (and one hopes, politely) to point this out.

● If you contact other researchers with the same family interests, think carefully about what you want from them and what you can offer in return. If you have only just started your research, you don't want to ask them to send you a copy of their entire family tree by return of email. They may have spent years and a fair bit of money on their research. While people are generous with their time and help, it is sometimes useful to put yourself in their position (as will no doubt be the case a couple of years from now).

● If someone does contact you, either with a query or with information, then respond quickly, even if it's only with a holding email. It may help to say that, while there seems no obvious link between the two families at present, you will keep their email on file in case your future research uncovers a possible connection.

● As with postings to an email group, be clear about what you are asking and how much information you are providing for the other person.

Links list

Nearly all genealogical websites have links to other family history resources. You will soon discover which are the most useful and which you should bookmark in your Favorites list. One of the most comprehensive sites is Cyndi's List at **www. cyndislist.com**. Started in 1996, it now has over 250,000 links to worldwide genealogical topics. Although it appears heavily geographically focused, the General UK sites link from this page has everything that you would expect: vital records, census, gazetteers, directories, newspapers – another of the genealogical treasure chests that are such a great help in your research.

Research tasks: General research for the Fischer/Smith family

Wills

> **FISCHER** Frederick Charles 60 Greenfield Gardens, Cricklewood, Middlesex died 5 Jun 1934 at the Central Middlesex County Hospital, Acton Lane, Middlesex. Probate London 29 June to Elsie Dorothy Fischer spinster. Effects £600 11s 8d

1. Who might Elsie Dorothy Fischer be?

2. How could you find this out?

3. When was she born?

4. Roughly how much is the estate worth in today's money?

Research tasks: General research for your family

Wills

1. Find out where you can search the National Probate Calendar locally and whether it is a partial index or the full national index.

2. Note whether information pre-1858 is available in your area (though if your ancestors came from a different place, you would need to check in these localities).

3. Make a list of people from your family tree whose probate index information (and possibly their will) might help you in your research.

4. Copy this information from the index if it can be found.

5. Add data from the entries to your research log and undertake follow-up research where you now have new names, relationships or addresses.

Research task: Fischer/Smith suggested answers

The will shows the following:

1. As Elsie Dorothy Fischer is a spinster, she could be either Frederick Charles Fischer's daughter or his granddaughter. Niece (daughter of his brother) is also a possibility.

2. Check her date of birth on FreeBMD. Follow up on the 1911 census and see which members of the Fischer family are living with her. (It turns out she is Frederick's daughter, though there is another Elsie Fischer of the same age living in West Ham.)

3. 1902 September quarter.

4. £22,200

Summary

- Wills and newspaper archives can supplement basic research with BMD and census records.

- Detailed information about the places where your ancestors lived can be found in gazetteers.

- Directories, the pre-cursors of phone books, have entries for people offering goods and services, as well as the more wealthy inhabitants of a town.

- Joining a family history society is a good way to link up with others if your research develops in a more specialised way.

- Mailing lists on a number of topics put you in touch with researchers worldwide on a daily basis.

- Use Cyndi's List and other links to help you develop your own list of sites relevant to your research.

Brain Training

1. What was contained in the 'court section' of a directory?

a) Businesses

b) Law firms

c) Names of young women who had been presented at Court

d) Well-to-do people living in an area

2. What are letters of administration?

a) Copies of wills

b) Instructions from the testator to a solicitor

c) Letters from executors to the probate court

d) Probate court instructions about how an estate should be divided

3. What is the National Probate Calendar?

a) Dates when the probate court is in session

b) Dates when wills were written

c) Index of wills granted probate or letters of administration

d) Opening times for the Probate Office

4. Where is the British Newspaper Library located?

a) Colchester

b) Colindale

c) Muswell Hill

d) St Pancras

5. Which of these places has an official gazette similar to the London Gazette?

a) Belfast

b) Birmingham

c) Glasgow

d) Manchester

Answers

Q1 – d   **Q2** – d   **Q3** – c   **Q4** – b

Q5 – a

PART IV
Recording your research

He's been insufferable ever since his online research suggested a distant link with royalty.

Using spreadsheets

9

Equipment needed: Computer with spreadsheet program.

Skills needed: Recording and analysis of research facts.

A spreadsheet is a computer program that allows you to enter figures and data in a tabular format, that is, in columns and rows. In a stationery shop, there are specialised printed books for accountancy and bookkeeping. These are the paper-based versions of the spreadsheet. While most people think of these as tools for managing figures for financial purposes, they have a range of other uses, mainly where you want to keep lists. These lists may or may not contain numerical data.

You've seen earlier a few brief examples of spreadsheets used to produce a table or act as a log for your research. There are many books whose aim is to teach you how to make full use of a spreadsheet and the many features that such programs contain. This chapter only covers those functions most relevant to recording and reviewing data from your research. If you are new to spreadsheets and it all starts to seem a bit heavy, a cup of tea and a bun can sometimes help.

Choosing software

In Chapter 2, spreadsheets were mentioned as part of suites of office programs which might be included in your computer set-up package. If not, you need to buy one or pay to download one from the Internet. The following are the most commonly available:

- Excel is part of the Microsoft Office suite but can also be purchased separately. Information can be found at **http://office.microsoft.com/en-gb/excel/**.

- Microsoft Works is a suite of programs (word processing, database and spreadsheet) which is often included with new computers. The full package can be bought if you don't have it on your computer. You can see details at **www.microsoft.com/products/works/**.

  The spreadsheet in Works is a streamlined version of Excel, with fewer features, but it is more than adequate for most purposes.

- OpenOffice is a free suite of programs that you can download from **www.openoffice.org**. Apart from the immediate benefit of it being free, you can open and save documents in different formats, which means they can be read by researchers with other spreadsheet programs. For the purposes of the examples in this chapter, the OpenOffice spreadsheet (called Calc) will be used. Other spreadsheets can be used in a similar way. If there are any major differences that affect the way they can be used for your purposes, these will be noted.

Understanding basic spreadsheet terminology

Figure 9.1 shows the blank page you get when you open a spreadsheet. As with many such programs, there are a range of menus, options and icons at the top of the page. These can appear intimidating if you are not familiar with spreadsheets. If you ever need to find out what an icon does, just hover the mouse cursor over it and a temporary text description should appear. You can ignore most of the icons for the moment (possibly even forever).

The page is set out like graph paper. There are:

- **Rows** numbered on the left-hand side from 1. In Figure 9.1 you can see 20 rows. In fact, you can go down as far as row 65536 (enough to hold anyone's family data).

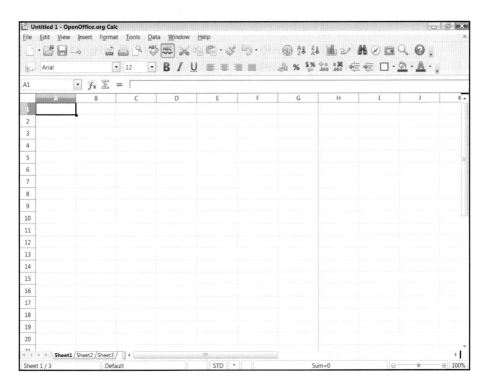

Figure 9.1

- **Columns** across the top labelled alphabetically from A. Since the alphabet runs out fairly quickly, after 26 columns the labelling becomes AA, AB, AC etc and ends at AMJ which gives you 1024 columns. Some spreadsheets have more, some fewer. Again, don't worry about this. You are unlikely to need as many columns as you need rows.

- **Cells** are the squares where each row and column intersects. You enter your data (words or numbers) into the cells. Each cell has an 'address' made up of the row and column reference. In Figure 9.2, the highlighted first cell is A1. This address also appears in the small box above the grid. If you move around the spreadsheet and click random cells, you see that this cell address changes. The main use of the cell address is if you want to set up the spreadsheet to calculate dates or ages automatically.

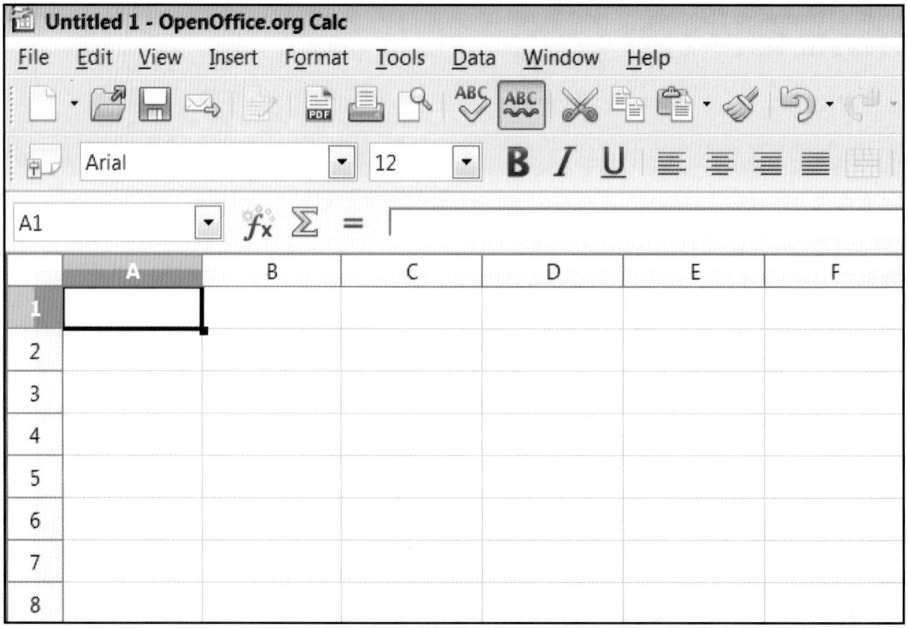

Figure 9.2

Creating data lists from research findings

The examples in this chapter use the Fischer/Smith data. You can either set up a spreadsheet and start with the same data or enter your own family information.

Setting up the spreadsheet

The purpose of the spreadsheet is to act as a research log, showing the resources searched and the information found. By viewing it in a grid format, you can see quickly whether there are any anomalies, such as dates that vary significantly, or where an individual was sometimes known by another name. This will help you decide which data is probably the most accurate. You can then create a record for this person in specifically designed family tree software (Chapter 10).

For this research log, you need to allocate 14 columns. You may not be able to see these all at one time and may need to scroll across the page. This is one reason why you should limit the number of columns you use. It can be time-consuming to keep scrolling across the page and difficult to keep track of where you are.

The following headings will each be entered in a single cell in the first row, starting with cell A1 and finishing in cell N1. Type the word and then highlight (click) the next cell. If you make a mistake, click in the cell again and retype the word.

A1.	Year
B1.	Source
C1.	Forenames
D1.	Surname
E1.	Spouse
F1.	Age
G1.	DOB
H1.	Birthplace
I1.	Registration
J1.	Quarter/date
K1.	Reference
L1.	Address
M1.	Occupation
N1.	Other

Figure 9.3 shows the left-hand side of the spreadsheet with the first eight (all right, eight and a half) column headings. Scrolling across would reveal the rest.

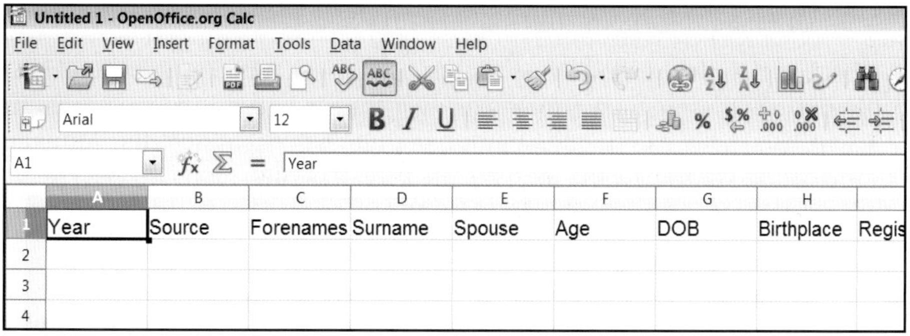

Figure 9.3

Saving your work

It is never too early to save work in progress. Everyone has had the experience of creating a document or perhaps editing a photograph and then closing the program without saving the new version. Many programs autosave as you go but it doesn't hurt to do this yourself as well.

Another reason to save early in the process is that it lets you have some control over how the document in named and where it is saved. In Figure 9.3, the name of the document is in the title bar at the top of the page. By default, the program has called this Untitled 1. If you were to start another new spreadsheet during this session, it would call it Untitled 2. The names are not going to be very useful to you like this. You next step is, therefore, to save the document.

● Click the File menu near the top left of the page. (The File menu is nearly always found in this location in any computer program where you are dealing with documents or images.)

● You are offered options to Save and Save As.

● Save As is the option you want. (Save will use the existing name of the document which, at the moment, is Untitled 1).

● The Save As menu opens (Figure 9.4). This menu may look slightly different in different spreadsheets. If you can't see the Folders list, find an option to Browse Folders.

● Use the Folders menu to navigate to the Folder where you wish to save your document. In this case, there is already a folder created called Family History.

● Give the spreadsheet file a new name, one that lets you find it easily when you have many files from your research. This one will be called Fischer.

● The last thing to decide is what type of spreadsheet file this should be. By default, the program chooses its own format which uses .ods as its file extension. (A file extension is a group of three letters that tells the computer what program should be used to open it.) For the moment, accept the OpenOffice spreadsheet extension (.ods).

● Click the Save button.

If you look at the top of the screen, you will see that the spreadsheet is now called Fischer.ods. When you want to save this next time, either while you are working

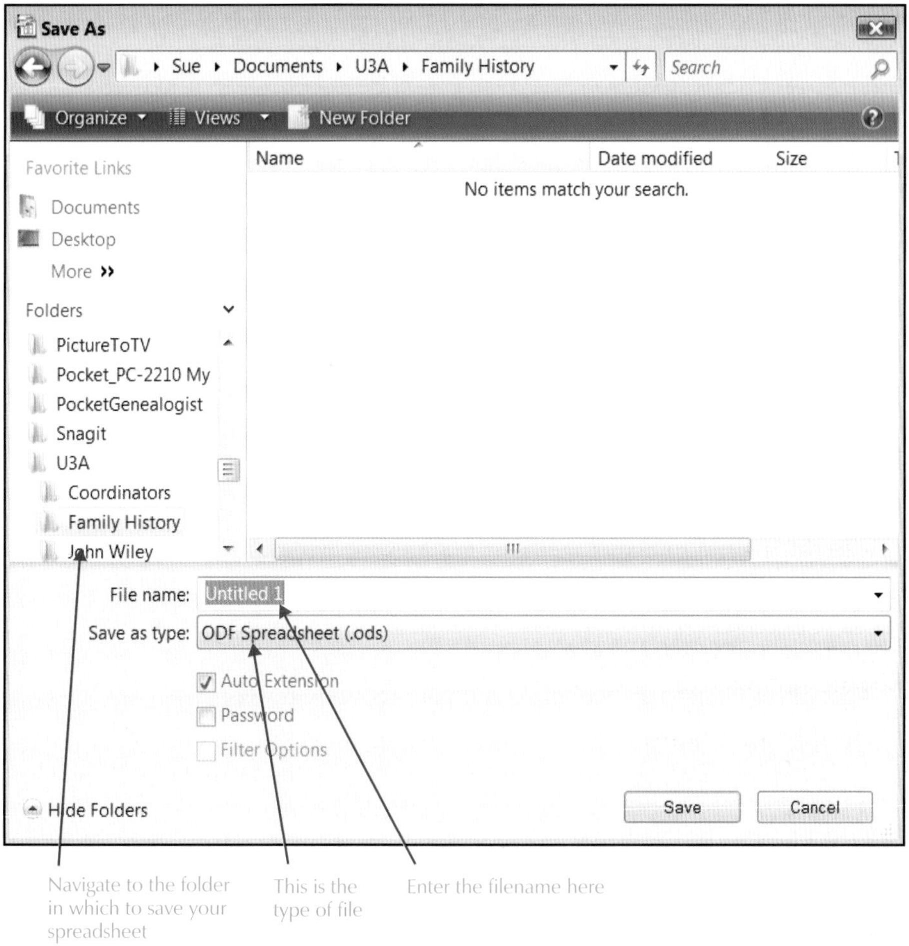

Navigate to the folder in which to save your spreadsheet

This is the type of file

Enter the filename here

Figure 9.4

or when you have finished a session, you can use File ➤ Save. This automatically saves the document with the new file name, in the selected location and with the chosen file extension.

The principles outlined here for saving files apply to all programs that handle documents, such as spreadsheets, graphics, word processed documents and databases.

Entering data

As you get data from different sources, you should enter it in a new row on the spreadsheet. Although you are trying to work back logically in time, documents may present themselves to you out of their chronological sequence. Unlike a paper system, this can be easily rectified later by sorting the document electronically.

The first document seen for the case study family was the marriage of Carl and Maria in 1890 (Chapter 1, Figure 1-1). The data should be entered in row 2 as follows:

Year: Enter *1890*.

Source: Enter *marriage certificate* (abbreviate if necessary).

Forenames: Enter *Carl Robert*. (Copy exactly what is in the document, even if you think it may be in error. You will have other opportunities in the family tree software to indicate alternative names or spellings.)

Surname: Enter *FISCHER* (start using upper case for surnames).

Spouse: Enter *Maria SMITH*.

Age: Enter *Of age* (no age given but you know he is over 21).

DOB (date of birth): Not given on a marriage certificate though you could work out the latest year in which he could have been born. Even if you know the date from other documents, do not enter it here.

Birthplace: (Not given.)

Registration: Usually for the district where the registration was recorded. In this case, use *Feering*, which is the local parish.

Quarter/date: If the data is from a BMD index, it will probably only have the quarter (March, June, September or December). As this is the actual document, you have the full date, *18/10/1890*.

Always write the year in full. Since you will be dealing with data from more than one century, both you and the computer will need to distinguish between 1890 and 1990.

Reference: For the BMD index, the reference will allow you to get the certificate. The reference here, *244*, is the certificate number in the records of Feering Church. It is not the primary reference number when a certificate copy is ordered, though it may help if you are searching for it in the parish registers themselves.

Address: Enter *20 Harrington Street*. (Subsequent research showed this was in the Camden Town/Regents Park area but this is not shown on the document, so should not be included here.)

Occupation: Enter *house decorator*.

Other: Anything else that is important. With some documents, there is too much extra information to fit here, which is why you might decide to set up more columns. Add *Father: Frederick FISCHER, house decorator*.

The second source you looked at for this family was in the FreeBMD indexes (Chapter 3, Figure 3-3). You can now enter the data from this source on the second row in the spreadsheet. If you compare the two rows, you can see that this is the same person, even though the two sources contain slightly different data.

The logical place to look, after the marriage, is the next census, which is 1891 in this case. Carl and Maria are living in 247 Stanhope Street, St Pancras. Maria will now be Maria Fischer, not Smith. An age will be given for Carl. The reference number should be the census reference RG12/118, which is on the transcription and on the census form. You can add a schedule number (412) to help other researchers find their way to this record. A page and/or folio number would have done the same thing.

Figure 9.5 is in the best traditions of '. . . and here's one I prepared earlier'. It shows the main documents found for Carl during the research process. The only document not yet found is his death record. This is probably not yet in the years that have been transcribed and so will involve searching through each quarter of each year.

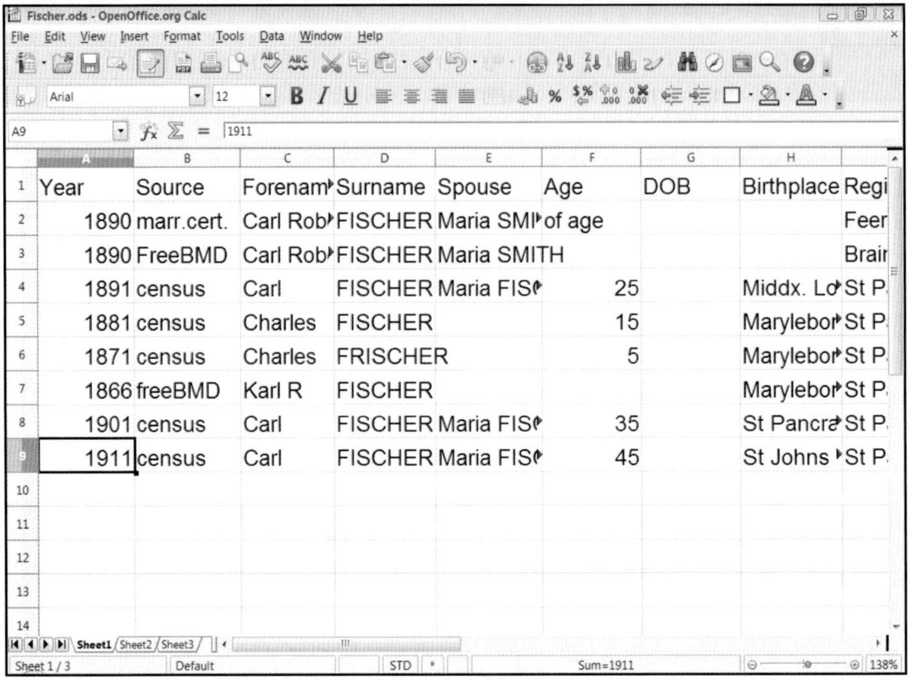

Figure 9.5

Moving round the spreadsheet

Although you can move round a spreadsheet by using your mouse and highlighting individual cells, a much more effective way is to use the four navigation arrows on your keyboard. If you have a desktop computer with a full size keyboard, these keys will be towards the right, at the bottom, next to the numeric keypad. If you have a laptop that doesn't have a numeric keypad, the arrow keys should be at the bottom right.

These arrow keys can also be used to move around text documents created using a word processor and in your filing system.

Making the spreadsheet easier to read

The data as shown in Figure 9.5 is perfectly usable but could do with some tidying up. Figure 9.5 is the 'before' version; Figure 9.6 shows the spreadsheet after the cosmetic makeover.

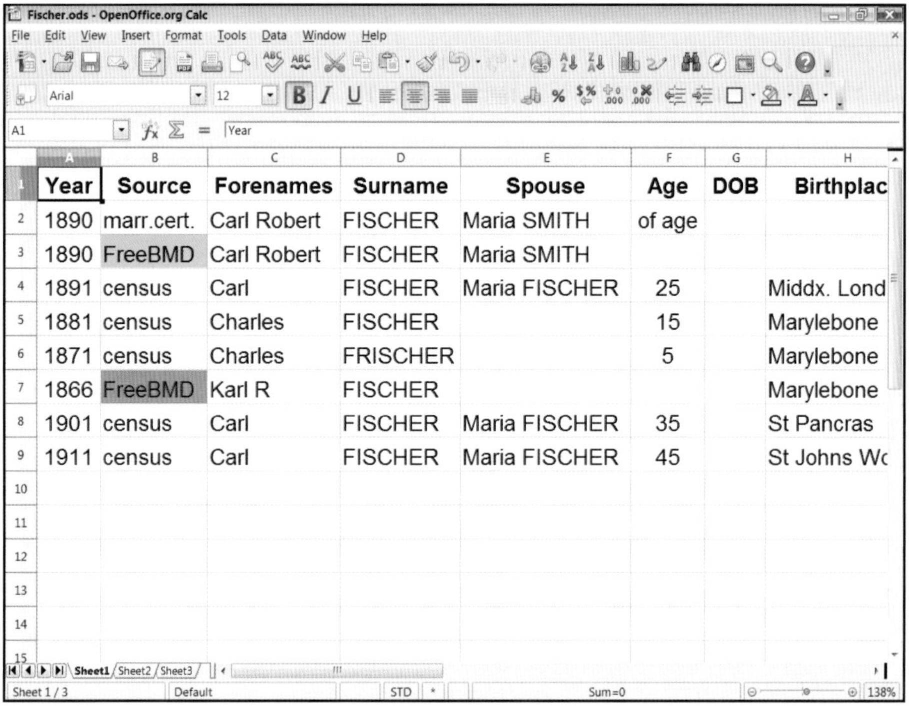

	A	B	C	D	E	F	G	H
1	Year	Source	Forenames	Surname	Spouse	Age	DOB	Birthplac
2	1890	marr.cert.	Carl Robert	FISCHER	Maria SMITH	of age		
3	1890	FreeBMD	Carl Robert	FISCHER	Maria SMITH			
4	1891	census	Carl	FISCHER	Maria FISCHER	25		Middx. Lond
5	1881	census	Charles	FISCHER		15		Marylebone
6	1871	census	Charles	FRISCHER		5		Marylebone
7	1866	FreeBMD	Karl R	FISCHER				Marylebone
8	1901	census	Carl	FISCHER	Maria FISCHER	35		St Pancras
9	1911	census	Carl	FISCHER	Maria FISCHER	45		St Johns Wc

Figure 9.6

Tidying things up makes the spreadsheet easier to read on the screen and improves the look of the printed version. This process of changing the way things look is called formatting. The following changes have been made:

- **Column widths adjusted**: The columns were initially all the same width. A column with a year will only need to be four characters wide; more space must be allocated for columns with longer text entries such as names and addresses. If you don't adjust the width of a column, then part of the entry may get hidden by text in the next cell.

  To change the width, move your cursor over the dividing line between two columns in the heading row with the letters (eg between columns A and B, or B and C). The cursor should change to a double headed arrow. Double click and the column will automatically be adjusted to the width of the longest entry.

  (This is one of those phenomena more easily recognised than described, so try it on whatever data you have entered in your spreadsheet and see how it works.)

- **Text alignment changed**: This refers to whether the text and numbers line up with the left or right edge of the cell or whether the text is centred. In the new version, columns A and F are centred; the others are left aligned. To make a change, click on the column letter. This highlights the whole column so that any alterations are made to all the cells in the column. You then need to use the relevant button in the Formatting toolbar (see Figure 9.7) to make this and other changes.

Bold   Left, Centre and   Background   Text
            Right align   colour   colour

Figure 9.7

- **Header row in bold**: To make the headings stand out from the rest of the data, click on the number 1 at the left of the first row. This highlights the whole row so that any alterations are made to all the cells in the row. Use the Bold button in the Formatting toolbar (Figure 9.7) to make the change.

- **BMD data cells colour-coded**: All the FreeBMD entries looked the same. Adding a colour background to the box can show at a glance whether the record is for a birth, marriage or death. The colours used are the same as the covers of the bound volumes that previously held the BMD indexes at the General Register Office, ie red for births, green for marriages and light grey for deaths. (Actually, the death indexes were bound in black but then you wouldn't be able to read the text in the box.)

  To make the change, highlight just the cell this time and use the dropdown arrow on the background colour button (see Figure 9.7) to select an appropriate colour (light enough so you can still read the text). In some spreadsheets, this function is called 'fill colour' rather than 'background colour'.

Sorting the data

The great thing about using a spreadsheet is that it lets you sort your data in many different ways. You can then save your re-ordered data or sort it again. This would be impossible with handwritten lists. Now that the spreadsheet contains most of the information collected about Carl Fischer, it would make sense to sort it by year so that there is a timeline of events connected to him. Additional data, such as his death record or entries in electoral registers, can be inserted as and when they are found.

To sort by year do the following:

1. Click and hold the second row to highlight it.

2. Drag the cursor down to the last row so that all the rows are highlighted except the first one containing the headings.

3. Click Data in the menu bar at the top of the screen.

4. Select Sort (see Figure 9.8).

Figure 9.8

5. In the Sort menu, choose the column by which you wish to sort. In this case, you want the data to be ordered by year, so use column A.

213

6. Click OK. The data is resorted.

7. Save the spreadsheet. (Use Save As to give it a new name; use Save to keep the original name for the newly-sorted data.)

There are two things to note when you do a sort. First, *you must select the whole row*. If you only select certain cells in the row, the computer sorts just those cells (remember how literal-minded it is). This mixes up your data so that, for example, the information about Carl's birth can end up in a row with the date of his marriage.

The first row acts as headings for each of the columns. You will want to keep this row out of the sort process so that it stays at the top. There are ways to include the header row but this involves much more detailed explanation about the workings of spreadsheets than is needed here.

If anything does go wrong with the sort (or with any other process that you try out), you can always reverse the last action by clicking Edit in the menu bar at the top of the screen and choosing Undo.

Calculating birth years

The spreadsheet can also help you by automatically calculating a birth year. This involves subtracting the age recorded in a document from the year in which the document was created. You have seen this in census transcriptions. The age of the individual was recorded on the census and this was subtracted from the census year. There were occasionally problems with this, where a birthday was after the census date or when the recorded age was misread. However, it is useful to have a list of birth years extrapolated from the information collected. Even if these are not identical, it at least gives a possible range for future searches.

In 1752, Britain changed from the Julian to the Gregorian calendar so the day after 2 September 1752 was 14 September. Catholic countries had been using the Gregorian calendar since 1582.

Setting up the spreadsheet to calculate a birth year involves the following:

● Putting a formula in the spreadsheet cell where you want the result to appear. The formula refers to other cells already containing data.

- Making the result in the cell a different colour to other data you have collected. This reminds you that this has been calculated from other information and was not in the original document.
- Copying the formula to other cells in the same column.

Look again at Figure 9.8. The formula goes in column G (DOB – date of birth). It tells the computer to take the number in column A (Year) and subtract from it the number in column F (Age). You can then change the text to red.

Figure 9.9 shows what you need to do. (This is the spreadsheet, which has been resorted in chronological order of events.)

	A	B	C	D	E	F	G	H
1	Year	Source	Forenames	Surname	Spouse	Age	DOB	Birthplac
2	1866	FreeBMD	Karl R	FISCHER				1866 Marylebone
3	1871	census	Charles	FRISCHER		5	=a3-f3	
4	1881	census	Charles	FISCHER		15		Marylebone

Figure 9.9

1. Type 1886 in cell G2. The event is a birth recorded in the March quarter so you don't have to work out the year.

2. Move the cursor to cell G3.

3. Type **=a3-f3** (The = sign tells the computer that this is a formula it needs to work out. The cell reference letters don't need to be in capital letters.)

4. Press the Enter or Return key. The year appears in the cell.

5. Move the cursor back to G3 (pressing Enter usually moves it to the next cell).

6. On the formatting bar, use the dropdown arrow next to the Font (text) colour icon to select a red colour. The date is now in red. (The colour appears only in this cell as no other cells were selected for this operation.)

   You could now repeat steps 2 to 6 for each of the cells in column G. However, the quicker way to do this is to copy the formula which is now in G3 and paste it into the other cells in the column. (Copy and Paste are terms that are often used in computing. They refer to taking a copy of a picture, word, phrase or complete file and putting an identical copy of it somewhere else. This could be in the same document, or in another document or folder.)

7. Make sure the cursor is highlighting cell G3. Click the Copy icon in the toolbar at the top of the page. (The Copy icon usually looks like two identical pieces of paper). You won't notice any change yet.

8. Move the cursor to cell G4. Click the Paste icon in the toolbar. (It is next to the Copy icon and looks like a miniature clipboard.)

9. The year now appears in cell G4, with the text in red.

10. Copy and paste in the same way into cells G7, G8 and G9. (G5 and G6 won't work as there was no specific age given in the documents.)

Figure 9.10 shows the final result. It may look as if the spreadsheet has just copied the number 1866. However, if you highlight cell G8 and look at the cell contents

This is the formula that generated the date 1866

	Year	Source	Forenames	Surname	Spouse	Age	DOB	Birthplac
1	Year	Source	Forenames	Surname	Spouse	Age	DOB	Birthplac
2	1866	FreeBMD	Karl R	FISCHER			1866	Marylebone
3	1871	census	Charles	FRISCHER		5	1866	Marylebone
4	1881	census	Charles	FISCHER		15	1866	Marylebone
5	1890	marr.cert.	Carl Robert	FISCHER	Maria SMITH	of age		
6	1890	FreeBMD	Carl Robert	FISCHER	Maria SMITH			
7	1891	census	Carl	FISCHER	Maria FISCHER	25	1866	Middx. Lond
8	1901	census	Carl	FISCHER	Maria FISCHER	35	1866	St Pancras
9	1911	census	Carl	FISCHER	Maria FISCHER	45	1866	St Johns Wc

Figure 9.10

area just under the toolbars, you will see that it has actually put a revised formula into each cell, taking account of the change of row number. It's this ability to work with a formula plus the sorting function that makes the spreadsheet such a powerful tool for recording and then reviewing your family research.

Adding other family members

The accountancy pad or bookkeeping ledger you buy in the stationery shop has a fixed size for each page (though it will have a number of pages.) The spreadsheet has a much greater size and so can accommodate a lot more data on a single sheet.

There may be times, however, when you don't want to put all the data you collect on a single sheet. In your example, a worksheet has been created with data relating to Carl Fischer. Although his wife, Maria, appears in some of the events, you would probably want to create a separate sheet for her. Such a sheet will include the events that overlap with Carl but also events that just relate to her.

At the bottom left of the spreadsheet (Figure 9.11), you will find a number of tabs labelled Sheet1, Sheet2 and so on.

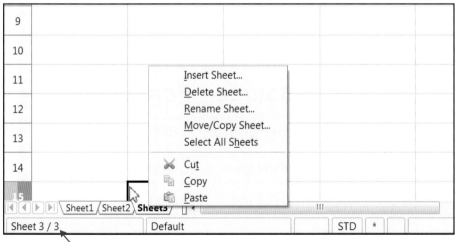

Figure 9.11

This facility is not found in Microsoft Works, where you have to create a separate spreadsheet with a different name for each member of the family. The alternative is to include the research on a single sheet but lower down the page.

Sheet3 (which is blank) is currently highlighted. If you right-click on the tab, a menu allows you to insert, move, delete or rename sheets. If you have previously copied a sheet, you can paste it here. To help you keep track, there is a counter in the bottom line, which tells you that this is Sheet 3/3.

Right-click on the Sheet1 tab and rename it *Carl*. Do the same for Sheet2 but rename it *Maria*.

You could set up Maria's sheet from scratch, as you did for Carl. However, you could Copy and Paste Carl's sheet and then delete rows and information that were incorrect or not needed for Maria.

Click Carl's tab to return to his sheet. Click the blank cell near the top left, at the intersection of the row and column headings (see Figure 9.12). This selects the whole sheet. Right-click Carl's tab and select Copy.

Click in this blank cell to highlight the whole spreadsheet

	A	B	C	
1	Year	Source	Forenames	
2	1866	FreeBMD	Karl R	F
3	1871	census	Charles	F
4	1881	census	Charles	F
5	1890	marr cert	Carl Robert	F

Figure 9.12

Select Maria's tab. Make sure the cursor is in cell A1. Right-click Maria's tab. Select Paste. Click anywhere in Maria's sheet to take off the highlighting. You can now change things to reflect Maria's life events. Where these were shared with Carl, you can keep the rows but change the information in some of the cells (census and marriage references and some addresses can stay the same).

Figure 9.13 shows the sheet for Maria after the necessary data changes have been entered. If you do use this copy and paste method, make sure you check the whole line for data changes. You may have seen that, when you entered a different age in the census rows, it automatically changed the DOB column information. The other thing that shows clearly is that Maria's birth was registered in the December quarter of 1867. This is one of those cases where transcription information or extrapolating from the data can be misleading. Whenever you search for information about Maria, use the date range 1867–1868 to have a better chance of finding her.

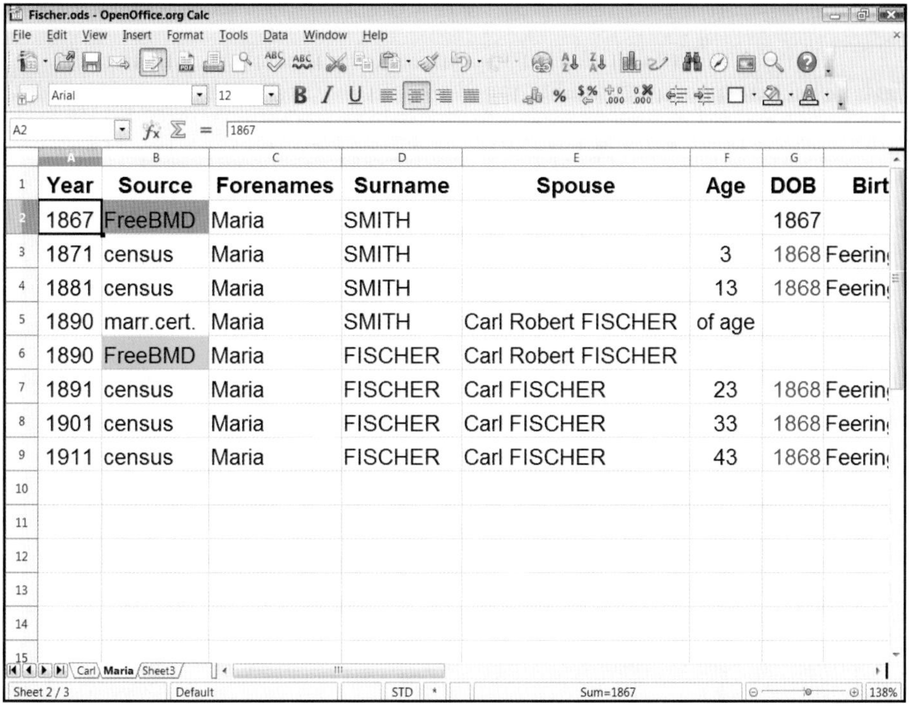

Year	Source	Forenames	Surname	Spouse	Age	DOB	Birt
1867	FreeBMD	Maria	SMITH			1867	
1871	census	Maria	SMITH		3	1868	Feerin
1881	census	Maria	SMITH		13	1868	Feerin
1890	marr.cert.	Maria	SMITH	Carl Robert FISCHER	of age		
1890	FreeBMD	Maria	FISCHER	Carl Robert FISCHER			
1891	census	Maria	FISCHER	Carl FISCHER	23	1868	Feerin
1901	census	Maria	FISCHER	Carl FISCHER	33	1868	Feerin
1911	census	Maria	FISCHER	Carl FISCHER	43	1868	Feerin

Figure 9.13

Indexing projects

The spreadsheet can be used for other projects related to family history. So far, you have used it as a research log to review data about a particular individual. There will be occasions when you have access to an archive and want to extract information about all the individuals with a particular name. You may not be sure at the time whether they are all related to you. However, by creating your own database index, you can sometimes identify them as relatives through information that subsequently becomes available. You therefore do not need to return to the same archival source to search for them.

This was probably more useful when the main source of data was in paper-based documents located in archives. Figure 9.14 shows the extraction of my own family name from the bound index volumes that were located at the Family Records Centre. Each volume contained the records for one quarter of one year. Since my surname is not very common, it was not a problem to note the names and record them later on a spreadsheet. It did, however, take many visits to go through all the volumes and then do the same for marriages and deaths.

	A	B	C	D	E	F	G	H
1	Family Record Centre: Record of Birth, Death and Marriage Information for FIFER Family							
2	Year	E	Name	Forenames	Mother/Spouse Age		DOB	Registrat
3	M=1 J=2 S=3 D=4				Maiden Name			Distric
61	1903q1	b	Fifer	Judith				Whitechapel
62	1903q1	b	Fifer	Solomon				Whitechapel
63	1903q4	b	Fifer	Betsy				Whitechapel
64	1904q1	b	Fifer	Harris				London C.
65	1904q1	b	Fifer	Joseph	Lodker			Birmingham
66	1904q2	b	Fifer	Joseph	Schwatzburg			Birmingham
67	1905q2	b	Fifer	Albert				Whitechapel
68	1906q1	b	Fifer	Morris				Whitechapel
69	1907q1	b	Fifer	Sadie				Kings N.
70	1908q3	b	Fifer	Samson				Mile End
71	1911q3	b	Fifer	Dora	Botinsky			Whitechapel
72	1913q3	b	Fifer	Isaac	Fashinsky			Whitechapel
73	1913q3	b	Fifer	William H.	Foxwell			Leigh
74	1916q4	b	Fifer	George Henry	Foxwell			Leigh
75	1917q1	b	Fifer	John	Foxwell			Leigh
76	1917q2	b	Fifer	Doris	Fifer			Bristol
77	1918q1	b	Fifer	Stanley A.	Glass			Croydon
78	1919q1	b	Fifer	Harold	Shellingsby			Holborn

Figure 9.14

There are three worksheets in this file. If you look at the sheet tabs at the bottom, you will see that there is a sheet for each of the birth, marriage and death records. If I see that the mother's maiden name is Shellingsby, I can then instantly check the marriage record sheet to find the first names of both parents. I could create similar lists for other major names within my family. If you decide to do a one name study, the spreadsheet with its 65,000+ lines will be very useful.

The terms 'brother' and 'sister' in some older records may, in fact, refer to brother-in-law or sister-in-law.

The other use of the spreadsheet is in indexing projects, which may involve a number of different people transcribing various years within the records. Since most people can access a spreadsheet, there is no need for specialist software. The transcribers are all given a template that shows the columns and how they should be formatted. Their instructions would also tell them how to record dates, whether surnames should be in upper case letters and other things that would ensure that all the data collected will look the same and can be collated relatively easily. Figure 9.15 shows some indexing work on Jewish records from nineteenth century Poland, transcribed from LDS microfilms as part of a co-operative

AKT	Surname	Forename(s)	Town	Type	Year	LDS film #	Commen
1	PECH	Laie Ruchel	Kalisz	B	1834	743143	
2	FLATTO	Elle	Kalisz	B	1834	743143	
3	FEYL	Hanusia	Kalisz	B	1834	743143	
4	POŁACKI	Hersz Matis	Kalisz	B	1834	743143	
5	POŁACKI	Berek	Kalisz	B	1834	743143	
6	LEWI	Wolf	Kalisz	B	1834	743143	
7	FAUST	Moritz	Kalisz	B	1834	743143	
8	NOMBURG	Fraidel	Kalisz	B	1834	743143	
9	LEWI	Fabis	Kalisz	B	1834	743143	
10	TRAUBE	Michle	Kalisz	B	1834	743143	
11	LUSTIG	Haie Liebe	Kalisz	B	1834	743143	
12	BOHM	Laib Ahren	Kalisz	B	1834	743143	
13	TRAUBE	Icek	Kalisz	B	1834	743143	
14	WĄKCZESKI	?achie	Kalisz	B	1834	743143	
15	NELKEN	Zanetta	Kalisz	B	1834	743143	
16	PRASZKIER	Hinde Dmeyral	Kalisz	B	1834	743143	
17	EILENBERG	Tobe Fraindel	Kalisz	B	1834	743143	
18	MOZESSOHN	Haie	Kalisz	B	1834	743143	
19	WALOCH	Ruchel Laie	Kalisz	B	1834	743143	
20	ZAIFFE	Efroim	Kalisz	B	1834	743143	
21	WAIS	Tobe	Kalisz	B	1834	743143	

Figure 9.15

volunteer project. Like FreeBMD, this is an ongoing activity, which places a database of the transcribed material online as it becomes available. This particular project now has over 3.5 million index references online from 500 Polish towns.

Printing your spreadsheet

The most common printer paper size is A4 and this presents certain challenges when you want to print a spreadsheet. If you have a large number of columns, then they won't all fit on the width of the page. (It is possible to force the printer to do so, but then you probably won't be able to read the results.)

There are a number of things that can help you produce better printed lists. These can be accessed through the File menu, which is where printer options are usually found. Take some time to find out where these options are in the spreadsheet program you are using. Many of them you can ignore for the moment (for example, references to Headers and Footers).

- Use Print Preview first to see what the document would look like when print- ed. Close this and then make changes. Each time, go back to Print Preview to see if things have improved.

- Page Setup usually lets you change the 'orientation' of the paper from Portrait to Landscape. This will let you see more columns (but fewer rows). Landscape is usually better unless you have only two or three columns.

- Page Setup is also where you can change the width of the margins (top and bottom as well as left and right). This will let you see more, but be careful if you want to hole-punch your papers for putting in a folder.

- Although you can see grid lines on the screen, they will not print out unless you tell the printer that this is what you want. The option for this is usually in the Page Setup/Page Style menu on a tab marked Sheet (though in Works it is on a tab marked Other Options). There is a box marked grid/gridlines, which needs to be ticked.

You may decide that, for printing purposes, you only want to print out a few columns. You can highlight these columns and then tell the computer that this is the print area. In OpenOffice Calc, this is done again in the Format menu, this time by defining the Print Range.

Once you have the page looking reasonably well presented, you can go to the Print menu where you will be offered options about what to print. Some are common to all printers; others will be specific to your printer.

> If you are going to be printing out a long list, you might want to do a test run first on the back of printer paper you want to recycle. You can also use the print options to restrict the output to a single page or a set of pages.

Being kind to your eyes

Using the computer screen for long periods can be tiring. I've always had glasses for distance vision and now have glasses for reading and close work. The computer screen sometimes seems to me to require yet another set of lenses. If you are finding things a bit small on the screen there are various things that you can do.

- Increase the font (text) size. If you look towards the top of Figures 9-13 and 9-14, you will see, towards the left of the formatting toolbar, a box with the number 12. This is the font size at which the document will be printed. A higher number means bigger text. Many spreadsheets have an initial setting of 10, which is rather too small to read comfortably (if you have older and wiser eyes). Size 12 is much more comfortable for printed reports. You can change the size before you start entering any data by using the dropdown arrow next to the font size.

- You can also change the size of the text that you view on screen while keeping the printed font size to 12. In Figure 9.14, there is a toolbar box towards the top which reads 125%. This made the text on my computer screen 25% bigger than the normal viewing size.

  If there is no box on the toolbar to change the size, find the View menu. This should let you change the viewing size in various ways so that you can read comfortably what you are entering on the screen. The only disadvantage to increasing the viewing size is that you may have to scroll across the screen more frequently to see what is in other columns.

- Avoid over-elaborate typefaces. Most people generally use the Arial font for spreadsheets because it has clean lines and is easy to read.

- If you do use a coloured type, then make it one that is easy to read both on screen and when printed. If using a coloured background for certain cells, make sure it is light enough for the text to remain legible.

- Take frequent breaks if you have to do a lot of typing. Try to avoid having a direct light source shining on the screen.

- Some programs let you increase the size of the icons. If you are using a program for the first time, it is often useful to go to the Tools ➢ Options or Customize menu to change the setup for the spreadsheet.

Research tasks: Recording your family using a spreadsheet

Take the person for whom you have found the most records or references and set up a spreadsheet for him/her. Put in BMD and census records first and then sort the sheet into chronological order. Don't forget to save your work frequently as you go along.

If you have other references, for example, from newspapers, think if they could also provide corroborative or additional data for you. They may have names, ages, occupations and addresses, all of which could fit the template you created. Other more formal records, such as pension or military records, could also be included.

Print out the list to take with you to record offices when you undertake further research.

Summary

- Spreadsheets allow you to create lists of data so you can review and compare information collected about an individual or a family.

- The electronic format allows you to sort data in many different ways.

- You can use a formula to get the computer to work out things like year of birth from other given data.

- Some programs let you have multiple worksheets rather like the pages in a pad of graph paper.

- Take time to set up the screen so that you can view it comfortably when entering data.

- Formatting allows you to change the appearance of text in the individual cells of the worksheet.

- Copying and pasting lets you fill the sheet quickly with similar information rather than needing to retype everything.

Brain Training

1. In a spreadsheet, what does the icon that looks like a clipboard allow you to do?

a) Copy

b) Cut

c) Paste

d) Rename

2. If you click on a letter across the top of a spreadsheet, what happens?

a) A cell is highlighted

b) A column is highlighted

c) A row is highlighted

d) The whole spreadsheet is highlighted

3. In which menu option can you find a feature to undo the previous action(s)?

a) Edit

b) File

c) Format

d) Tools

4. If you type = before the rest of the entry in a spreadsheet cell, what are you wanting to achieve?

a) Change the text colour

b) Create a duplicate cell

c) Create a formula

d) Delete the information in the cell below

5. Which menu allows you to change how text is seen on the screen without changing how it will appear in print?

a) Edit

b) File

c) Format

d) View

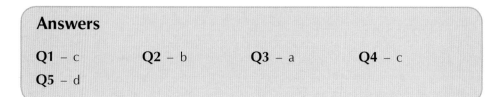

Answers

Q1 – c   **Q2** – b   **Q3** – a   **Q4** – c

Q5 – d

Using family history software   10

Equipment needed: Computer with family history program (Personal Ancestral File, Family Tree Maker, Brother's Keeper, Roots Magic, Legacy etc).

Skills needed: Recording of facts and sources.

The lists that you created for your family data in the previous chapter were produced using multi-purpose software. So far, most of the data has related to individuals, with the occasional mention of other family members in documents such as census returns. The goal for the genealogist, however, is to look at how all these individuals fit into the complex web of family relationships, whether within their own, previous or later generations.

To do this properly requires more than generic office software (although some people have created 'drop-line' family trees using spreadsheets). Family history software allows you to enter your research findings and then use the computer's data handling abilities to work out family relationships, create reports and charts, incorporate images and audio clips and generally help you manage the process in a more efficient and satisfying way.

The programs work on the very simple basis that every individual has a father and mother (whether or not you know the names of these people) and that every person is either male or female (see Figure 10.1). Not everyone gets married and not everyone has children but the parents/gender criteria apply to all.

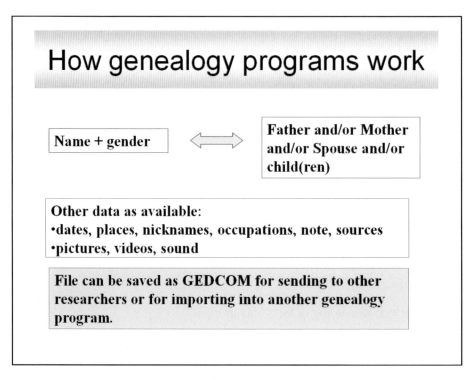

How genealogy programs work

| Name + gender | ⟷ | Father and/or Mother and/or Spouse and/or child(ren) |

Other data as available:
•dates, places, nicknames, occupations, note, sources
•pictures, videos, sound

File can be saved as GEDCOM for sending to other researchers or for importing into another genealogy program.

Figure 10.1

What this means in practice is that, if two individuals are linked to the same parents, the program knows automatically that these two are siblings and this knowledge extends to being able to work out instantly the relationship between any two individuals in the family tree by tracking back and forwards (and often sideways) through the threads linking individuals to parents (and, as appropriate, to spouses and children).

The data is usually saved in a file format that can be read by the particular program used to create it. However, because of the requirement for family historians to share data with other researchers, a generic format, called GEDCOM, has been developed. You can export your data to a GEDCOM file and it can then be opened in nearly any other family history program. Similarly, you can import such a file into your software, even if it was created using a different program.

It is very rare, nowadays, for a family history program not to support the GEDCOM format. If this is the case, you would be well advised to avoid it. Online family tree services, such as GenesReunited and Ancestry, allow you to upload your tree to their websites using GEDCOM files.

This chapter looks at what you can expect when putting your research data into a family tree program, and works through the process of setting up a family file for the Fischer/Smith family.

Benefits of using a family tree program

The main advantage of using a family tree program, as with many computer programs, is that you have to enter the data only once. You can, of course, update it, add to it or amend it but you are not required to start all over again if changes are needed.

Once you have an individual on the tree, you can add other information as and when this arises in your research. The computer can store more data, and organise and retrieve it more efficiently, than is possible using research notebooks and hand-drawn trees.

Family historians want to be able to produce reports with the data they have collected. For many people, this report takes the form of the traditional family tree with boxes containing names, places and dates for each individual. Before there was widespread access to computers and printers, such charts were handwritten on pieces of paper and stuck together to form a scroll. As well as the problems with adding or amending data, they were not always practical or hard-wearing. The more research done, the more numerous the side branches of the tree and the wider and more unwieldy the scroll became.

Not surprisingly, the computer has changed all this. Such formats are still possible but can be easily updated and then printed out again. Multiple copies are possible, meaning that the finished product can be distributed more widely within the family without looking dog-eared through repeated unrolling and handling. In addition, programs offer a range of other reports and lists tailored to research or presentation requirements. This flexibility extends to incorporating pictures, video and audio clips, and even links to external websites.

You can keep all your data in one tree but, if one branch of your family wants to start its own family research, most programs let you split the tree. This is usually achieved by saving a separate file containing all the descendants of a common ancestor.

The programs have very detailed facilities for entering your sources. You should try to get into the habit of doing this as you go along. (Experience shows that this is unlikely to happen retrospectively, however good your intentions.) The reason for including sources is to help those with whom you share your research and also future generations who may wish to continue your work. Knowing the source of a piece of data means that other researchers don't have to repeat your work. If they do wish to examine the original material, then your references make life much easier for them.

Some problems with family tree programs

There are a few things to consider when choosing and using a family tree program. These would probably come under the heading of precautions rather than disadvantages.

- As with all software, there is a learning curve. Nearly all computer programs seem to have more features than anyone could be reasonably expected to want or use (though thinking about it, the same could be said of microwaves and washing machines). Put in the basic data and build the outline of your tree. Fancy formatting and embellishments can come later.

- There are many programs on the market and, although they all have the same basic functions, they differ in ease of use, number and type of reports and functionality. As you can transfer your data easily between programs using the GEDCOM standard, you might be tempted to maintain parallel trees in different programs. Avoid this if possible. If you are entering a large amount of new data, you will have to do this more than once and you can lose track of where it has been updated. It is best to keep one program as your main tree and make all changes here. Then, should you wish to use a report format in another program, just export a GEDCOM file for that purpose and print out the report or the chart.

  Of course, you can always 'move house' and use different software on a permanent basis as your main program. Like moving house, there may be some pieces of furniture that need a little adjusting if they are to fit properly. This won't be the main pieces of data such as names, dates and places but you may find that any special tags you have created for data in one program may have some problems getting through the door of their new home.

- Many family tree programs have trial versions that allow you to enter a limited number of either individuals or generations. They may be time-limited. If you do make full use of them to enter a lot of data, make sure that you can transfer this to another program at the end of the trial. Sometimes, this transfer can only be made to the full-priced version of the trial software, which effectively locks you in to that program unless you wish to rekey your data.

● The ease of sharing data electronically was mentioned earlier in the context of finding other researchers through their online trees on websites such as Ancestry. Before adding data from another source to your tree, be comfortable that the other research is adequate and well referenced. All researchers have, on occasion, drawn the wrong conclusions from information gathered during their research. While they can change this on their own tree once they are aware of the error, it is often impossible to work out how far the data has been shared, once you give it to someone else. This is not to discourage the sharing of data but just to advise some caution.

Deciding which program to use

You may wonder which program is best. It's a difficult question and one that many experienced researchers are reluctant to answer. It's the same with cars; you may love the make and model you've been driving for years; someone else wouldn't have it as a gift.

The advice is usually to find a free or trial program and play about with it, entering your data, looking at the features and seeing how easily you can find your way about. The program you start with may remain more than adequate for all your needs. If you later decide that you want something that is simpler or more fully-featured, then you can try this out by exporting a GEDCOM file, without losing any of your hard work.

Much software is designed for the US market. If your research is exclusively UK-based, you might want to look for a UK version. This is not simply a question of spelling and date formats but it may be better geared to the vital records and census formats used in the UK.

Most of the CDs given away with the monthly family history magazines have trial versions of the software. The other place to look is Cyndi's List at **www.cyndislist. com/software.htm**. This has links to specific programs and more generic information about software. A UK-based site to visit is **www.genealogysupplies.com**. Click the software link to see the range of programs on offer.

It's best to get started with something as soon as possible, rather than agonising over the merits of different programs. The examples in this chapter will use Personal Ancestral File (PAF), the program produced by the LDS. It can be downloaded from the home page of the FamilySearch website **www.familysearch.org**. It has a number of advantages:

● It's free.

● It's designed for a wide range of people to use and is therefore simple enough for beginners while offering a range of features for more experienced users.

● There are links from the program to tutorials on the FamilySearch website.

● It has a fairly clean and uncluttered look, which is less intimidating for new users.

● There is a companion program which allows additional reports to be produced.

Getting started with Personal Ancestral File

If you haven't already done so, download Personal Ancestral File from the FamilySearch website **www.familysearch.org** and install it on your computer. If you don't have much experience of downloading and installing programs, ask for help from a family member. He/she has, after all, something of a vested interest in getting this up and running.

Unfortunately, if you are using a Mac computer rather than a PC, you may find that versions of PAF for the Mac haven't been updated over the years and won't run on your computer. The main family history program for the Mac is called Reunion and there are one or two others, but these can be quite expensive. It may be worthwhile seeing if you can get hold of an earlier copy of Reunion to see how it works for you. Alternatively, you might wish to build your family tree online at one of the Family History websites discussed in Chapter 13.

Work through this chapter to set up a file for the Fischer/Smith family. This takes you through the main features of adding and linking individuals, recording basic sources and looking at creating lists and reports. You may also want to take advantage of the tutorials available on FamilySearch at various stages during the process. In the research task at the end of the chapter, you can then create a new file; this time for your family.

Figure 10.2 shows the welcome screen you see when you first open the program. You need to click the New option, but before selecting it, you might want to click the Help button to see the range of topics that you can call up if needed. The first two options on the welcome screen list are for when you have previously started a file that has been saved in the PAF format. If you choose Search, the computer looks through all your files to find any in that format; the Open option takes you to the filing system and lets you browse for the file yourself. As with most filing, it is useful to keep files of a similar type in the same location, so that they are easier to find.

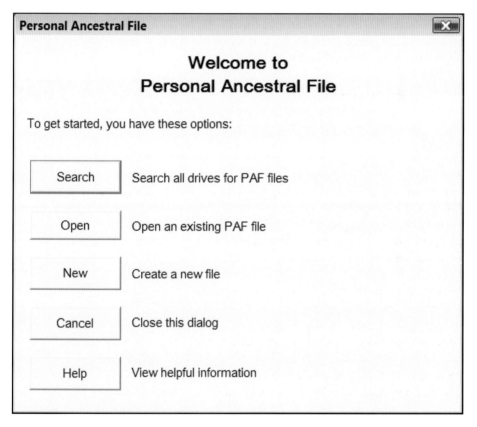

Figure 10.2

When you click New, a window opens in your filing system and you are invited to give a name to a new PAF file. Call the file *FischerSmith*. At the top of the window, it will give a suggested location for such files. If you want to change it, you could create a new folder called PAF in your Documents and save all family tree files there. If you do lose track of where they are, you can always get the program to search the system for you. Click Save when you are ready.

The Preferences window opens, as shown in Figure 10.3. Preferences allow you to specify how certain aspects of a program are handled: where files should be saved; how dates should be written; whether names are capitalised in reports; the size of fonts. In this case, you are asked to give information about yourself as the person preparing the data. This will be saved with the file, so that anyone receiving a copy of the data knows the owner of the material and how you can be contacted. You only need to put in your name as a minimum, particularly if you are not intending to share data at this early stage. You can always return to Preferences later (located in the Tools menu).

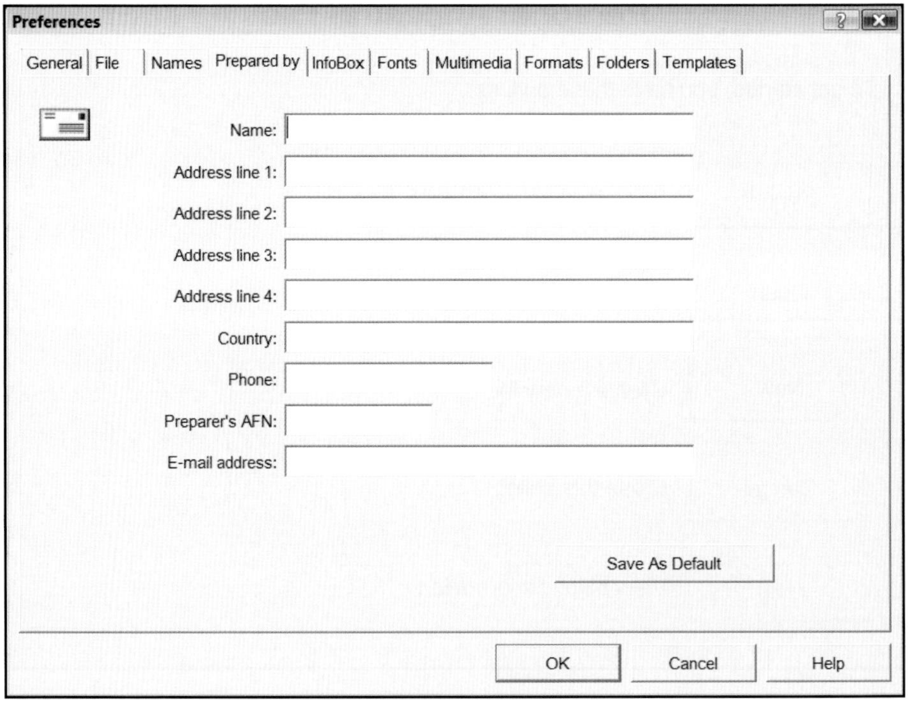

Preferences

General | File | Names | Prepared by | InfoBox | Fonts | Multimedia | Formats | Folders | Templates

Name:
Address line 1:
Address line 2:
Address line 3:
Address line 4:
Country:
Phone:
Preparer's AFN:
E-mail address:

Save As Default

OK   Cancel   Help

Figure 10.3

While in this menu, click the tab marked Formats. Ensure that Date Entry is set to European and that it will display as DMY (Day, Month, Year). In the Names tab, tick the Capitalize surnames on screens and reports option. Click OK.

Entering family members on the tree

There are three main ways of viewing data, by clicking the following tabs:

● Family (individual + spouse + children)

● Pedigree (individual + parents + grandparents → 5th generation)

● Individual (a list of everyone entered so far with their record numbers, name and a small amount of information).

Figure 10.4 shows the initial screen which has opened in the Family tab. The first person you add will go in the highlighted box. Before adding anyone, click the Pedigree and Individual tabs to see how these pages look. The Pedigree and Family pages are similar to those you saw in IGI and Pedigree Resource File results in Chapter 5. Return to the Family tab.

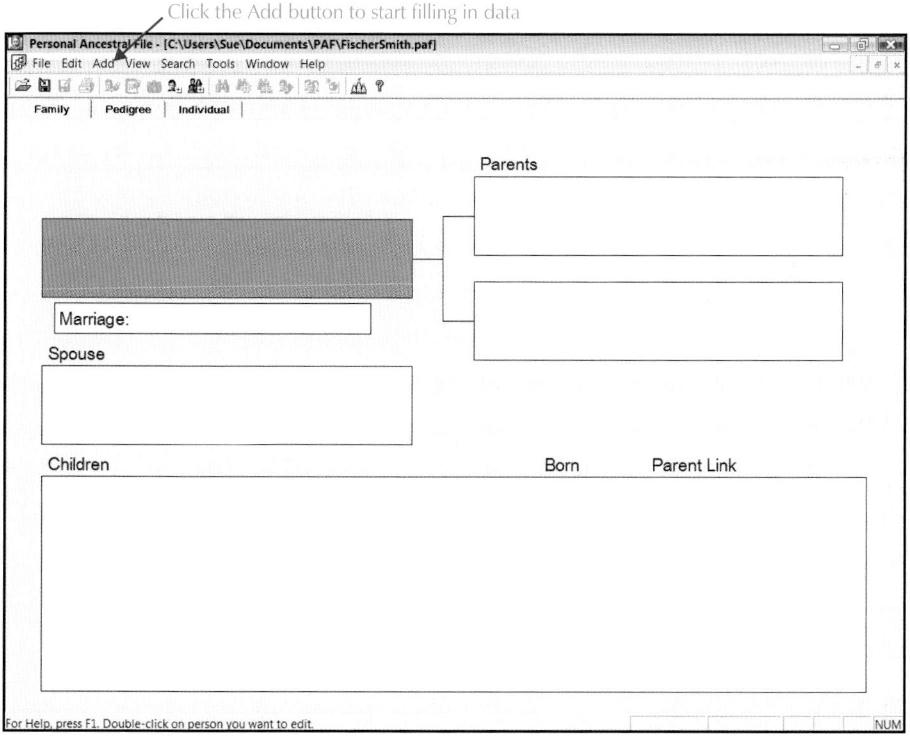

Figure 10.4

The menu bar button that you will use most frequently is Add. The options offered depend on who is highlighted and what family members have already been linked to this person.

Follow these steps to create the first entry:

1. Click Add.

2. Select Individual.

3. Enter *Karl Robert Fischer* in the name box. (You can leave it to the program to capitalise the surname in reports.)

Where someone uses different forms of their name over time, it is difficult to know which name to choose. The usual convention is to use the person's birth name. There is room to add other versions of a name, including nicknames, further down the page.

4. Use the dropdown arrow next to the box marked Sex to choose Male.

5. Enter *1866* in the Birth box. No records viewed so far have given an exact date of birth. The BMD index gave the March quarter but it could be misleading to put March in here. He might have been born in January or February and still have been registered in the March quarter.

6. For place of birth, enter *Marylebone, London*. Once you have created a place name such as Marylebone, it will be offered to you as an option from a list when you enter further individuals. This saves time typing and also means that entries are consistent.

7. Under Other, enter *Carl/Charles* in the box marked Also Known As. This will not show up on the main screens, but you can include it in reports. He will be referred to as Karl for the rest of this chapter to avoid confusion.

Figure 10.5 shows how the Add Individual screen should look. At the bottom left of the screen is a Record Identification Number (RIN). As Karl is the first individual in the file, he is allocated RIN 1 and is considered the 'Root person' on the tree. When you create your own tree, you should enter yourself first and become the Root person.

Add Individual

Karl Robert FISCHER

		Save
PERSONAL:		Cancel
Full Name:	Karl Robert /Fischer/	
Sex:	Male	Options
EVENTS:		
Birth:	1866	Help
Place:	Marylebone, London	s
Christening:		
Place:		s
Death:		
Place:		s
Burial:		
Place:		s
OTHER:		Individual
Title (prefix):		Sources
Married Name:		
Also Known As:	Carl/Charles	s = sources
Nickname:		
Cause of Death:		
Physical Description		
Ancestral File Numbe		
Custom ID:		

RIN: 1   Template: Default

Figure 10.5

You may also have noticed that the program has separated the surname from the other names in the top line. These slashes won't show up in the main screens or reports. They are necessary, particularly where there are double-barrelled names or surnames with prefixes. They help the program to create alphabetical lists based on surnames. If the program does not identify a surname correctly, you can adjust the slashes.

8. Click Save. (This is important to remember each time you make a change to the data held on an individual.)

Adding events

The spreadsheet data for Karl has more information than you were able to enter on his individual record. Potentially, there are dozens of events that could be included for an individual: graduation, baptism, divorce, emigration, retirement, house moves or census. The initial screen just gives the most common events. This stops it from being too cluttered. If you wish to add or create others, you are able to do so.

One piece of information gathered was that Karl, like others in his family, was a house decorator/painter. Occupation is one of the events that can be added.

To add an event, follow these steps:

1. In the Family View sheet, click Karl's name to highlight it

2. Double-click to open the Edit Individual window. (Apart from the window title, this is identical to Figure 10.5.)

3. Click the Options button on the right

4. Select New Event/Attribute

   Figure 10.6 shows the built in options list. You can select an existing option, edit an option or create a new one.

Select Event	? ✕
Karl Robert FISCHER	**Select**
Adoption	**Close**
Adult Christening	
Annulment	**New...**
Baptism	
Bar Mitzvah	**Edit...**
Bas Mitzvah	
Birth	
Blessing	Delete
Burial	
Census	**Help**
Christening	
Circumcision	
Confirmation	
Cremation	
Death	
Divorce	
Divorce Filing	
Emigration	
Engagement	
Excommunicated	

Figure 10.6

5. Scroll down to Occupation.

6. Click Select.

You are now back in the Edit Individual window, where a new section, Other Events, has been added. You can enter details of the event. Confusingly, the information to be entered in the Occupation box is the date rather than the actual occupation. If you look at other entries on the page, such as Birth or Death, you will see that they are arranged in the same way.

The spreadsheet data shows Karl as an apprentice in the trade in 1881 and still working as a painter/decorator in 1911. You don't know when he started work or when he retired. You should therefore put in a date range.

7. Enter *Abt 1881/1911* in the Occupation box. (Abt is short for About.) The program will warn you that the dual dates exceed 10 years. Click OK to tell it to accept the entry.

8. You still need to add a place of work and job title. Click the word Place in the Occupation details. A new entry window is opened. It is reasonable to assume that Karl worked in the Marylebone area, since this was where the family was located in each census. As you start to type in the place name, you will be offered place name options that you have previously created. Accept the Marylebone, London option.

9. Click description and type *a house decorator*. Include the indefinite article (a/an). This looks better in reports which are set up to read: 'He worked as . . .' (The reports in other programs may be tailored to work out themselves whether a/an should be included.)

Many occupations can be described in a variety of ways. There are fashions in this, just as in other things. Since 'house decorator' appeared on the census, this was probably the way that Karl described himself at the time, so you should use it (though you may need to check other categories, such as Artist, if researching in directories).

10. Click Save to confirm the changes.

Growing the tree

You are now at the point where you can link a new individual to Karl. (Remember, you can always go to any person on the tree, at any time, to add or amend information).

Click Add in the menu bar. This time you are offered options for Spouse, Child, Father and Mother. It is possible to add a new individual or a new family but these won't be linked to Karl. My own preference is to enter individuals only when I can link them to an existing person.

Select Father from the Add menu. This opens a new individual box. The program assumes that the father has the same surname as the son. It also knows that a father is male and so has already entered this data for you. Add the following information.

1. *Ludwig Frederick* in the name box in front of the first surname slash.

2. Birth date: *1836*.

3. Place of birth: *Stuttgart, Germany*.

4. Death: *22 Sep 1908* (If the information was from the BMD index, then it would only be possible to enter the year. Fortunately, the exact date and place of death were found in the Probate Calendar.)

5. Place of death: *At sea* (this lack of a specific place may produce some strange wording later in the reports).

6. Also Known As (AKA): *Frederick* (the name by which he is known in most documents).

7. Use Options to select an event and add Occupation, as you did for Karl. Make the date *Abt 1860/1890* as he is shown as retired in later events. The screen should look as in Figure 10.7.

8. Save the new information.

Before the program returns to Family View, you are offered the option to add marriage information. Since every individual has two parents, the assumption made is that Karl's father had a wife and was married. Even though there is no named wife yet, marriage details can be included.

Fleet marriages were clandestine marriages performed in the Fleet prison without the calling of banns or the need for a marriage licence. They were stopped after Hardwicke's Marriage Act of 1754.

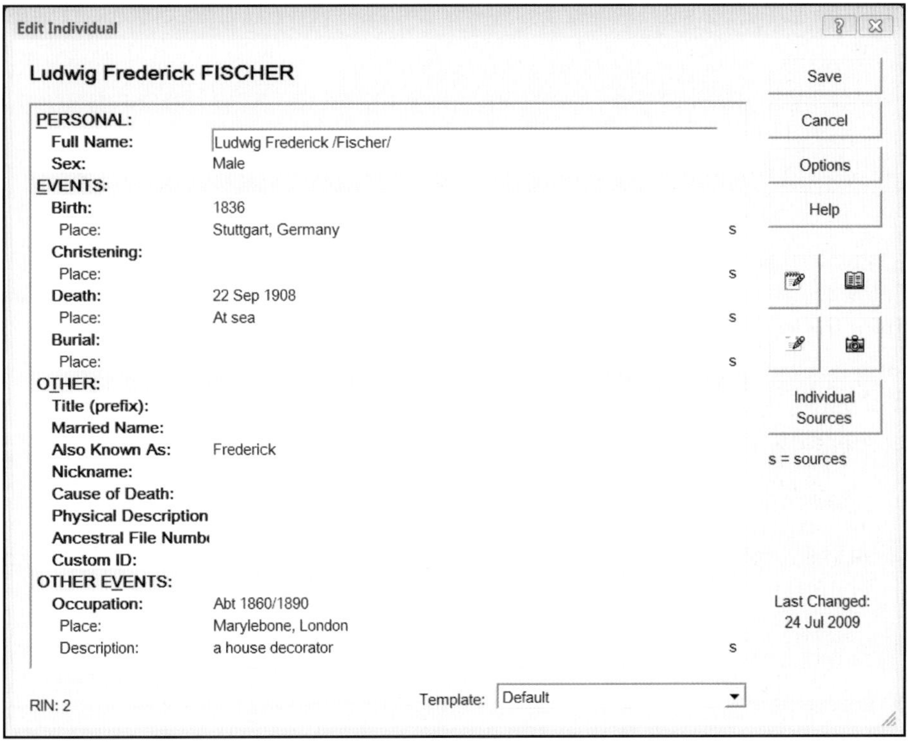

Figure 10.7

This raises the issue of how to deal with the wide and complex range of family relationships that exists today and which also existed in the past (even if not discussed publicly). Some programs offer you a range of options to cover this; others tend to have a more traditional view of family relationships and you may have to work round the options, perhaps through the use of notes and events.

In this case there is no problem, as you have information from Frederick's marriage certificate (Chapter 4, Figure 4-15). Add the date *12 Aug 1860* and the place *All Saints, St John's Wood, Marylebone, Middlesex, England*. You can see that Middlesex and its relationship to London can be problematic. Many parts of east London were designated as Middlesex at that time. Even today, when the county has no administrative existence, the name still exists in the postal addresses for many north London boroughs. There will be many similar problems elsewhere in the country as a result of boundary changes over the years.

> If you do decide to publish your research in some form, you might add a chapter on locations, past and present, where your ancestors lived. Explanations about boundary/name changes can then be included, perhaps with maps and photos showing variations over time.

As always, click Save. Family View now shows Karl and his father, Frederick. An 'unknown' mother to Karl/wife to Frederick is shown. As you have information about this person, this could be entered now.

1. Highlight Karl.

2. Click the Add button and select Mother.

3. Select Add New Individual from the two options offered.

4. Add information about Sophie. You have her maiden name from her marriage certificate and her age and place of birth from census records. (If you haven't yet found a woman's maiden name in your research, then use her married name, and add the search for the maiden name to your to-do list.)

5. Full name: *Amelia Johanna Sophie Rubardt*.

6. Birth date and place: *1839/Oldenburg, Germany*.

7. Death: *1895/Marylebone, London*.

8. Married name: *Fischer*.

9. AKA: *Sophie*.

10. Save.

When you looked at pedigrees on IGI and other FamilySearch results, you could go back through the generations by following the arrows on the right of the page. Where the arrow is a solid colour, this means that there are family members from earlier generations that can be viewed. Transparent arrows mean that this is currently the earliest person in that branch. Family View now shows two such arrows, one from Frederick and one from Sophie (Figure 10.8).

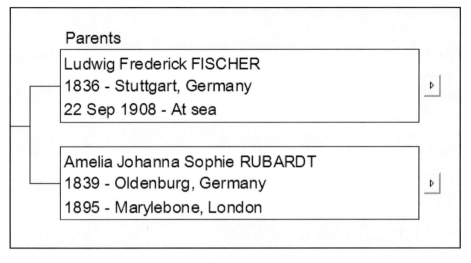

Figure 10.8

Click the arrow from the box with Frederick's name. You are now in a Family View sheet where the individual is Frederick, his spouse Sophie and Karl is now shown as their child. The only research information gathered about Frederick's ancestors was his father's name and occupation, recorded on Frederick's marriage certificate. There are three other bits of information that you could deduce from this:

- The father was alive at the time of the marriage (otherwise he would have been shown as deceased).

- The father was probably born before 1816 (Frederick is 36 and you can guess that his father was at least 20 at the time of his birth).

- The father was probably born in Germany.

Any of these assumptions could ultimately be proved false but they provide a reasonable starting point in the absence of any other evidence. Further research into the Fischer family will then require access to German records. (Note that Frederick is an anglicised version of Friedrich, which is what you may need to look for.) Material is available online and a group such as the Anglo-German Family History Society would be able to point you in the right direction.

For completeness, you can add a father to Frederick and include the following information:

1. Name: *Ludwig Frederick Fischer*. (Does this show that Frederick is the eldest son in the family, since he shares his father's name?)

2. Birth date and place: *Bef 1816, Germany*. (You don't know whether he was born in Stuttgart.)

3. Death: *Aft 1860*.

4. Occupation: *a vintner*.

5. When shown the window for marriage details, click Cancel as you have no information.

   There doesn't appear to be a facility in the current Family View to enter Sophie's father. Figure 10.9 highlights a double-headed arrow, which allows you to switch between the Family View for the husband and wife.

Move between views

Figure 10.9

6. Switch to Sophie and add her father. Christian Nicholas Rubardt, a Government Officer in Oldenburg, Germany was probably born before 1819 and probably died after 1860.

If you wish and if you have the data, you can go back to Karl and enter Maria Smith and her father. Other family members who have appeared in the census are Maria's siblings and mother, Karl's siblings (including his brother Frederick's family), and Karl and Maria's children. There is also a potential line of enquiry into William Christian Rubardt, a witness to Sophie's marriage and of an age to be her brother. From the apparently unpromising beginning of a single 1890 marriage certificate, there is now a small but well-researched family tree.

Sources

The menus for adding sources are almost as detailed as those for individuals. While it is tempting to skip this part of the work, it helps to have some idea of what sources there are and what they can document of your research. You may wish to set up a few general sources at the same time that you create your family tree. If necessary, you can then add to these as you go along.

A source usually consists of two main parts:

● **Source**: an overview of the document, record or person providing you with the information. This could be a published source such as a census, an index, family records, a website, newspaper or personal knowledge.

● **Citation**: the specific location within the source of the information cited.

For the Fischer/Smith family, you have used a limited number of sources, mainly census and BMD records. For your own family, there will be additional references to family records (letters, invitations and photographs) and personal knowledge (interviews with relatives).

To set up a basic source, follow these steps:

1. Go to Edit in the menu bar at the top of the main screen.

2. Select Source List.

3. Click New.

4. Source Title: *BMD indexes* (tick the box to print title in italics).

5. Author: *General Register Office (GRO)* (tick the box to print in parentheses/brackets).

6. Call Number: *www.freebmd.org.uk*.

   Note that, as you type, the Sample Footnote at the bottom of the screen changes to show how it will appear when printed in a report.

   In the middle of the page, there is a Repository button. This allows you to put contact details for an archive or (with permission) an individual.

7. Click Repository.

8. Choose Add.

9. Type *FreeBMD* in the name box. Click OK.

10. Click Select and then OK.

The source list now contains an entry for BMD indexes. Where you have found an item of data in the FreeBMD indexes, you can use this source to reference it.

For census records, you can set up a single record and then copy it, changing the year each time. For all censuses, the author is the Registrar General and publication is Kew, The National Archives. All censuses from 1841 to 1891 are found on the Ancestry website. The official site for 1901 is **www.1901censusonline.com**; for 1911 it is **www.1911census.co.uk**, run by **Findmypast.com**.

Figure 10.10 shows the Edit Source screen for the 1841 census.

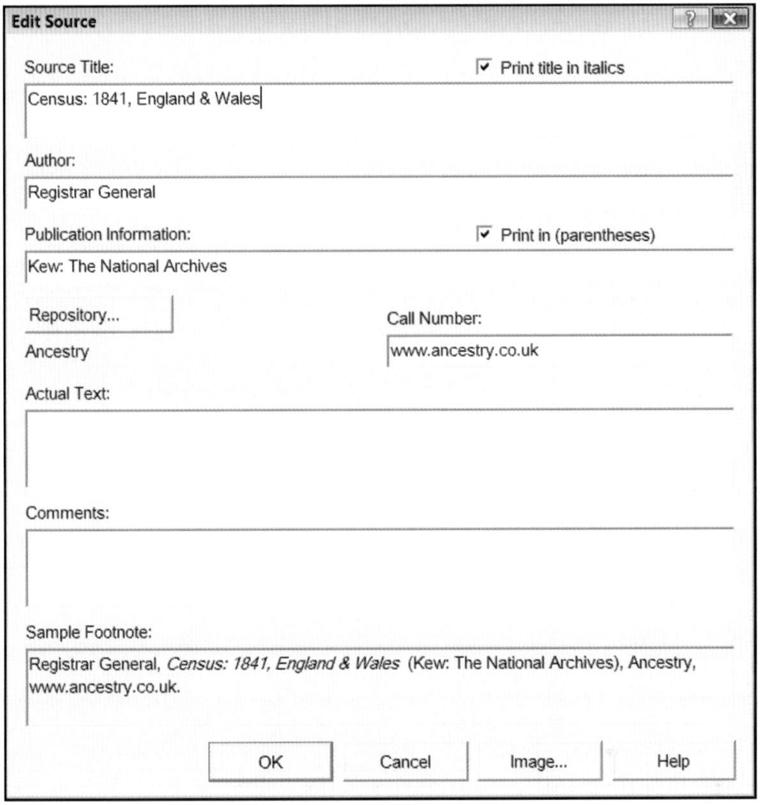

Figure 10.10

If you want more advice on how various sources could be set up, then help is available. At the top of the main PAF screen, click Help and then select Lessons. This takes you to the FamilySearch website pages, which has guides to using various aspects of Personal Ancestral File. Read the navigation instructions and then select Notes and Sources from the menu on the left. Although most of the examples are US-oriented, you can easily adapt them for UK purposes, as you saw with the census example. You might want to come back to the Lessons page to review other aspects of using PAF, such as printing reports.

Back in the program, create a basic source list (shown in Figure 10.11). A similar list will probably be a useful starting point for any family tree.

Edit Source List

Title

BMD indexes

Birth certificate
BMD indexes
Census: 1841, England & Wales
Census: 1851, England & Wales
Census: 1861, England & Wales
Census: 1871, England & Wales
Census: 1881, England & Wales
Census: 1891, England & Wales
Census: 1901, England & Wales
Census: 1911, England & Wales
Death certificate
Marriage certificate
Probate Records (Post 1858)

Title

BMD indexes

Author

General Register Office (GRO)

Publication Information

Comments

Close   New   Copy   Edit   Delete...   Help

Figure 10.11

Using the sources

The next task is to allocate resources to key data items and provide references so that other researchers can replicate your search if necessary. You will also find it personally useful to be able to recall what you have searched and the sources you have used. Most family historians will tell you that the problem is not always carrying out the research, but organising it and not duplicating work at a later date.

To add sources to an individual, follow these steps:

1. Highlight Karl Fischer in the Family View screen.

2. Double-click to open the Edit Individual window.

3. Certain events (birth, marriage, occupation) have a small 's' to the right of the entry box. Double-click the first one next to the birth information.

4. From the Source List, highlight BMD indexes. Click Select.

5. Enter *Mar 1866, St Pancras, 1a 560* in the Citation Detail box as shown in Figure 10.12.

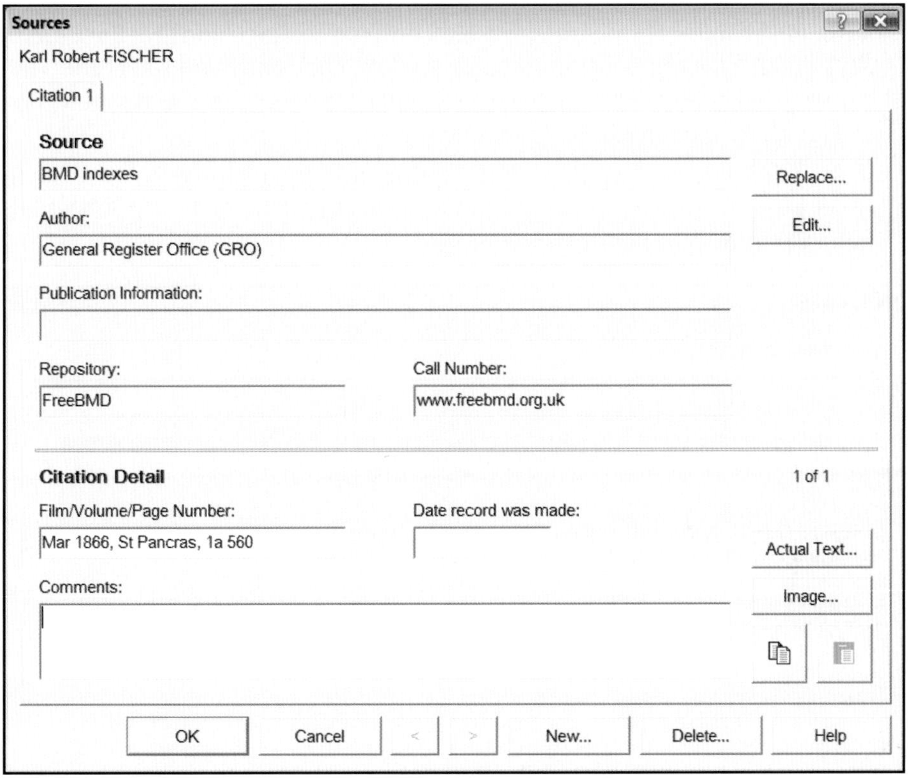

Sources

Karl Robert FISCHER

Citation 1

Source

BMD indexes   Replace...

Author: Edit...

General Register Office (GRO)

Publication Information:

Repository: Call Number:

FreeBMD   www.freebmd.org.uk

Citation Detail   1 of 1

Film/Volume/Page Number: Date record was made:

Mar 1866, St Pancras, 1a 560   Actual Text...

Comments: Image...

| OK | Cancel | < | > | New... | Delete... | Help |

Figure 10.12

The title of this window shows that it is for the Birth of Karl Robert Fischer and that there is currently one citation for this event.

At the top right of the window, next to the Close icon, there is a question mark. If you click it and hover the cursor over parts of the window, the program will give you information about these features. Try it with the items in the Citation Details section. (You need to click the question mark each time you want to check out a different item.) This feature is available in many windows.

6. Click OK to return to the Edit Individual window. You will see that the 's' is now 's*', showing that a source has been added and can be viewed. Click Save and return to Family View. There should be a small black triangle in the top left corner of the name box. This indicates that the record has sources attached.

7. Repeat the process to attach a source to the Occupation data. Apart from his birth record, nearly every resource you have looked at has shown Karl as a painter/decorator. You can add more than one source, as this provides additional confirmation. Add the 1911 census as a source and give the Citation *RG14/662 schedule 81*. Before you click OK, click New and select the 1901 census source. You will now have a second citation tab for Occupation. Type in *RG13/131 schedule 171*. Click OK.

8. In the Edit Individual window, click Options and then Sources to view the list of all sources currently attached to the individual (Figure 10.13). Click Save before returning to the main screen.

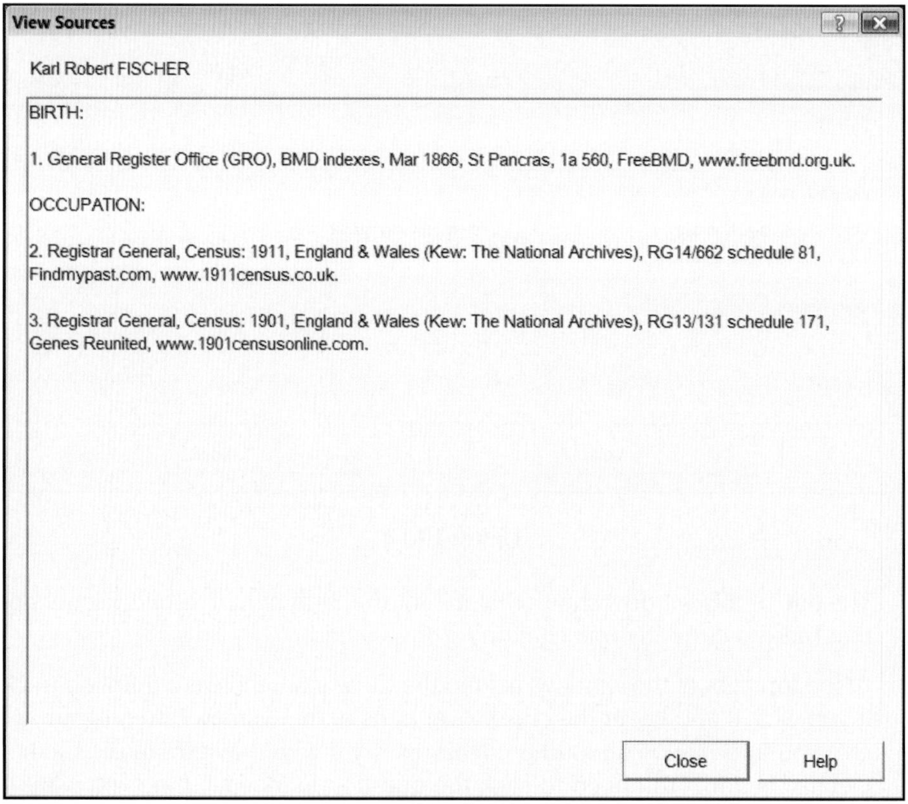

View Sources

Karl Robert FISCHER

BIRTH:

1. General Register Office (GRO), BMD indexes, Mar 1866, St Pancras, 1a 560, FreeBMD, www.freebmd.org.uk.

OCCUPATION:

2. Registrar General, Census: 1911, England & Wales (Kew: The National Archives), RG14/662 schedule 81, Findmypast.com, www.1911census.co.uk.

3. Registrar General, Census: 1901, England & Wales (Kew: The National Archives), RG13/131 schedule 171, Genes Reunited, www.1901censusonline.com.

Close   Help

Figure 10.13

Now that you have set up and attached the sources, you can add new sources or edit existing sources at any time. (For example, you could add the census address in the Citation Comment box.)

Adding notes

Notes allow you to record biographical information that does not fit easily into the standard event format used by most family tree programs. This can include stories, descriptions of people and places, detailed explanations, and further research to be followed up. If you find sensitive information, this can be recorded as a note but tagged so that it will not print out in any reports. You can also attach tags to certain items so that they can be searched for and viewed as a group.

To create a note, follow these steps:

1. Highlight Karl Fischer in the Family View screen.

2. Double-click to open the Edit Individual window.

3. There is a notepad icon on the right of the window. Click to open it. (You can also select Notes from the Options button.)

4. Add the following two entries, separated by a blank line. Each entry should start with an exclamation mark.

    ! Although the German name Karl was anglicised to Charles on both the 1871 and 1881 censuses, all subsequent records, including his marriage, show him as Carl.

    ! An apprentice painter/decorator in 1881, he may have worked in a family business, since both his father and brother were in the same line of work.

5. Save the Notes and click Save again to exit the Edit screen.

The notes for an individual (or for a marriage) will be on a single screen. Where you have more than one note, they should be separated by a single blank line. You will need to consider whether a note is confidential and whether it can be shown on a printed report. It may be that it is not confidential but primarily for your information (for example, a to-do list). Starting the note with a symbol allows you to tell the program what to print or the status of the item.

    ! An exclamation mark as the first character of the first word (no space) means that this note will always print.

    ~ A tilde (usually found to the right of the @ key) marks a note as confidential.

A tag is a word followed by a colon at the start of the note (eg Census: or Education:), which lets you search for, view or print certain groups of information. The tag can also have a confidential mark in front of it so that it will not print out. If the tag has two words, eg To-Do or Military_Service, these should be connected with a hyphen or an underscore so the program recognises that they are both parts of the tag and not part of the note.

When setting up reports and views for printing, there is usually an option relating to whether or not confidential items should be shown.

To view the notes at any time, highlight the name of an individual and right-click. One of the options is Notes. Click Open to view the note. You can also edit in this screen (as with most programs, there are usually several ways to achieve the same result).

Adding multimedia

One feature that makes using a family history program so enjoyable is the ability to add multimedia – photos, images of scanned documents, video and sound clips. Your research will uncover data but it will also give you a range of other materials that you might want to include. If you have your grandfather's medals, for example, these can be scanned to produce images to add to your reports (Figure 10.14).

Figure 10.14

Photos and images of scanned documents

There are few images currently available for the case study family. You might want to practise the techniques using any photo from your own albums. In the next chapter, you look at how to build up a collection of photos and scanned images to use in your family history program.

You have seen that a quick way to edit information about an individual is to right-click on the name box in the Family View screen. Do this now for Karl and select Multimedia. Figure 10.15 shows you the initial screen which lets you set up a collection of materials relating to this person.

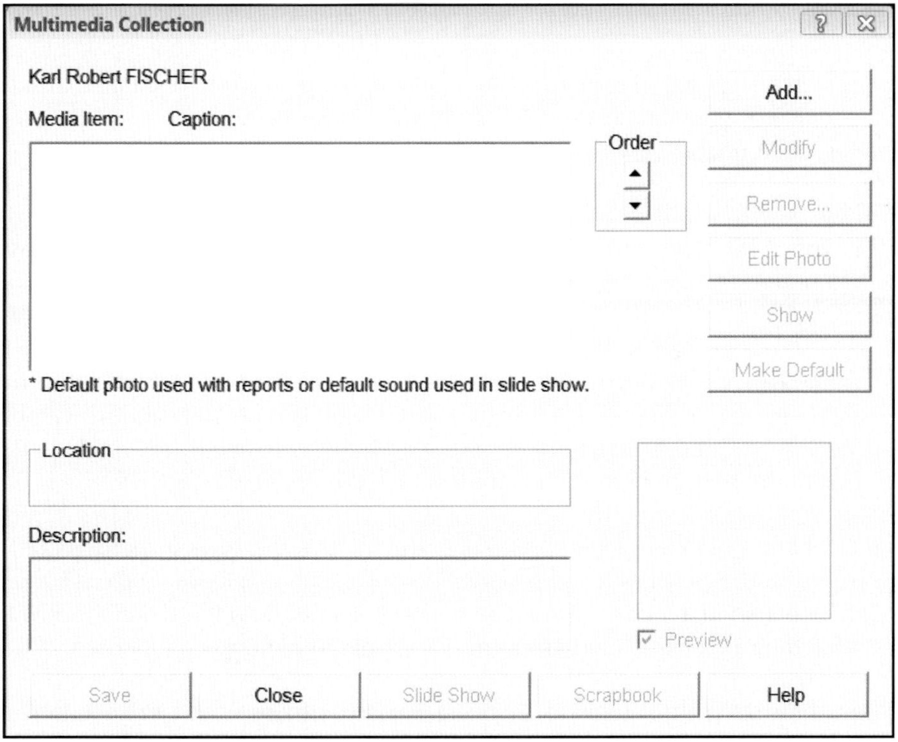

Figure 10.15

Before you add a picture, use the help question mark icon at the top right of the screen to find out what the various buttons and parts of the screen are for. (You used this feature earlier to view information about citations in Figure 10.12.)

Here are the steps you would take to add an item to the Multimedia Collection:

1. Click Add. A new window opens for details of the item.

2. Select item type (photo, sound or video). Choose photo for this example.

3. Use the Browse button to open your filing system and navigate to where you are holding your images.

> It will help if you keep all the multimedia material you want to include in one folder. If you ever want to move to another program, it will make it easier to recreate the links to these images.

4. Select an image. (I will use the scanned image of the original marriage certificate; you should use any photo of a male, possibly one you have, as yet, been unable to identify.)

5. Give the item a brief but meaningful caption.

6. If you wish, you can add some more detailed comments for your own reference.

7. Click OK.

   Figure 10.16 shows you the updated screen. All the option buttons on the right are now available. The item is shown with its type and caption. The file location and the description are also shown. If the image is not visible in the box at the bottom right of the window, tick the Preview box.

You can have a number of items in this list, and it is possible to view them as both a Slide Show and as a Scrapbook (the latter looks like a photo album). Although there is only one item in the collection at the moment, try out both these options now to see what they look like. The buttons for this are at the bottom of the screen.

When there are more items in a collection, you can use the Order button to move highlighted items up and down the list. You might, for example, want to put the pictures of an individual in chronological order, so that the Slide Show goes from childhood to later life.

There is an option to nominate one item as a default photo, which will appear in report printouts and on the Family View screen in the name box. The default is

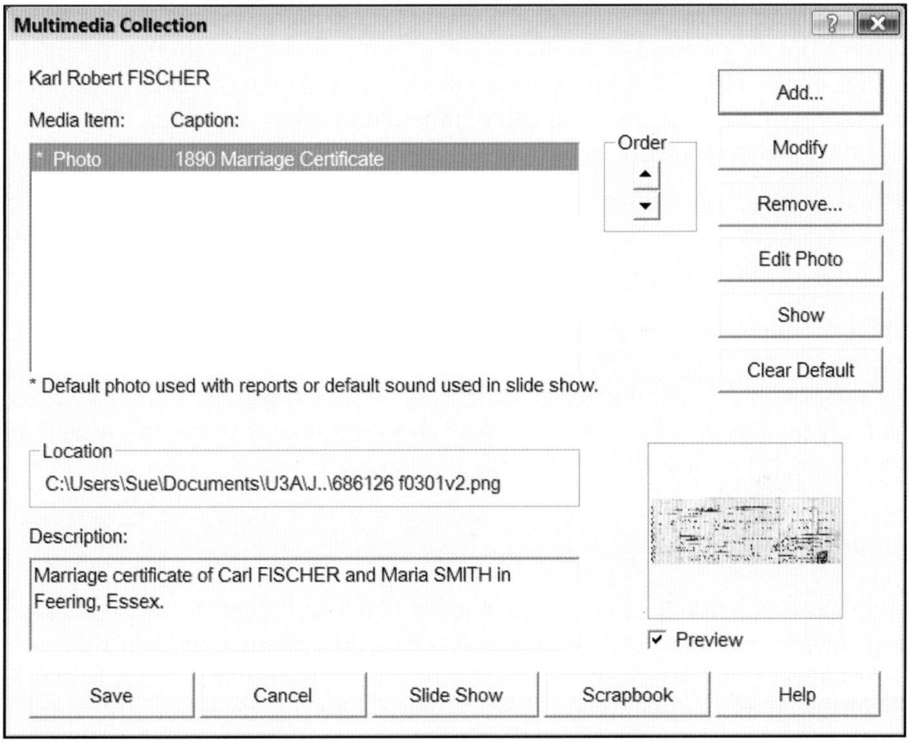

Figure 10.16

marked with a star (*). The program has automatically marked the item just added to the collection as the default photo. If you have added the picture of a person, then leave the default set to see how it works. As I have added a document, this would look a little strange (and rather small) in a printout, so I will clear the default using the last option in the right hand list. The button then reverts to Make Default, which would allow you to select another item and create a new default image.

The options on the right show the degree of flexibility you have in customising material for the program.

- **Add**: Add further multimedia items to the collection.

- **Modify**: Change the location, caption or description of an item.

- **Remove**: Delete the item from the collection (this only removes the link to the image, and does not delete the image from your computer).

- **Edit photo**: A basic screen that allows you to crop the image and flip it vertically, horizontally or through 90 degrees. You can also decide whether to include this image in the Slide Show and/or the Scrapbook. For the Slide Show, there is an option to change the length of time the image is on screen. (The default time for all slides is set using Tools→ Preferences → Multimedia.)

- **Show**: Opens the image in a new window. With a document, this may be sufficient to allow you to read it (depending on the size of the original). The images in printed reports are much smaller versions, known as thumbnails.

When you are done, you must click Save to keep the changes.

It is also possible to add images to sources, either at the general source level or at the individual level. Wherever a window gives you Image as one of the options, you can click it to find and attach a file to the source.

Including audio files

Although most of the initial material in your collection is likely to be photographs or scanned images of letters, certificates and other documents, you may want to develop a collection of sound files to include with presentations. Chapter 12 covers this in more detail but you may want to start thinking about the range of material you could collect or create.

- Favourite pieces of music as a background to a collection of pictures about an individual.

- Mood or themed music to accompany images of places connected to the family.

- Clips from recorded interviews with family members.

- Newsreel clips available on the Internet, which put family events against the backdrop of world events.

- Spoken commentary describing people and family events.

Audio files in PAF need to be in WAV or MIDI formats. If you don't have much experience of sound files, talk to someone who downloads music from the Internet or who uses sound to accompany photographic presentations.

The audio files are added to the multimedia collection in the same way as image files. Once a sound file has been added, your options are to play it, modify or remove the link. You can set one audio file as the default, which will play during the Slide Show sequence. When you are editing photos, there is an option to add a sound file to an individual image in the Scrapbook. When you view the Scrapbook, such images will have a small speaker icon in the top right hand corner. Clicking the icon will play the sound file.

Audacity is a free piece of software you can use to record commentary or to save files in the WAV format. You can download this from **http://audacity.sourceforge. net/**. Audacity will do all the things you are likely to want to achieve with sound files in your family history program.

Viewing data

You can use the various data entry screens to view details about individuals and their families. At some point you may want to see an overview of the entire data set and also create reports for yourself and for family members. Your reports may start with and include different subsets of your family data. It is helpful to look at how you can change the starting point (person) in a report.

Root person and Home person

You have seen that the first person entered into a new PAF file is given the index number RIN 1 and is considered the Root person of the tree. A slightly different concept is the Home person. Just as a website has a Home page to which you can return at any time, so an individual can be nominated as the Home person, to whose record you can return at any point. This is useful if you have a large family tree and you get stuck down one of the branches. Rather than navigating back through every member of the family, you can click on the icon for the Home person and return there immediately.

By default, when you first set up the file, the Root person and the Home person are the same. To see this working, go to Family View and navigate back to Sophie's father, Christian Rubardt. In the menu bar at the top of the page, find the icon of a person, with a red arrow. If you hover your cursor, you will be told that this will take you to the Home person (rather like the House icon in Internet Explorer which returns you to the Home page). Click the icon and you will be back with Karl Fischer.

You do not have to keep the Root person the same as the Home person. You may decide to make the Home person the oldest or the youngest person on the main branch of the family tree. You can then work forwards or backwards in time from this person. If you are doing a lot of work on one person and his/her immediate family, you might temporarily make that individual the Home person.

The other use for the Home person designation is that this will also be the individual that you will see when you open the file (similar to the web home page concept). Since many things are customisable in this and other programs, you won't be surprised to learn that this, too, can be changed so that the program can be opened at the last record that you viewed before closing.

To make these changes, select Tools and then Preferences from the menu bar. This is the same menu that you saw in Figure 10.3. This time, select the File tab in the Preferences window (Figure 10.17).

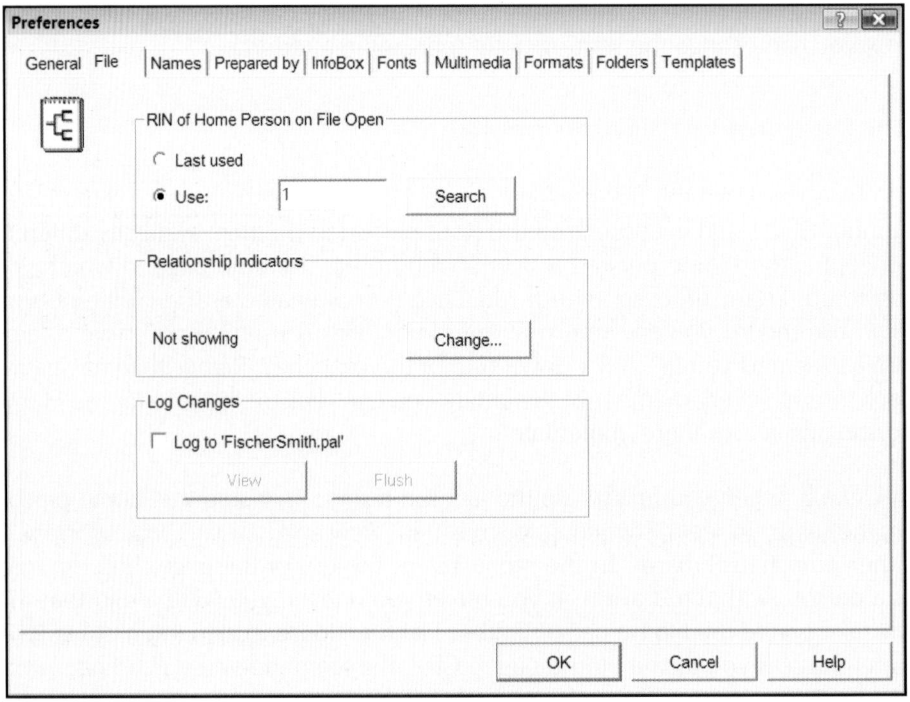

Figure 10.17

In this figure, the program is set up always to open the file at RIN 1. Should you wish to change this, click Search and select another RIN. (If you don't know the number you want, you are offered the option to look at a list of all the people in the file and make your selection there.) The alternative to opening at the file with a specified individual is to select Last used instead. This opens the program with the same person you were viewing just before you closed the program. For the moment, leave this section as it stands.

It can be useful and interesting to show the relationship of people in the tree to the Root person. Click the Change button. Make sure the Root person is showing Karl Robert Fischer. (If not, click Search and enter 1 in the Record Number box.) Tick the Show relationships on status bar box. Click OK and then again to return to Family View.

Karl Fischer should be the person currently highlighted on the screen. In the lower-left corner of the screen it should say Root Person. If you now highlight his father Frederick, this changes to Father, showing the relationship of the highlighted individual to the Root person. Highlight Sophie and see it change again. Move back to his grandfathers. Each time, the program calculates and shows the relationship.

You do not have to keep the RIN 1 individual as the Root person. If you are showing the family tree to a relative, it can be a good idea to make them temporarily the Root person. That way, they will see their relationship to any individual you show them in the file. To make the change, select Tools → Preferences → Relationship Indicators → Change → Search → Individual List. Find the person and highlight the name. Click OK (three times in all) and view the results. (Don't forget to change the Root person back to yourself when your relative has gone home.)

Other data views

So far, most of the work you have done with data has looked at the Family View page. This shows an individual with parents and, where applicable, spouse and children.

There are two other tabs that allow you to view the information in the tree in different formats. Pedigree shows the direct ancestry of an individual. From the family page showing Karl, chose one of his daughters and follow the arrow left from her name. Now select the Pedigree tab just above her name. Figure 10.18 shows the Pedigree chart for Lilian Alice Fischer.

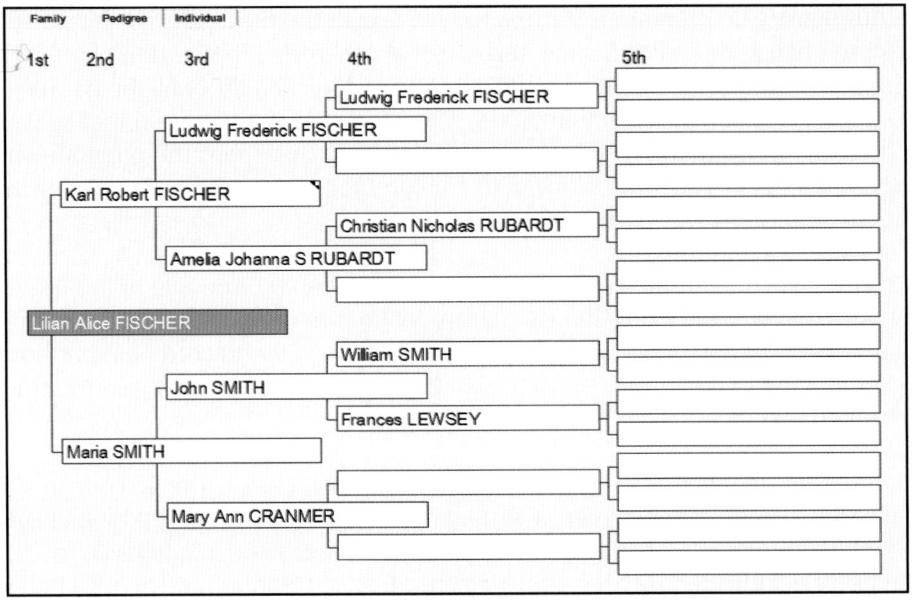

Figure 10.18

The Pedigree chart shows only names. This slimmed down data potentially allows a further four generations to be shown, the last of which needs space for 16 names.

There is a way to show a floating information box over a name by hovering the cursor. Try it for one of the names in the Pedigree chart. If nothing comes up, go to Tools → Preferences → InfoBox. You can select whether to see no information, dates only or dates and family information. It is also possible to change the amount of time you have to wait for the box to appear. Select Dates and Family Information and leave the time setting as it stands.

The other option in this window is to create a Locked box. Normally, if you hover your cursor and then move it, the pop-up information box disappears. Sometimes it may be useful to keep it on the screen for a while. Set up the Locked box to show the same information as the Floating box. Click OK. When you want to use a Locked box, hover your cursor until the box appears and then press the Space Bar. This will leave the InfoBox open until you press any key.

The final tab, in the main screen, allows you to see a list of everyone entered in the tree. Click this Individual tab and move to the top of the list. Figure 10.19

shows the list in numerical order. If you click the word RIN at the top of the first column, the order reverses, showing Frederick Arthur Fischer (RIN 32) at the top and Karl Robert Fischer (RIN 1) at the bottom. Clicking the heading once more reverses it again.

▾ RIN	Full Name	Sex	Birth - Date	Death - Date
1	FISCHER, Karl Robert	Male	1866	
2	FISCHER, Ludwig Frederick	Male	1836	22 Sep 1908
3	RUBARDT, Amelia Johanna Sophie	Female	1839	1895
4	FISCHER, Ludwig Frederick	Male	Bef 1816	Aft 1860
5	RUBARDT, Christian Nicholas	Male	Bef 1819	Aft 1860
6	SMITH, Maria	Female	1867	
7	SMITH, John	Male	1828	1908
8	CRANMER, Mary Ann	Female	1827	
9	SMITH, Jonah	Male	1849	
10	SMITH, James	Male	1850	
11	SMITH, Elijah	Male	1852	
12	SMITH, Joseph	Male	1861	
13	SMITH, Charlotte	Female	1874	
14	SMITH, William	Male	1806	
15	LEWSEY, Frances	Female	1807	
16	SMITH, William	Male	1832	
17	SMITH, James	Male	1834	
18	SMITH, Sarah	Female	1835	
19	SMITH, Joseph	Male	1837	
20	SMITH, Maryann	Female	1839	
21	FISCHER, Lilian Alice	Female	1892	
22	FISCHER, Freda Olive	Female	1897	
23	FISCHER, Doris Margaretha	Female	1905	
24	FISCHER, Friederich Carl	Male	1861	
25	FISCHER, Arthur	Male	1862	
26	, Mary Ann	Female	1867	1896
27	FISCHER, Nellie	Female	1889	
28	WOODFORD, Emma Sarah	Female	1867	

Figure 10.19

To make the list alphabetical by surname, click the Full Name heading at the top of the second column. Any entries where a surname is not known are placed first, followed by the alphabetical list. To reverse the list, click again on the heading.

You can customise the Individual View. Right-click one of the headings (eg RIN). Choose Add or Modify Columns. A menu displays possible fields for inclusion on the left and the actual ones used on the right. You can select options from the left and move them to the right using the arrows between the two menus. You can also remove headings from the right side in the same way. It is better not to have too many columns showing; otherwise, as with the spreadsheet, you need to keep scrolling across the screen. RIN, Full Name, Birth, Death and Sex are probably sufficient.

Highlighting any name in the list takes you to that person's family. Try selecting any individual and then click on the Family tab. If you need to return to the Home person, use the icon in the toolbar with the red arrow.

Relationship calculator

You have set up the preferences so that the relationship of any individual to the Root person is always shown. You may sometimes wish to calculate the relationship between any two individuals, without changing the Root person.

Go to Tools→ Relationship Calculator. Whoever is currently highlighted in Family View will appear in the top box by default. This can be changed using the Search button. Click Search and enter 5 in the RIN box (you can look in the Individual list if you don't know the number of the person). Click OK.

Now click Search in the lower box. Enter 1 as the RIN and click OK. Now click Calculate to see the relationship between the two people.

Try this again using RIN 1 and 24. This time, because you have selected two people with common ancestors, these will also be shown in the result (see Figure 10.20).

Relationship Calculator	? ☒

First Person

Line of Descent to Common Ancestor	Search	Karl Robert FISCHER
Karl Robert FISCHER b.1866		RIN: 1 Sex: M b.1866
Ludwig F FISCHER & A J S RUBARDT		Father: Ludwig Frederick FISCHER
		Mother: Amelia Johanna Sophie RUBARDT
		Spouse: Maria SMITH
		Spouse:

Second Person

Line of Descent to Common Ancestor	Search	Friederich Carl FISCHER
Friederich Carl FISCHER b.1861		RIN: 24 Sex: M b.1861
Ludwig F FISCHER & A J S RUBARDT		Father: Ludwig Frederick FISCHER
		Mother: Amelia Johanna Sophie RUBARDT
		Spouse: Mary Ann
		Spouse: Emma Sarah WOODFORD

Relationships

Common Ancestors

Ludwig F FISCHER & A J S RUBARDT	Bro	Karl Robert FISCHER is the brother of Friederich Carl FISCHER. Their common ancestors are Ludwig Frederick FISCHER and Amelia Johanna Sophie RUBARDT.

| | Calculate | Close | Help |

Figure 10.20

Creating reports and charts

Most people tend to think of family trees in chart format – in fact, as highly stylised trees with branches. This format works well if you are working backwards through your direct ancestry; that is, two parents, four grandparents, eight great-grandparents and so on. There is a mathematical progression that means that such charts can be of known dimensions (even if you are currently missing some names from the boxes on the chart).

If you reverse the process and look for the descendants of an individual, you can see that the size and scope are greatly increased, since even in the first generation, there may be many children. Repeat this process only four times and the number of descendants will make it a very leafy tree. Even if not all the children have descendants themselves, you still need to accommodate them on the chart.

Your research has also turned up information that can't be neatly included in a small box on a chart (or at least, not one that is easy to read). The data collected on occupation, military service, schooling and a range of other activities can be seen in your family history program but you will also want a means of sharing it with other family members.

For these reasons, you want additional options, which will allow you to produce lists and narrative based reports as well as charts. Family tree software is often judged on the number and flexibility of the reports and charts offered. The flexibility may relate to what data can be included, how the report is structured (for example, can it have an index and include photos?) and more cosmetic issues relating to typeface options and size, text and box colours and backgrounds.

In PAF, the main program has a number of reports, whose features you may want to explore. You can preview all these on screen, before deciding whether you wish to print them or whether some further adjustments are needed before they look as you want them to.

Printing reports

In most computer programs, print options are in the File menu and this is the same in PAF. Choose File → Print Report. (In other family tree programs, there may be an additional or separate menu for reports.) Figure 10.21 shows the Reports and Chart window. It has ten tabs at the top of the window, arranged in two rows.

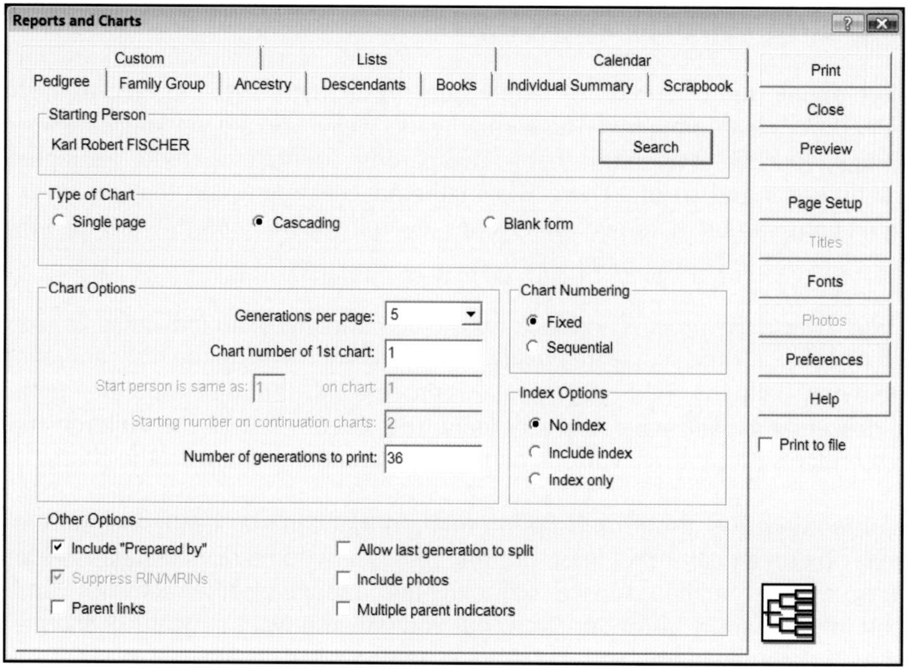

Figure 10.21

Because you are presented with so many options, all of which have multiple possibilities for customisation, these windows can sometimes seem quite bewildering and it is difficult to know where to start. The best approach is to change as little as possible and just keep previewing the report using the same highlighted individual and see what happens. If the Preview report is hard to read, clicking magnifies what is on the page.

You can use the Help question mark icon at the top left of the window to see what the options mean. As the Fischer/Smith family tree is not very large, you may decide to print out some of the reports and charts and keep them as sample copies. After a time, you will decide which reports are of more use and interest to you. You may want to start by looking at the following:

● **Individual Summary:** This gives the main events of the person's life, showing his/her parents, spouse and marriage details. If set up to do so, notes and sources are also printed. Photos can also be shown.

264

- **Ancestry Chart:** There are two options, Standard and Wall charts. The latter allows you to stick together multiple sheets for display. As this tree is quite small, this is not very labour-intensive at the moment, but it could be once the tree starts to grow. The Standard chart contains less information about each person but fits more on a single page.

- **Descendants Chart:** This works in a similar way to the Ancestry Chart. The descendants of the first child of the identified ancestor are shown by their generation number and their descendants are included until the end of that line is reached. Then the second child is shown, together with their descendants. This can look confusing with a large family chart. The thing to remember is that everyone with the same number is the same generation (ie children are second generation, grandchildren third generation and great-grandchildren fourth generation). Figure 10.22 shows this for the earliest Ludwig Frederick Fischer on the family tree.

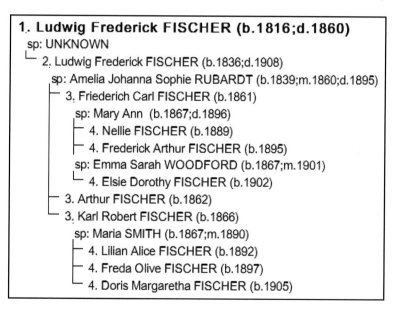

Figure 10.22

- **Books:** This produces a narrative format and can be either an ancestor or a descendants report. There is an option to start each generation on a new page. An individual appears first as a child. If he/she married and had children, then that person appears again in the next generation as the head of a family. Figure 10.23 shows the second page of a descendants report that started with Karl's grandfather. The report is set up to show the links back from a person to the first ancestor (these are the names in brackets after Karl's name).

---

5. **Karl Robert FISCHER**[1] (Ludwig Frederick, Ludwig Frederick) was born[2] in 1866 in Marylebone, London.

Karl was employed[3,4] as a house decorator about 1881/1911 in Marylebone, London.

> Although the German name Karl was anglicised to Charles on both the 1871 and 1881 censuses, all subsequent records, including his marriage show him as Carl.

> An apprentice painter/decorator in 1881, he may have worked in a family business, since both his father and brother were in the same line of work.

Karl married[5] **Maria SMITH** daughter of John SMITH and Mary Ann CRANMER on 18 Oct 1890 in Parish Church, Feering, Essex. Maria was born in 1867 in Feering, Essex.

Maria was employed as a servant in 1890.

They had the following children:

   9 F   i.   **Lilian Alice FISCHER** was born in 1892 in St Pancras, London.

   10 F   ii.   **Freda Olive FISCHER** was born in 1897 in St Pancras, London.

   11 F   iii.   **Doris Margaretha FISCHER** was born in 1905 in St Pancras, London.

Figure 10.23

Using a PAF Companion program

Some family tree software has report and chart options contained in the main program. Others have additional programs for these options. PAF has a Companion program that can be used alongside the main program. You can download a limited generations version of this free from the FamilySearch website. Upgrading to the full program currently costs $6.75.

You will probably want to familiarise yourself with the reports in the main program before moving on to PAF Companion. One report in the Companion which is very useful is a Kinship list. This prints every person in the family tree and shows how they are linked to a named individual. In the main program you were able to show the link between two people, but not print a list showing everyone as a relation.

Figure 10.24 shows part of the printout for everyone as they are related to Karl. You can see that it takes the hard work out of deciding how people are related, something that gets very taxing when you start including second cousins three times removed.

Kinship of Karl Robert FISCHER		
Name	Relationship	Common Ancestor
(---), Mary Ann (b. 1867 d. 1896)	Sister-in-law	FISCHER, Ludwig Frederick
CRANMER, Mary Ann (b. 1827)	Mother-in-law	CRANMER, Mary Ann
FISCHER, Arthur (b. 1862)	Brother	FISCHER, Ludwig Frederick
FISCHER, Doris Margaretha (b. 1905)	Daughter	FISCHER, Karl Robert
FISCHER, Elsie Dorothy (b. 1902)	Niece	FISCHER, Ludwig Frederick
FISCHER, Freda Olive (b. 1897)	Daughter	FISCHER, Karl Robert
FISCHER, Frederick Arthur (b. 1895)	Nephew	FISCHER, Ludwig Frederick
FISCHER, Friederich Carl (b. 1861)	Brother	FISCHER, Ludwig Frederick
FISCHER, Karl Robert (b. 1866)	Self	FISCHER, Karl Robert
FISCHER, Lilian Alice (b. 1892)	Daughter	FISCHER, Karl Robert
FISCHER, Ludwig Frederick (b. 1836 d. 1908)	Father	FISCHER, Ludwig Frederick
FISCHER, Ludwig Frederick (b. bef 1816 d. aft 1860)	Grandfather	FISCHER, Ludwig Frederick
FISCHER, Nellie (b. 1889)	Niece	FISCHER, Ludwig Frederick
LEWSEY, Frances (b. 1807)	Grandmother of the wife	LEWSEY, Frances
RUBARDT, Amelia Johanna Sophie (b. 1839 d. 1895)	Mother	RUBARDT, Amelia Johanna Sophie
RUBARDT, Christian Nicholas (b. bef 1819 d. aft 1860)	Grandfather	RUBARDT, Christian Nicholas
SMITH, Charlotte (b. 1874)	Sister-in-law	SMITH, John
SMITH, Elijah (b. 1852)	Brother-in-law	SMITH, John
SMITH, James (b. 1850)	Brother-in-law	SMITH, John
SMITH, James (b. 1834)	Uncle of the wife	SMITH, William
SMITH, John (b. 1828 d. 1908)	Father-in-law	SMITH, John
SMITH, Jonah (b. 1849)	Brother-in-law	SMITH, John

Figure 10.24

A good use for this relationship list is when you are trying to interest a more distant family member in your research. While a list showing how you are related to everyone may be interesting, printing a personalised list showing how that family member links to everyone on the tree is guaranteed to fascinate them and may provide you with an invitation to tea and a look at their family photographs.

Saving your work

Once you have started to create a family file, you have the option at the end of a session to save your work and then close the file or save and close the program, leaving the file open. If you choose the latter option then, the next time you open the program, it bypasses the Welcome screen and takes you back to your file.

Backing up your work is very important. If you make major changes to your data, then you should make another copy. For additional security, make a backup on a memory stick. That way, if something bad does happen to your computer, you have not lost your data. Remember, you can always buy a new computer or a new software program. What you cannot recreate is your hours of hard work inputting data into your own family tree.

If you want to upload your family tree to a website, such as Ancestry, or share your data with someone, you will need to create a GEDCOM file. Select Export from the File menu. Choose the GEDCOM option and click Export. If you have not entered your address as the owner of the data, then you will be prompted to do so. Give the file a name and ensure that it is being saved in the location you designated for such files (if not, navigate through your filing system until you find the correct folder).

If someone wants to share their data with you and sends you a GEDCOM file, be careful to save and close your existing file before you open theirs. It is possible to import a GEDCOM file into your PAF file but you should check out their data first before merging it with your own. The way to deal with this is to open a new, empty PAF file, with a different name to your own. Then use the Import option on the File menu to bring in the data. You can then view it separately and decide whether to merge it with your own PAF file or use it as a source for adding data manually to your family tree.

Research tasks: Recording your family using family history software

Once you have explored the data entry, sources, notes and report options with the Fischer/Smith data, close that file and start a new PAF file for your own family. Enter your own personal details as the first person and then start adding parents, spouse and children as appropriate. Remember to link each new individual, in some way, to existing people on the family tree. Save and backup frequently as you work.

Summary

- Most family tree programs work in the way described for Personal Ancestral File.

- Add individuals, linking to others in the tree (parents, spouse or children).

- Create sources and references to allow others to follow up your research.

- Use notes for confidential information and for other data collected in addition to basic life events.

- Use photos and sound to enhance your reports.

- Investigate the report and chart options to decide which you like and see how they can be customised.

- Save and backup your work frequently.

- Don't import a GEDCOM file into your own until you have checked out the data it contains.

Brain Training

1. **Which of these file formats allows you to transfer data between family tree programs?**

a) DOC

b) GEDCOM

c) JPEG

d) PDF

2. **What does RIN stand for?**

a) Record Identification Number

b) Relationship Identity Number

c) Relationship Identification Name

d) Root Identification Name

3. **What name is given to small copies of photo images included in your family reports and shown on screen?**

a) Graphics

b) Icons

c) Miniatures

d) Thumbnails

4. **You can add parents to a child in the family tree even if you don't know both their names. True or false?**

5. **What type of software is Audacity?**

a) Audio editing program

b) Family tree program

c) Spreadsheet

d) Video editing program

Answers

Q1 – b   **Q2** – a   **Q3** – d   **Q4** – true

Q5 – a

11

Working with family photos

Equipment needed: Family photographs, multifunction printer or scanning facilities, image editing software.

Skills needed: Using image organising and editing software to add pictures to your family history material.

One of the features you looked at in the previous chapter was the way that images could be included with the family data you have researched. These images, whether photographs or scanned documents, give an additional dimension to your research and improve the quality of the output – whether in printed, web or presentation format. In this chapter you look at ways of acquiring, organising and editing images to fit with the requirements of your genealogical research.

Sorting your family photos

One overdue task, for most people starting their research, is to sort out the family photos stored at home. Some people are already organised in this respect with photos in albums, labelled and easily to hand. However, they appear to be in a minority. Think of your new-found interest in family history as an opportunity to get round to one of those tasks that everyone always intends to do, but that never quite makes it to the top of the current to-do list.

If you have started to create a tree using genealogical software, you already have a numbering system that you can use. The RIN (Record Identification Number) automatically allocated to each individual allows you to search in the family tree program. It's also useful if you share data with others and have a number of people on the tree with the same or similar names. If someone wants to update or extend information about an entry, it's easier for them to use the RIN as a reference so that you are both clear you are talking about the same person.

Print out two lists from your program showing RIN, full name and dates of birth and death. The first list should be in alphabetical order by surname; the second should be in numerical order for cross-referencing.

Take your collection of pictures of people whose names you know. On the back of each, using a pencil, write the word RIN and the relevant number in the top right hand corner. This allows you to identify each photo and tag it but you won't get bogged down in writing all the details on each picture.

For those pictures of people whose names you are not sure of, do the same thing but put a question mark after the RIN. Any pictures of people you have no idea about will have to stay that way for the moment.

Hosting a picture-tagging party

If you can organise this, then you might be able to achieve several things at the same time:

- Have your identification of known people confirmed
- Have doubtful identifications confirmed or challenged
- Have unknown photos identified
- Get help writing the information on the back of each photo
- Interest other members of the family in your project and get them to do the same for their photos
- Give them photocopies of pictures to take away to show to other family members for identification
- Find out about other photos and documents held elsewhere in the family.

Invite over two older members of the family on a Sunday afternoon. Explain that you want to sort out family photos and would like some help. If you have a multifunction printer, set it up with a good stock of paper. (You will be using it as a photocopier, so it doesn't need to be connected to your computer.)

Give each person a copy of the numerical list, a pencil (HB or softer) and a rubber. Divide the first group of pictures between them. Ask them to check the RIN on the back against the list. If they agree that it is the correct person, ask them, on the back of the photo, to write the name as it appears on the list, eg SMITH, John (1828–1908).

A few issues arise from this:

- The convention by which women are shown with their maiden names, may come as a surprise to your guests. The chances are that they will have known her by her married name (assuming she was married). If the picture was probably taken after her marriage, ask them to add in brackets the words '(later xxx)', where xxx is the married name.

- In some cases, you won't know the maiden name of a woman, who will appear on your list either with no surname or with her husband's surname. In this case, the information should be entered as on the list. If your guests know her maiden name, ask them to add '(nee xxx)', where xxx is the maiden name. Ask them also to enter this on the numerical list so that you can update your records later.

- Where a photo is of a couple, you can have two RINs to work with.

- Where the photo is of a number of people, you will find it hard to include all their details on the back and for anyone to work out who is who. The best way to deal with this is to make photocopies of the pictures beforehand (enlarging them if practical and if your copier has a zoom function). You can then give the photocopies to your guests and ask them to draw arrows to individuals and give them a RIN. (This time, they will need to have the alphabetical list to work from to identify the people and find the relevant number.)

By this time, everyone will probably be ready for some refreshments. It is tempting to feel that you will get all the photos identified and labelled in one session but this is probably over-optimistic. What is useful is the discussion about family members that will inevitably arise, and which may give you further information and ideas for research. While they are confirming and labelling photos, you can be making notes and prompting with questions.

If they say they like a particular photo, offer to send them a nicely-printed version. If they don't know who someone is but think that another member of the family might know, make a quick photocopy and give it to them to take away and find out.

At the end, ask if a repeat session is possible. Encourage them to bring some photos of their own. You might give them some photocopies from the unidentified group to take away and think about.

Sorting photos is a good winter task, as someone in my family history group reminded me. Otherwise all you do is sit in front of the television on a Sunday afternoon and fall asleep during reruns of old films. Hope it works for you.

Handling and preserving photos

Some of the photos you come across are likely to be old and/or fragile. Others will have been stuck in frames and photo albums and cannot be removed without potential damage to the picture. You can find specialist photographic services to help you deal with these, though this can be expensive. If there is only one copy of a photo that is of particular significance to the family, you might be able to persuade others to join you in getting pictures restored. As with old and fragile documents, the best thing is to handle them as little as possible, store them in archival quality plastic wallets and scan them so you can work with copies rather than with the originals. For online purposes, you need things in an electronic format in any case.

Scanning photos and other documents

Even if you have a scanner, scanning the accumulated photos from several generations of hoarders can take a long time. You might want to do the most important ones yourself and then see if you can find a local service that will scan the others for you and put them on a CD. If you are prepared to part with the photos, you will find online services that will scan photos, slides and negatives for you. Depending on the resolution of the image (something you'll look at later), the cost can be £17–£27 for a batch of up to 150 pictures and £90–£100 for a batch of between 500 and 1000 photographs. Negatives and slides work out at 34p–44p each depending on their resolution.

Most books on digital photography will give you detailed information on how to scan photos and this can be extended to scanning other documents, such as letters, wills and certificates. A good place to look at this in more detail is *Digital Photography for the Older and Wiser* by Kim Gilmour, John Wiley & Sons Ltd. ISBN 9780470 687024.

The main thing that you need to consider when using photographs is the resolution. All digital images are made up of tiny boxes (pixels) that contain information about colour, brightness and other light-related matters, which together create an image for you to view on the screen or printout. If you've ever looked at a newspaper picture that has been blown up to make an advertising poster, you will have seen that it is made up of tiny dots. When viewed at regular newspaper size, the eye is not aware of the dots and sees the picture as smooth. Digital images work in a similar way. The more pixels you cram into the available space, the better the image looks. Using fewer pixels makes the picture look more 'blocky' and you lose the crispness of the photographic image.

You may be wondering, therefore, why you shouldn't scan all images to have the greatest number of pixels. There are a number of factors to take into account:

- The greater the number of pixels (ie the higher the resolution) the bigger the electronic file size.

- If your ultimate aim is to make photographic quality prints of a reasonable size, then high resolution is a must.

- If your aim is to show images on the screen (in a family history program, on a web page or in a web album) then you can and should use images of a much lower resolution. On screen the images are usually viewed at 72 dpi (dots per inch) and having more pixels just means that the images take a much longer time to appear on screen.

If you are planning to send photos as email attachments, make sure that you reduce the resolution and therefore the file size. If attachments are too large or there are too many of them, they will take a long time to download. Some recipients may have restricted downloaded limits and you don't want to create problems for them.

- The challenge for most family historians is that they often require images for both purposes. Low resolution is fine for onscreen viewing and for the tiny thumbnail images used in reports. Sometimes, however, a family member will ask for a copy of a picture for framing and this will need to be of a much higher quality.

- The advice would be to scan images at a high resolution (particularly if you are going to keep the originals on a CD so they are not taking up valuable space on your computer hard drive). Make lower resolution copies from these originals and use these for the majority of your online family history activities.

If you have a digital camera, you can take pictures yourself of family members, buildings and locations where people lived and worked, gravestones and churches. You can use a flatbed scanner to create images of small objects such as medals.

There may be images of places on the Internet, or you can find old postcards at antique fairs. Local libraries may have reproductions of old photographs as postcards. If your research is likely to be circulated more widely, you will need to check out copyright issues relating to these materials.

Using software to edit and organise photos

There are many different programs that will allow you to organise, search and edit your images. Digital cameras are usually sold with software that allows you to perform all these functions. You can also buy a range of products, from expensive, professional image editing programs such as Photoshop CS to more modestly priced but powerful software such as Paint Shop Pro and Photoshop Elements. Most digital photography classes that you might attend will probably use one of the latter. There are also free programs available, such as GIMP and Picasa.

Programs have two main functions:

- To help you organise photos, tag them in groups (useful for different branches of a family), give them captions and titles.

- Editing options that allow you to crop photos, change the resolution, adjust colour and brightness and generally improve on the original so that it works optimally for the purpose you require.

Some programs focus primarily on one or other of these functions; others have them running as two separate, though linked, activities. Increasingly, the functions are combined, particularly as the use of digital cameras becomes more widespread and people want to be able to manage the large number of photos they are now able to take at relatively low cost.

Using Picasa

For the purposes of this book, the program selected to demonstrate the basics of organising a family photo collection is Picasa, produced by Google. Like PAF, it is free, and therefore a good place to start practising techniques, many of which you will be able to transfer to other software should you decide that you require something more fully-featured. Again, as with PAF, Picasa may be all that you require to manage your photographs. The website from which you can download the program is at **http://picasa.google.co.uk/**.

If you have a Mac computer, you may wish to use iPhoto for editing and organising purposes. Check out **http://picasa.google.com/mac** as well.

Figure 11.1 shows the Picasa home page. There is a video introduction which is worth watching (possibly twice, since it covers a lot of ground in quite a short space of time).

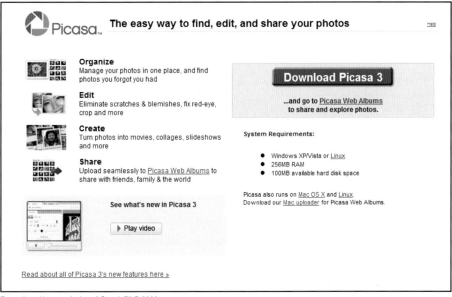

Figure 11.1

Picasa is primarily an organising program with good editing capabilities. When you install it, it scans your computer for images. If you have carefully saved all images to the Pictures folder, then you can restrict it to looking for files here. If not, you may need to get it to search more widely and then you can end up with many pictures of software logos and icons, which you don't really need. Whenever you edit an image elsewhere or save one in your computer, it will bring it into the program.

The Folder system mimics, to some extent, the file and folder system on your computer. You can have the folders in a Tree View containing sub-folders or a Flat Folder View which lists each folder individually. Folders can be sorted by name, size, date they were created or by recent changes. If you prefer to see a similar view to your filing system, choose Tree View sorted by Name.

Figure 11.2 shows the main screen (known as the Library) showing the folder with some of the images for this book. There is a slider bar at the bottom right which enables you to change the size of the thumbnail views.

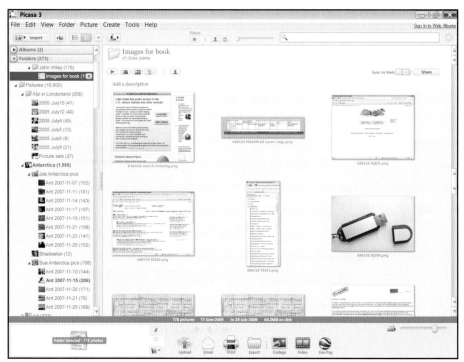

Reproduced by permission of Google™ © 2009

Figure 11.2

Understanding picture locations

What can be confusing at first is to understand why you can edit a picture in Picasa (for example, change a colour picture to sepia) and why this change doesn't show up in your main filing system.

Think of Picasa as making a virtual copy of your filing system. You can make changes to the virtual copy (turn it sepia), print out the new version and include it with projects created in Picasa. All this leaves the original in your filing system intact. Deleting a picture from the Library will, however, also delete it from your computer's filing system.

When you make changes to pictures in a folder, Picasa logs this. If you decide that you want the changes reflected in the main filing system, then click the Save to Disk button at the top right of each set of folder images. Even then, you have not lost your original. Picasa creates hidden folders in the filing system containing the originals of any images you have changed. You can make these folders visible by changing the file and folder view options in your filing system. This means that you can access the originals if you wish.

Using albums to group photos

Albums allow you to make yet another virtual copy, this time drawing in pictures from a number of folders. For family history purposes this is useful as you can create folders with different branches of the family, with all the images relating to one individual or to pictures relating to a single event such as a birthday party. The great thing about the album system is that you can have the same picture in more than one album at a time. Any changes you make in the Library copy are shown in the album versions and vice versa.

You create a new album in the File menu. If you want to add an image to an album, right-click the photo and select Add to Album. This shows you the album list and allows you to select one. All the images in a folder can be selected and moved to an album in one go.

Facilitating searches with tags

Rather than creating multiple albums for every purpose, you can tag individual images and then search for them using the tag. In Figure 11.3, a search for weddings has found three images from a family album tagged with this word. It has also found a folder whose main title included the word wedding, although the images in the folder were not tagged.

Reproduced by permission of Google™ © 2009

Figure 11.3

To tag a photo, highlight the image. Go to View in the menu bar and select Tags. Type in the keyword (for example, *weddings*) and add to the list. An image can have a number of different tags.

Basic editing

Double-clicking a picture takes you straight to the editing window. You may want to select a group of images for editing, however. A single click on any picture puts it in the selection box at the bottom left of the screen. Clicking another picture replaces the first selection. If you want to add more than one picture to the box, you need to hold them there. Figure 11.4 shows the selection box with five images. Each was held by clicking the green pin icon on the right of the box. The images themselves have a small green circle to show they have been 'pinned'.

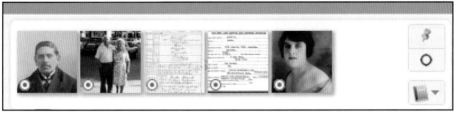

Figure 11.4

To clear an item from the box, highlight it and click the red circle. Note that this does not delete the image from your system, just from the selection box. Clicking the circle without highlighting an image offers you the option to clear the whole box.

Items in the selection box can be added to an existing album or a new one can be created for them. Click the blue Album icon on the right.

The selected items can be edited. Double-click the first image and you will be taken to the editing window (Figure 11.5).

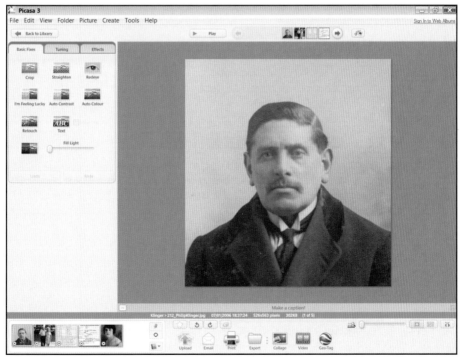

Figure 11.5

The image selected now appears in the editing window. Above this picture are thumbnails of the other selected images. Clicking any one of these puts it in the editing window. The arrows allow you to scroll through the images. The Play button runs a full screen slideshow of the selected pictures. The image in the editing window can be resized using the slider bar at the bottom right. This is useful if you have a document image that you need to magnify to read.

The editing functions are held on three tabs to the left of the window. Figure 11.6 shows the Basic Fixes tab, which contains the main tools that you would expect to find in most image editing software.

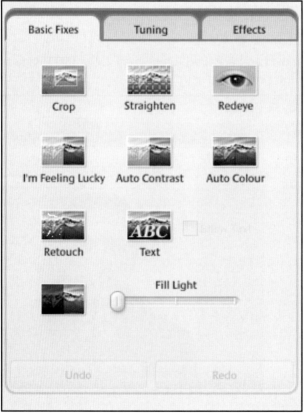

Figure 11.6

Play around with these options to see the effect they have. You can always undo previous actions if you don't like the results. More than one edit function can be used on a picture. Sometimes it makes sense to carry these out in a certain order. For example, you may want to straighten an image and then crop out any problem areas.

Retouching allows you to repair any blemishes in the picture. This can be quite painstaking and time-consuming work but you might want to try it on an old photo that has cracks and spots. You can zoom in and change the size of the brush you are working with. You highlight an area you wish to change, and click. Move the brush away to view the effect. If you are satisfied, click again. Help on all the features can be found on the Picasa site at **http://picasa.google.com/ support/?hl=en**.

In addition to Basic Fixes, there are two other editing tabs offering a number of options relating to light and colour. These are Tuning and Effects. Tuning is useful for improving under-exposed images. You can sometimes see backgrounds and even people that you hadn't known were there. Over-exposed originals are more difficult as you can't put back what isn't there. Try these options and see how pictures can be improved.

The Effects tab is fun to mess about with. Some of the effects are useful for family history presentations; others are probably better with more artistic and creative endeavours.

Printing

At the bottom of the main and editing windows are icons that allow you to use your pictures in different ways. They can be emailed to family members, uploaded into a Picasa web album viewable on the Internet, or made into a video or a collage. This is also where you will find the print menu. Click the Print icon to view the available options (Figure 11.7).

All the pictures in the selection box will be printed. In Figure 11.7, the option highlighted is Full Page. If you click any of the other options, different sizes are selected, which will allow you to print more of the images on screen. Figure 11.8 shows the 5 x 8cm option. Use the Border and Text Options menu to change the appearance of the printed document. These include whether the file name and/ or caption are printed.

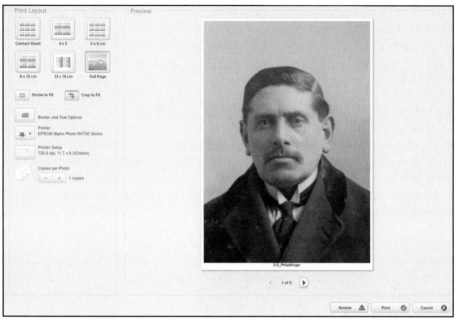

Figure 11.7

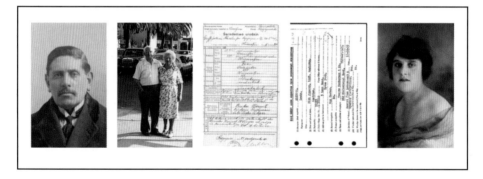

Figure 11.8

One very useful feature is the ability of Picasa to decide whether the resolution of your pictures is high enough to print out at the size you have selected. In Figure 11.7, there is a Review option at the bottom of the screen next to the Print button. It is coloured orange and has an exclamation mark alerting you to the fact that the resolution (quality) of some of the pictures is not good enough to print out at Full Page. Figure 11.9 shows the window you see after clicking the Review button.

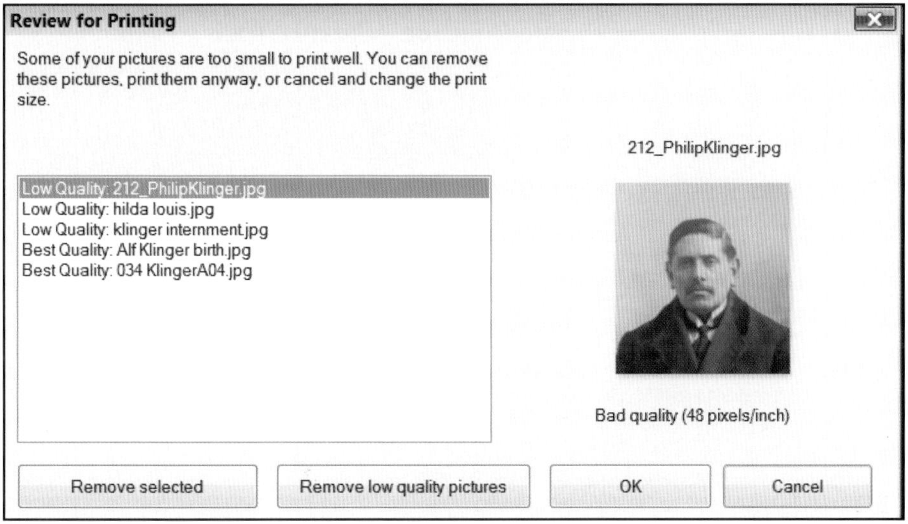

Figure 11.9

You can then decide whether to print them anyway, remove them from the selection or cancel the print request and change the print size. The low quality images were being used in the family tree program where they were perfectly adequate for viewing on screen. As you saw earlier, a better quality image is needed if you want a large size print.

For the 5 x 8cm size selected in Figure 11.8, clicking the review button would show that all the images will print acceptably at this size.

> When printing out black and white photographs, change your printer settings to grayscale. This will save the coloured inks, which are used by default to create black and gray shades.

Other options on the page (Figure 11.10) allow you to select another printer (assuming you have access to more than one), change the printer setup (including the resolution at which you want pictures to print out) and the option to print multiple copies of each image. If you only want to work with one image at a time, then you should delete the others from the selection box. You can also Crop or Shrink to Fit the image so that it fits the page.

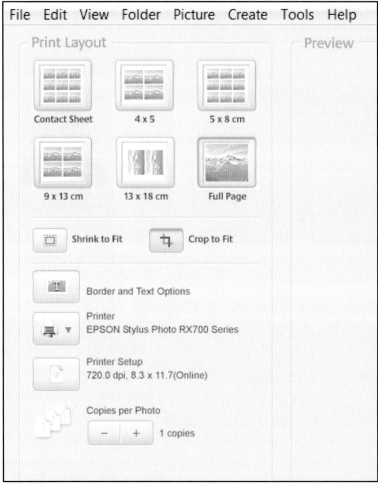

Figure 11.10

There are six print layouts you can choose from but you can customise this list and select others. Choose Tools from the menu bar and then Options. Select the Printing tab. Under Available Print Size, there are five boxes that you can configure using the dropdown arrows. The Full Page option cannot be changed.

Projects

Picasa has some other options that allow you to present images in a variety of ways. You can create a collage from images in the selection box. In Figure 11.11, a number of family members in uniform, from the First and Second World Wars, have been selected. These images are arranged in a mosaic to fit automatically on the page.

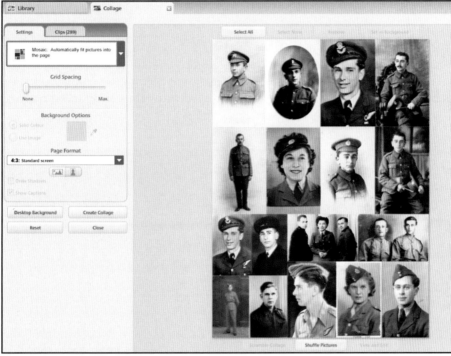

Figure 11.11

The Settings option on the left allows you to choose other arrangements for the pictures. Picture Pile scatters them at random on the page. You can then click a picture to drag it and any picture can also be rotated. A background for the pictures can be selected. This can be a solid colour or an image. There is a button underneath the collage that lets you shuffle the pictures randomly on the page.

Click Create Collage when you are ready. The collage is saved as a JPEG file which can then be printed out like any other picture.

As always, enjoy yourself with this program. You'll come back to it later, when you look at how to create presentations of your family history research.

Research tasks: Finding and using images for your family

If you already have an image organiser/editor on your computer, explore some of its features to see how this could help you manage family photos. Check the options for albums, tagging and editing.

If you don't already have such a program on your system, download Picasa and let it import your images into its Library. Create an album with family pictures and tag them (possible tags include weddings, military, buildings etc). Tag key individuals for whom you have many images. Practice making simple editing changes and printing pictures.

Summary

- A wide variety of editing programs is available. Software is usually provided when you buy a digital camera.
- More fully-featured programs are available to purchase.
- Try Picasa as it's free.
- Programs have organising and editing functions.
- You may need two versions of a picture: one at low resolution for viewing on screen; one at a higher resolution to make good quality prints.
- There is a wide variety of printing and project options. These will vary according to the program used.
- Most editing allows you to crop, adjust lighting and tint photos. Red eye reduction and blemish retouching options are very useful.

Brain Training

1. **What does dpi stand for?**
   a) Digital Photography Image
   b) Digital Picture Inventory
   c) Dots Per Inch
   d) Dual Paper Image

2. **If you are viewing an image on screen, what resolution should it be?**
   a) 45 dpi
   b) 72 dpi
   c) 100 dpi
   d) 300 dpi

3. **What is the name for the process of identifying images with a common theme?**
   a) Creating a collage
   b) Cropping
   c) Retouching
   d) Tagging

4. **What is the technical name for the small dots of which digital images are composed?**
   a) Bits
   b) Bytes
   c) Pixels
   d) Thumbnails

5. **In the Picasa basic editing menu (Figure 11.6), which option gives you a one-click fix for lighting and colour adjustments?**
   a) Auto Colour
   b) Auto Contrast
   c) I'm Feeling Lucky
   d) Retouch

Answers

Q1 – c	**Q2** – b	**Q3** – d	**Q4** – c
Q5 – c			

PART V
Sharing your research

... and here's another 100 pictures of our grand-daughter, which I downloaded this morning...

Creating presentations

12

Equipment needed: Data and images from your research, computer software that allows you to make presentations (for example, Personal Ancestral File, Picasa, OpenOffice, PowerPoint).

Skills needed: Understanding your audience and managing your material to leave them wanting more.

There comes a time when you decide that you'd like to present and share your research with other people: relatives, other researchers, people in different social and leisure groups you belong to who'd like to hear what you've been doing. In this chapter, you look at how to put a presentation together, using the data and images you are collecting.

Understanding your audience

What you choose to include in any presentation (whether for business, academic or family history purposes) is going to depend on your audience. A group made up of family members will probably find details of kinship and anecdotes about people who were related to them fascinating. Compare this with someone who wants to research his/her own family and wants to know about research techniques.

A good rule for any presentation is always to leave the audience wanting more. One of the best presentations I've seen was created to achieve a Distinction from the Royal Photographic Society. Go to **www.martinanddoreen.co.uk** and click the link to Doreen Addison's Family History ARPS panel. (Click each small image to take you to a larger version.) There are only 15 images but they tell the story of a family home and the people who lived there. Scanned objects, maps and documents are mixed with family and other photographs. This is a real object lesson in how to create a presentation and keep your audience interested. For family history presentations, you could make a brief commentary to accompany each slide or use music.

In addition to the usual question, 'How far back have you got?', researchers are often asked if they have finished their family histories. Given that you could potentially go back many generations, the answer must always be 'No'. You've probably seen royal lineages, drawn up in earlier times, which have managed to map lines of descent back to Adam and Eve and thus to God. Biblical material is full of genealogical references. While scholars may argue about the real or relative timescales involved, those who drew up the royal trees would probably have argued that they had finished.

For those with more modest aspirations, much will depend on the location of a family over time and the availability of records. You may also want to expand information beyond the pedigree of individuals, looking at their social circumstances and trying to gain a better understanding of how they lived their lives.

Creating slideshows

You can present your research in a slideshow in a number of ways. If you are going to a family gathering, you might want to produce a show made up of photographs and some scanned images of documents to which you have added music. The slideshow will act as a background to the event, rather than the focal point. Any documents you include should not be too detailed. The presentation should be set up to play automatically as you are not really expecting people to read details from the screen. You can set up the presentation to start again (loop) when it has finished, so you don't need to worry about restarting it yourself. Depending on the size of the event, it can be shown on a computer screen or projected onto a larger screen or white surface.

The other alternative is where you want to make a presentation to an audience. Here you will probably be explaining things as you go along, so you want more control over the transition from one slide to another. You won't want background music as you will be providing a commentary.

It is also possible to produce a presentation with a pre-recorded commentary, which then does not require you to make a formal presentation to an audience.

Most software that handles graphics or multimedia should have the facility to produce a slideshow. The features available to you will depend on the software. Specialist programs will have more options than something like Personal Ancestral File, whose primary function is to handle data in a family group/pedigree format.

These are some of the things you may be able to do:

- Include a caption or a title with an image
- Reorder the sequence of images so the presentation flows more easily (based on chronology, location or individuals)
- Create title slides and add text
- Add music or recorded commentary
- Change the way that slides appear on the screen (sometimes called transitions)
- Add a common background to all the slides.

Three of the programs already covered will allow you to create a slideshow.

Personal Ancestral File (PAF) slideshows

In Chapter 10, you saw how the multimedia option allows you to add photos, scanned documents and audio files to the data held on any individual. This collection can then be played as a slideshow. The options for customising the presentation are limited. You can adjust overall features such as the background colour against which the slides are shown and the length of time each slide is on the screen.

The main limitation of the PAF slideshow is that you can only show the images attached to a single individual at any one time. There is no overarching pool of images that you could use to create a slideshow covering multiple family members. The only way to do this is to add all the other images you wish to show to the collection of one person, which is not a particularly satisfactory solution.

Picasa slideshows

Picasa (**http://picasa.google.co.uk/**) offers you two options: a slideshow and a video.

Setting up a slideshow

Before you start, decide which images you intend to use and put copies (edited as necessary) into a separate folder, or use Picasa's Album feature. This ensures that you don't use unedited versions by mistake and that you discipline yourself to select the best and most appropriate pictures rather than just including everything you have managed to collect so far.

1. Select the images you want to include and 'pin' them into the image selection box at the bottom left of the main screen.

2. Go to Tools ➤ Options ➤ Slideshow. Decide whether you want the show to play in a repeating loop (you can break out by pressing the ESC (Escape) key at the top left of your keyboard). Choose whether or not to play music. Browse to select the folder holding the music you want to play. Click OK.

3. Go to View or Folder on the menu bar. Both have options to play the slideshow. You can also use the Play button at the top of the editing screen.

The slideshow will play in a full screen. If you move your mouse, a toolbar appears at the bottom of the screen (see Figure 12.1), the slideshow stops and you can customise it to your requirements.

Reproduced by permission of Google™ © 2009

Figure 12.1

From the left of the toolbar you have the following options:

- **Exit**: Leave the slideshow.

- **Fit screen and magnify**: The slider allows you to zoom in and out. The small image icon lets you move quickly to 100% and Fit on Screen views.

- **Rotate**: Turn images by 90 degrees left or right.

- **Previous image/Play slideshow/Next image**: The three arrows in the centre of the toolbar.

- **Star**: Marks an image as a Favorite.

- **Slide transitions**: The dropdown menu offers you Dissolve, Wipe, Circle, Push, Rectangle, Cut and Pan and Zoom. Whichever you choose applies to the whole slideshow.

- **Captions**: If you have added a caption to an image you can turn these on or off. A caption can be added to a picture in the main edit screen using the option in the grey bar just under the image.

- **Timings**: Change the amount of time an image is on the screen. If there are things to be read on screen, you may wish to make the timing longer. Again, whatever you choose will apply to the whole slideshow.

Experiment with the settings, perhaps just using a few pictures to see what works well.

Creating a video

The video option allows you some more sophisticated effects such as scrolling captions, title and text screens. It also lets you change the order in which slides appear.

1. Select your pictures in the same way as for the slideshow.

2. Select Create and then Video from the menu bar. In the editing screen there is an icon for Video creation at the bottom of the screen.

3. The Video Maker tab opens and creates an editable introductory slide for your show (Figure 12.2).

Figure 12.2

The selected images are along the bottom of the screen. You can drag them to rearrange the order in which they are shown (unlike the slideshow, where it depends on the order in which they were selected).

The menu on the left has three tabs, Video, Slide, and Clips. The Video tab is where you can load music, choose a transition style and decide how long each slide will be on screen. You can also change the amount of overlap between one picture and the next. This can be very effective in creating a smooth presentation rather than one that jumps between images. Captions can be shown if available.

You can change the dimensions of the image on screen. For the moment, stick with 1024 x 768 pixels, which should work well on most screens. You also have the option to crop the image so that it fills the entire screen. Try it and see how you feel about the results.

The Slide tab lets you make adjustments to individual pictures. You can edit the Introductory text slide, changing the background and text colour, font style and size as well as the wording. The Template option allows you to change the way the text appears on the screen. You can have a scrolling caption as in TV credits or a typewriter option. You can also edit the text itself. More text slides can be added throughout the sequence by using the New Text Slide icon, which is in the section at the bottom of the screen. Such slides might be used to introduce a different branch of the family or a different stage in an individual's life.

The Clips tab allows you to bring in additional pictures from the selected folder or from other folders. You can delete any items from the show by highlighting and then pressing the delete key or using the red cross at the bottom of the editing screen. The pictures are not deleted from your system, only from the Video selection.

Use the green play arrow under the main image to preview the video. When all the features are adjusted to your satisfaction, click Create Video on the left-hand side of the screen. If there are many pictures in the presentation, it will take a while to compile the video. When it has finished, it will start playing. A copy of the video is stored in your folder system. You can run it from Picasa again and edit it. If you right-click the video file icon in the Picasa folder system, you have the option to open it with another program, for example Windows Media Player.

OpenOffice – Impress presentations

Impress is the OpenOffice equivalent of Microsoft's PowerPoint Program, and presentations created in one can be opened in the other; just check you have the correct format when saving your file. OpenOffice can be found at (**www.openoffice.org**). This type of software is primarily used for business and academic presentations to an audience, using a digital projector and with a commentary delivered by the presenter. However, its flexibility allows you to use it for a variety of purposes:

- Looped slideshow as a background presentation at an event
- Printing images and text in a landscape format booklet where you would prefer not to use a word processing program
- Printing handout and note sheets for your audience. (This could be used at a larger version of the 'photo identification' event, where you present the photo on screen and ask those present to fill in on their handout sheet the name of the person they think is shown – a pub quiz in your own home.)

When you open the program, you see a screen similar to the one in Figure 12.3. Exactly what is shown will depend on how you have instructed the program to start.

Figure 12.3

Most of the features allow you to customise the presentation in various ways. For the moment, you'll just look at how to import pictures and run a slideshow. Once you have done this and saved your presentation, then you can explore some of the other features available.

Before you even start to create slides, save the presentation, giving it a name and location that will make it easy for you to find. As in other programs, use the File ➤ Save As option.

Figure 12.3 has opened with a Title Slide. If you click in the areas indicated, you can add a main title and a subtitle. Figure 12.4 shows what this will look like.

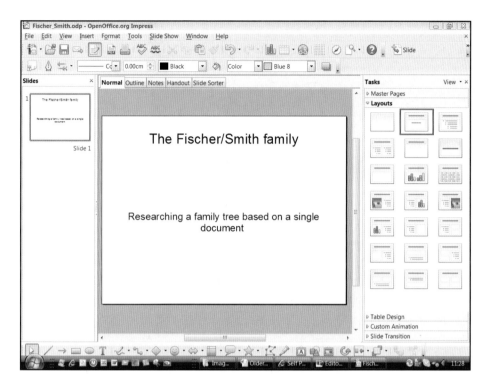

Figure 12.4

The panel on the right of the screen allows you to select different slide layouts. At the moment, the title slide layout is highlighted. Go to Insert in the menu bar at the top of the page and choose Slide. A new slide opens in the central screen area. In the Slide panel on the left, both slides are now shown. You can use this panel to move quickly between slides.

The new slide still uses the title slide layout. Select the blank layout from the options in the right panel and the format will change. As there are currently no pictures available of the Fischer/Smith family, I have added a collage image created in Picasa. To add a picture, go to the Insert menu again. This time select Picture and then choose the From File option. This takes you into your filing system. Browse to find the folder and file containing the image you want. Click to highlight the file name and then click Open (Figure 12.5).

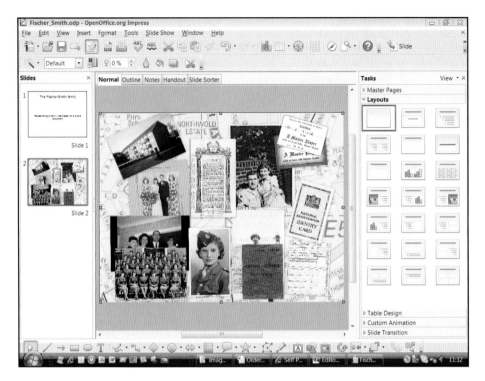

Figure 12.5

The image appears in the slide. Sometimes you may want to resize the image (it may be too large for the slide box or you may want to add a second picture). The picture you inserted may have very small boxes at each corner and along each side. (If not, click the picture and these should appear.) If you click and hold one of the corner boxes, you can move these in or out to resize the image.

 This resizing feature is available in most programs where you are handling images. (It also works in word processing, where an inserted image is often initially too big for the page layout you are using.)

Insert a new slide. Change the layout to one that has a title and text. The layout will let you use bullet points or numbering. Whatever the purpose of your presentation, don't try to include too much on screen and don't make the font too small. A good rule of thumb is a maximum of six lines with six words in each line. Figure 12.6 shows how the text slide can be used.

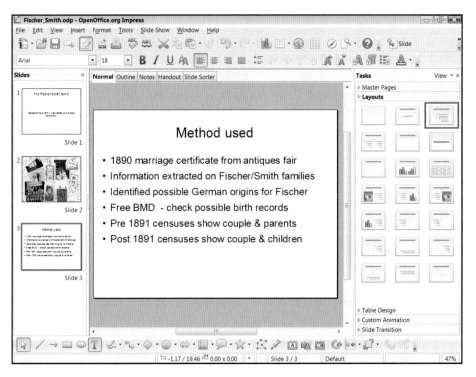

Figure 12.6

Insert a new slide. Change the layout to one that has both text and image settings. Double-click the picture side to insert an image. Create a title and text for the slide. The results should look as in Figure 12.7.

If you want to change the order of the slides, this can be done through the Slide Sorter, which is in the View menu (menu bar at the top of the screen). Click and drag to move the slides. If you are managing a large number of slides, then the Slide Sorter is the best place to do this. If you only want to change the order of a couple of adjacent slides, you can do this in the left-hand slide panel on the main screen. Try this now, moving the last slide (number 4) above the previous slide. Resave the presentation if you haven't already done so.

Figure 12.7

Running the slideshow

Make sure the first slide in your presentation is highlighted. Click the Slide Show option in the menu bar at the top of the page. Choose Slide Show. The first slide appears, filling the whole screen. By default, the show runs in manual mode. This means that you need to click the left mouse button or the space bar to move to the next slide. This is the best option when you are making a personal presentation to an audience and want to keep the material on screen while you explain additional points or answer questions. When the last slide is finished, the screen goes blank and you are instructed to Click to Exit, which takes you back to the main program.

If you need to exit the program at any point, click ESC (top left-hand button on the keyboard). To move forward and backwards between slides during the presentation, you can also use the navigation keys (the four keys with arrows).

Automating the slideshow

There are dozens of possible combinations for customising and automating the slideshow. Different timings can be assigned to each slide. This allows you to keep a slide with text on screen for longer than a slide with just a picture, for example. You can also adjust how you move from one slide to the next. This is known as a transition. These can be simple (fade out/fade in) or rather more spectacular (spirals, chequerboard, curtains). You can also allow these effects to be chosen at random by the computer. Although they are fun to play with, like font styles they should be used sparingly and with care, otherwise they can distract your audience from the content of the presentation.

For the simplest automation, you need to decide on the following:

● Is the Title Slide on screen at the beginning until you click to start the presentation? The alternative is to make it last for the same duration as all the other slides.

● How long should each slide remain on screen? Should they all be the same or do some need longer if they contain text that the audience will want to read?

● What kind of transition do you want between each slide?

● Will the presentation repeat at the end until the ESC key is pressed?

The Fischer/Smith presentation will have the following features:

● All slides (including Title Slide) to remain on screen for five seconds.

● Transition between slides is simple fade out.

● Presentation is repeated with no pause.

These effects can be achieved in Impress as follows:

PowerPoint may use slightly different wording or menu layouts but the principles will be the same.

1. Go to the Title Slide. Click Slide Show on the Menu bar and select Slide Show Settings. Adjust options as in the window shown in Figure 12.8.

Slide Show ☒

Range
- ⦿ All slides
- ○ From: | Slide 1 ▾
- ○ Custom Slide Show

| ▾

OK

Cancel

Help

Type
- ○ Default
- ○ Window
- ⦿ Auto

  00:00:00 ▲▼
- ☐ Show logo

Options
- ☐ Change slides manually
- ☐ Mouse pointer visible
- ☐ Mouse pointer as pen
- ☐ Navigator visible
- ☑ Animations allowed
- ☑ Change slides by clicking on background
- ☐ Presentation always on top

Multiple displays

Presentation display | ▾

Figure 12.8

2. The Auto option under Type is set to zero. This moves immediately from the final slide back to the first slide. If you want a longer pause at the end of the show before it repeats, you can set the timing using the up and down arrows next to Auto. Click OK.

3. Click Slide Show again in the menu bar. This time, choose Slide Transitions. The transitions options should now be open in the right-hand panel (see Figure 12.9).

4. Go to Edit in the File menu and click Select All. In the transitions panel, on the right of the screen, scroll to find the Fade Smoothly option. Further down the panel, change the Advance Slide option to Automatically After and adjust the timing to five seconds. Click the Apply to All Slides option. All the slides now have the same timing and transition.

5. If you want to change the settings for individual slides, you should highlight the slide and then change its options in the transition menu.

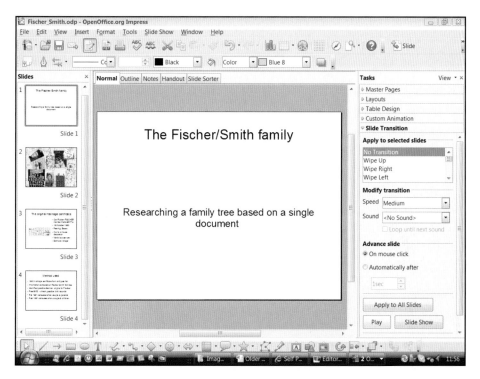

Figure 12.9

Save the presentation. Your new settings will be saved with the file. Preview the show by choosing the Slide Show option in the Slide Show menu. If you are not satisfied with the way it looks, you can tweak the options in the transitions menu, change the order of the slides or add further slides to your presentation. Remember to save it again before closing, to confirm your changes.

Printing

While you still have only a few slides in the presentation, take a look at Print in the File menu. In Impress, you are offered four options for printing content: Slides, Handouts, Notes and Outline. Ignore the Notes and Outline options for the moment.

- **Slides**: Prints one slide per page in landscape format unless you have altered the print layout settings. This gives you the nearest view to what was on screen but uses a lot of paper, ink and time if you want multiple copies.

307

● **Handouts**: Allows you to provide your audience with smaller versions of the screen shots. You can adjust the number of slides per page. Three per page gives the audience space for their own notes.

As with all print menus, you can determine which pages (slides) should be printed.

Research tasks: Developing a slideshow presentation

Collect some material on your family that you think would be suitable for a presentation. Using any of the programs mentioned in this chapter (or any other program you have that allows you to create a slideshow), put together a presentation for a small family gathering. The most useful programs are those where you can save your pictures and the settings. If saving is not an option, then put all the material you intend to use in a single folder and name the files so that you can run the slideshow in the correct order (eg 001family collage, 002marriage cert parents, 003Freds childhood pics, 004family house Brighton, 005family collage2).

Summary

● Most image editing programs have slideshow options.

● Decide on which images to show and make copies in a separate folder.

● Don't have too much text or make text too small.

● Leave images on screen long enough to be viewed.

● Use transitions to move between one image and another.

● The slideshow can be repeated in a loop.

● Music or a commentary can be added.

● Less is more!

Brain Training

1. **What is the optimum number of words you should have on a text slide?**

   a) 10

   b) 36

   c) 48

   d) 100

2. **Which menu option do you use to add a picture to a presentation?**

   a) File

   b) Format

   c) Insert

   d) View

3. **What name is given to the way in which you can move between slides?**

   a) Format

   b) Layout

   c) Master pages

   d) Transitions

4. **Which print format allows you to give your audience small versions of the slides shown on screen?**

   a) Handouts

   b) Notes

   c) Outline

   d) Slides

5. **What is the Microsoft Office equivalent of the presentation program Impress?**

   a) Access

   b) Excel

   c) PowerPoint

   d) Word

Answers

Q1 – b   Q2 – c   Q3 – d   Q4 – a

Q5 – c

Publishing a family tree

13

To some extent, the presentations produced in the previous chapter rely on your presence to give an audience further explanations and answer any questions they may have. These questions may be about research techniques or may specifically relate to the individuals in the family tree. However, you will also find you need to produce material that can be made available to relatives and other people you are less likely to meet, perhaps because they are located on the other side of the world. Here, the technology can again be of use. Among the various possibilities are two that will be looked at in this chapter: publishing your family tree online; and using computer and web facilities to produce a book on your family history, which relatives and other interested parties can then purchase.

Equipment needed: Computer and access to the Internet and Ancestry; a program that will enable you to create a PDF file.

Skills needed: Creating a GEDCOM file from your family history program and being able to upload it to a website; creating a PDF file and uploading it to a website.

Creating a family tree online

When you looked at family history software such as Personal Ancestral File, you saw that there were two ways in which the data files could be saved. The first was in a format specific to that program. This allowed you to open and edit your file and then produce reports. The second format was GEDCOM, which could be created using the Export function in the File menu. GEDCOM is a format recognised by most family history software and is therefore a way in which researchers can share data, even if they are using different programs.

Many of the websites that offer access to databases and indexes, such as census, BMD, passenger lists, military records and cemetery data, also allow you to create a family tree online. If you are just starting your research, you can build your tree from the beginning on the website. If you have already begun to create your tree in a software program such as PAF, the website often allows you to upload a GEDCOM file so that you have an instant online tree.

Implementing security and data protection online

Before looking at the mechanics of uploading a tree online, there are a number of issues that you should consider, particularly as people are increasingly sensitive about the availability of their personal data.

● Who will be able to access the data once it is online? You, your family, anyone who asks permission or anyone at all?

● Who can change or amend data? My own preference would be to restrict this and require changes to be sent to you so that they can be considered before inclusion.

● Does the website have options that allow you to conceal information about living people? These should be turned on.

● When you collected data about living people, did you ask for permission to include their details in your research? Were you clear that you might be publishing this in some form? The chances are that you didn't and you weren't. Some data will have come from other relatives and you may never have met the people concerned.

● Even if you hide details about living people in online material, what happens if someone asks you to send them a GEDCOM file? Do you have confidential notes included?

● What will you do if someone asks you to remove information? This can be done from your online file – but what about your own family history program? Much of the material you collect is a matter of public record (BMD, census, cemetery records and newspaper articles).

● What if someone wishes you to conceal information about a dead relative? Should you comply? What are the consequences if you don't?

For most researchers, these issues have achieved much greater prominence as developments in technology made it easier and quicker to share data with a potentially huge audience. If you are at the start of your research, you might want to consider these beforehand and draw up a list of criteria for yourself based on these considerations. The issues are both legal and ethical; however, even the legal issues vary from country to country. Cyndi's List has a series of links to genealogical ethics and etiquette topics, which you may want to browse. This can be found at **www.cyndislist.com/etiquette.htm**.

Be aware that there are some people who are happy for you to share your work with them but are less free in providing you with their own data.

The Fischer/Smith family online

For this exercise, I put the GEDCOM file for the case study family onto the Ancestry website. Since the material is all based on people born 100 years ago or more, issues about data on living people will not apply. You usually need to be registered with a website to upload your tree. For Ancestry, this can be the free account described in Chapter 6.

Once you are logged in to Ancestry, select the Family Trees option in the menu bar. This allows you to start a new tree (add your data directly to the site) or upload a GEDCOM file.

Once you have added a tree, it will appear on the home page when you log in to your Ancestry account.

You are asked for the location of your GEDCOM file in your system. Use the Browse button to navigate until you find the file. You can keep the file name as the Ancestry tree title or you can select a new name for the tree. Once you have clicked OK, the tree will be uploaded to the Ancestry site. The time this takes will depend on the number of people included in your tree. Once your tree is uploaded, you can view and edit it as required.

Figure 13.1 shows the pedigree view for the uploaded tree. There are tabs to show the family and the family group sheets. You can move between different family members and add data.

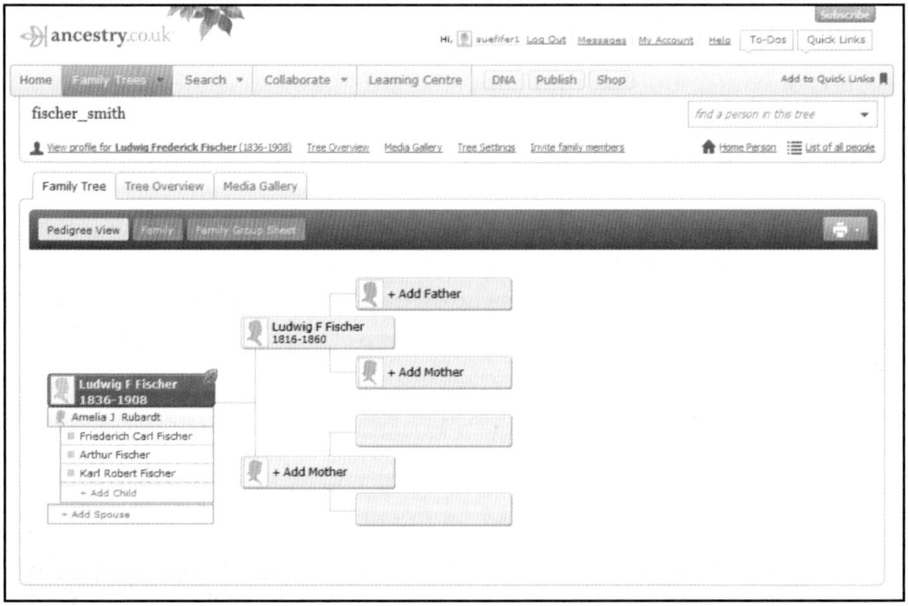

Figure 13.1

Just above these tabs there are a number of other options, one of which is Tree Settings. Clicking this gives you a general overview of the tree and the opportunity to adjust the privacy settings. You can also invite members of your family to come and view the tree. Whenever you make any changes to these settings, remember to save them before leaving that menu.

> **Research tasks: Putting your family tree online**
>
> You may decide that you are not yet at the stage of wanting to put your tree online. Use this task to review the options in websites such as Ancestry, GenesReunited, FindMyPast and any other sites you may have come across in your research.
>
> If you do want to start creating your tree online or to upload a GEDCOM file, set all privacy options to the maximum in the first instance.

Publishing your work

For many researchers and their relatives, there is a feeling that the end product of the research activity should be a paper-based publication. A CD on a shelf doesn't feel the same as a bound volume. So, even though the Internet and databases have proved useful in compiling the research, more traditional methods may be called for in telling the family story.

Even here, though, technology is changing the way books are printed. It was always possible to pay for your work to be printed. Self-publishing has a long tradition, whether for fiction or for specialised non-fiction where the market may be too small or uncertain for a publisher to take on the task. The problems in self-publishing have been the cost, distribution, advertising and storage of the books. Updating necessitated starting the process from the beginning and disposing of the outdated material.

Publishers themselves now use technology to work on a 'print on demand' model, which allows them to print fewer books for initial distribution but with the possibility of a fast turnaround time, should there be greater demand than expected.

As an individual researcher, you can also benefit from these developments. There are websites where you can upload your completed material (usually in PDF format) and where a single printed copy can be produced for you. You can then let relatives and others interested in your research know where they can acquire a copy of the book in the same way. You will have an arrangement with the website about how much you wish to charge for the book. The website keeps a certain amount to cover its costs and an agreed amount per book will be paid to you, possibly through an online account such as PayPal.

Benefits of this method include the following:

- No initial production costs
- Anyone visiting the site can see your book
- Email advertising by you can direct people to the site
- You don't have to store printed material in your loft, garage or garden shed
- Material can be easily updated
- You might even make some money in the process to fund further research

Consider the issues in the following list before committing to this publishing strategy:

- Security and data protection issues are the same as with putting your GEDCOM file online; it makes no difference that this is in book form.
- People who have bought one copy might be reluctant to buy another if you update the material.
- In addition to data, a book is likely to contain more images. What are the copyright issues relating to photographs and other materials you want to use?
- Editing is down to you (as with any self-publishing). Material has to be appealing to your audience. Plan it out in advance. What are you going to include; what is the logical sequence for the material; what and how many images will you need? What about an index? (Very useful, particularly to other researchers; unfortunately, an index is often not included with self-published material for some reason.)
- Will you include information on the whole family or will it be targeted at specific branches?

To see the way in which this works, visit **www.lulu.com/uk**. Check if there are any family history books published here.

There are a number of free programs that allow you to create PDF files. You can do a search for these on Google. There is also an article about PDF creators and convertors on Wikipedia. Some programs have advertising content as a trade-off for the free nature of the program; the payment of a small fee usually removes these messages.

You could also produce simple books using reports from family history software and images printed from graphics-handling packages such as Picasa. This might be a starting point and gives you more control over the process. It may be worthwhile investing in a comb binder and some clear plastic binder covers, which will let you produce some very acceptable results for distribution within the family. As with any book, report or presentation, it will be the content that keeps your readers turning the pages.

Research tasks: Publishing your family history

You probably don't yet have enough material or research completed to be able to publish something for distribution to your family. You might, however, print out for yourself some of the reports in your family history program and decide which you might want to include in any future publication.

Summary

- Security and data protection issues need careful consideration if you make personal information about living people available online.

- If you create an online tree, in addition to using a family history software program, you will need to ensure that both are up to date.

- Having an online tree increases the potential for you to find other people researching your family tree. The downside is that you may be contacted by many who are not related to you, particularly if you have a very common name.

- Draw up a list of criteria for the development of any online material. You could then show this to any people who are providing you with data so they know the rules you have set yourself.

- Self-publishing can now be undertaken online using the 'print on demand' model.

- You need to edit your own work; this requires care, as you may be too close to the material to see mistakes. Perhaps someone in the family can help.

- Base the content on your likely readership – important if you are dealing with many different branches of a family tree.

- Keep enjoying all aspects of your family history research; you never know who or what you might encounter on this journey.

Brain Training

1. What is the best way to upload a family tree to the Ancestry website?

a) Excel file

b) GEDCOM file

c) PDF file

d) Word file

3. What is the accepted cut-off point for document and data privacy issues in the UK?

a) 50 years

b) 75 years

c) 90 years

d) 100 years

2. What is the best way to send your family history book data to the Lulu website?

a) Excel file

b) GEDCOM file

c) PDF file

d) Word file

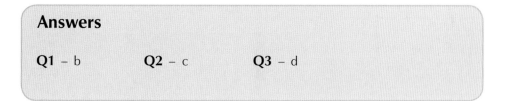

Answers

Q1 – b   **Q2** – c   **Q3** – d

Glossary

AgLabs A shortened form of Agricultural Labourers, the primary occupation of most people before the industrial revolution and the growth of large towns.

AKA Also Known As (used for stage names, aliases or where an individual is usually known by a particular version of his/her name).

BMD Birth, Marriage and Death records.

Boolean logic Technical term for using extra commands in a search query to tell the computer what you really want. Examples are AND, OR and NOT. They are always written in capital letters.

Browse Searching through Internet pages or a computer filing system. Sometimes viewed more in a spirit of seeing where it will take you and what it contains, rather than deliberately searching for something specific.

C (circa) Latin for 'about'; used when you are unsure of a date eg c1848; gives an idea of the timeframe rather than the exact date.

Civil registration Recording by civil (rather than religious) authorities of birth, marriage and death events.

Click For online searching, this means tapping the left mouse button once. Opening programs or documents usually requires a double-click of the left button.

Copy/Cut and Paste Taking a copy of a picture, word, phrase, or complete file and putting an identical copy somewhere else. This could be in the same document, or elsewhere in another document or folder. Copy and Paste leaves the original where it was (ie you end up with two versions). Cut and Paste moves the original to the new location (so you still have only one version, but in a different place).

Default The normal state in which a program or an option starts. For example, if you have more than one printer, one of them will have been nominated as the default printer. If you don't specify which printer you want to use for a printing job, then the computer uses the default printer. At any time, you can set another printer as the default.

Download Transfer a file or a program from a website to your computer. It may be a PDF document, an image or a music file. Uploading is the process in reverse; for example, you create a GEDCOM file in your family history software and then upload it to make it viewable on a website such as Ancestry.

dpi/ppi Dots per inch; pixels per inch – a way in which the resolution (quality) of an image can be measured. A higher dpi gives a better quality picture but the resulting electronic file is much bigger.

Dropdown menu A menu of options which appears when you hover your mouse cursor over a search, title or format box. There may be a small black arrow on the right of the box which you need to click to make the list appear.

Enumerator Person recording census information on behalf of the authorities.

FAQ Frequently Asked Questions; collections of questions that visitors to a site often ask. A good place to start even if you haven't thought of a question yet.

Fields Term used in databases for the various bits of information held and which you can search; for example first name, last name, date, age, address and occupation can all be fields in a database.

File extensions Three letters that come after every computer file name. They allow the computer to know which program to use to open the file. They all have a full stop (dot) in front of them. Examples of file extensions are .doc, .xls, .pdf, .jpg. Because they are mainly of use to the computer, sometimes your filing system doesn't show them to you (you can change this if you wish).

Files and folders The two main elements that you can see in the computer storage system. Just as in a filing cabinet for papers, you have folders set up and named to contain files (documents). Because the folder/filing system is electronic, you won't run out of space as quickly as you will with a physical filing cabinet. The downside is that you need to understand and manage the electronic system to ensure that files are placed where you want, rather than where the computer thinks you want them to be.

Folio A two-sided sheet in a ledger, such as a census, only one side of which is given a number. This will differ from the usual page numbering system. A record may therefore be referenced with a folio number and/or a page number and a record number.

In some wills, where probate was granted in London, an additional folio number has been handwritten in the printed Probate Calendar. The number is used when ordering a copy of the will or probate grant.

Font Another name for the text or typeface used. There are hundreds of fonts available. Use Arial for presentations and for text documents, reports and family history programs. Times New Roman is also good for documents. Too many fancy fonts and colours make things hard to read.

Gazetteer An alphabetical listing of place names for a district, county or country.

GEDCOM A standard format now used by most Family History software programs. It allows users to transfer data between different programs without the need to retype everything.

GOONS Guild of One-Name Studies. An overarching organisation for those who research a particular surname, whether or not it is related to their own family.

Hot key Using a single key on the keyboard instead of using the mouse. Hot keys are sometimes used in combination with other keys such as Shift, Ctrl (Control) and Alt.

Icon Small picture used to represent a program, document or menu option. To find out what an icon does or represents, hover the mouse cursor over it and a text description should appear.

IGI International Genealogical Index. A genealogical database created from birth, marriage and death records. Searchable on the LDS FamilySearch Website.

JPG/JPEG The most popular standard format for digital images. Used by most digital cameras and readable by nearly all graphics editing, family history, presentation and word-processing programs.

Keyword Word used in a search to find data. In image editing programs, where there is no text, you can create a keyword for a picture or group of pictures known as a tag.

LDS (Church of Jesus Christ of) Latter Day Saints (also known as the Mormon Church). Responsible for the FamilySearch website and many genealogical resources and materials.

Moderation The vetting process in an online discussion group which prevents unhelpful heated arguments from dragging on and minimises time-consuming off-topic postings.

National Probate Calendar Index of Wills and Grants of Probate organised by year.

OCR Optical Character Recognition. A process for scanning printed documents where the computer can read the individual letters. This allows the document to be indexed and searched.

PAF Personal Ancestral File – family history software produced by the LDS and available to download free from the FamilySearch website.

Palaeography The study and transcription of old handwriting.

Parent In the hierarchy of any computer filing system, this refers to the folder at the next level up from the current folder.

Patronymic Name derived from the father's first name, rather than based on a fixed family surname handed down in each generation.

Paypal Payment system, used extensively on eBay (the online selling and auction site). Offers a measure of security between buyers and sellers when either party is not willing or able to use/offer credit card facilities.

PDF Portable Document Format allows someone to create a file which looks exactly the same as the printed version. Anyone can therefore read and print this file, even if they don't have access to the program which originally created it. Often used for computer and software manuals, guidance notes and forms. Adobe Reader is required to view such files. Most computers already have the reader installed or it can be downloaded free from the Internet. You need additional software to create the PDF files. Free or low cost versions are available on the Internet.

Podcast Like a radio broadcast but available on the Internet. Can be listened to directly or downloaded for future reference. Can also be loaded into portable digital audio players. Developing to include video as well as audio.

Primary source The original record created at the time an event took place. It may not be error-free but is the best place to look for information.

RIN Record Identification Number – a numbering system used in family tree programs.

Schedule In the census, the paper given to the householder or filled in by the enumerator. The schedule number records each household in turn in the enumerator's book. It is not the same as a house number in an address.

Scroll To read a web page which is too big to fit on the computer screen, by moving up and down (as if you were reading from a rolled-up scroll). The easiest way to do this is to use the wheel on your mouse (if it has one); otherwise click and drag on the 'scroll bars' on the right of the screen.

Search engine A computer program that retrieves information from databases, web pages and indexes.

Secondary source Copies or transcriptions of original records created to maintain central records or for databases. May have errors where original records are difficult to interpret.

Software Another term for a computer program. Software is a series of instructions which allows the computer to carry out particular tasks such as organising images, creating a spreadsheet or managing a family history database. *Hardware* is the term used for any physical item in your computer setup (printer, screen, keyboard, mouse, CD drive).

Soundex A coding system for searching for names using what they sound like rather than how they are spelled. Many family history search functions use these automatically. If not, you should start keeping a list of possible alternative spellings and see if the database allows you to use wildcards to replace missing letters.

Strays People originating from one area who have moved to another place (or who may just be visiting another location on census night). The census in the new area will record their birthplace but you may not know where to look for them once they have moved. Some researchers create a database of strays in an area while they are looking for their own ancestors.

Submission (FamilySearch) A collection of family history material submitted as part of the Pedigree Resource File to the LDS/FamilySearch databases.

Tab Many menus have too many options to show in a single window. These are therefore shown in several windows grouped together with a small title tab at the top of each (rather like a card index system). Clicking a tab brings that window to the top of the pile.

Tag A label created in an image editing program which you can attach to a picture. This allows you to organise and search for images with common themes eg military, weddings, grandparents, locations.

Thumbnail A small version of an image used in file lists and in family history printed reports. Because the thumbnail has a small file size, it comes up quickly on the screen and doesn't take long to print out. This is an important consideration if you have many such images in your program. If you want to see a larger version of an individual image, (perhaps for reading or editing purposes), there is usually an option for this in the program.

TNA The National Archives, located at Kew.

Transition Moving from one slide/image to another during a slideshow or graphic presentation. Transitions can be simple (fade out/fade in) or more spectacular (curtains closing/opening, spirals, chequerboard, dissolve).

Transcription Copying the words from a handwritten or printed document to make it more legible or to create a database.

Transliteration Transcribing letters from one alphabet to another, eg from Cyrillic, Hebrew or Greek into a script readable by English speakers.

USB Universal Serial Bus: the standard for equipment which allows you to connect your camera, printer or flash drive to your computer.

Vital records Birth, marriage and death records.

Wildcard A system of replacing one or more letters with ? or * symbols when searching for names whose correct spelling is not known.

Will calendar See National Probate Calendar.

Index